LEARNING TO LIVE

LEARNING TO LIVE
Walter Russell Bowie

ABINGDON PRESS 🔊 NASHVILLE & NEW YORK

LEARNING TO LIVE

Standard Book Number: 687-21321-5
Library of Congress Catalog Card Number: 69-18450

Scripture quotations unless otherwise noted are from the Revised Standard
Version of the Bible, copyrighted 1946 and 1952 by the Division of Christian
Education, National Council of Churches, and are used by permission.

I am indebted to Harper & Row for permission to use material from my
Women of Light in my present discussion of the co-ordinate college (chapter
X), and to The Atlantic Monthly for permission to reprint in chapter XIX
portions of my article "The New Testament: A New Translation," copyright
© 1947 by The Atlantic Monthly Company.

TO JEAN

SET UP, PRINTED, AND BOUND BY THE
PARTHENON PRESS, AT NASHVILLE,
TENNESSEE, UNITED STATES OF AMERICA

Contents

Introduction... 7

I. The Early Days in Richmond... 9

II. A Child's World... 16

III. Conflict of Ideas... 24

IV. Boys, and Some Makers of Men...30

V. Harvard 1904... 44

VI. Enter, Jean... 54

VII. Life in the Virginia Seminary... 58

VIII. The Country Parish at Greenwood... 71

IX. The Beginning at St. Paul's... 83

X. Community Activities... 95

XI. In the First World War... 109

XII. Principles Worth Fighting For... 120

XIII. The Final Years in Richmond... 132

XIV. At Grace Church: Ideals and Aims... 140

XV. In the Rectory and the Rector's Study... 156

XVI. Some Not Unwelcome Combats... 166

XVII. Friends... 178

XVIII. A Hurdle Not Surmounted... 194

XIX. At Union Seminary... 205

XX. Changing Tides in Religious Thinking... 219

XXI. Lights and Shadows... 231

XXII. To Virginia Again... 239

XXIII. Too Little—and Too Late?... 253

XXIV. Clouds, and the Light Beyond... 263

XXV. The Heart of It All... 269

XXVI. The End, and the Beginning...277

Index of Names and Places... 285

Introduction

Is there any reason for a book which, being autobiographical, might seem mostly about one's self? One justifying reason, perhaps, and it is this: if the book can open out upon scenes and people and the crowded drama of our human relationships which go beyond a mere personal story.

For the great fact is that each one of us is part of a larger life. "No man is an *Iland,* intire of itself; every man is a peece of the *Continent,* a part of the maine." Each one of us is what he is because of the influences from many other lives which have flowed into him. If in some measure he can interpret them, he is dealing with what is much wider than himself. That is what I who begin to write this book am most aware of: aware that the *relationships* which I have had, and any of us have had, with those we know and love are what make life meaningful at last. And one man's associates and friends and inspirers do not belong to him alone. If he can make them vivid through the written word, then as he writes about them he may transmit not only the little that might have been his own, but that which in ampler measure has been given him, and belongs to all.

Also there may be a value which is not personal only and not presumptuous when one who has lived through a particular period of our changing affairs writes about events in which he has had some part. Samuel Pepys and John Evelyn were neither of them men of conspicuous consequence, but in their diaries they have made lasting contributions to our interest just by telling what they saw and knew. "Fourscore and seven years ago" were the words with which Lincoln began his Gettysburg address. I am not Methuselah, but I have been on this earthly stage for nearly fourscore and seven years, have watched the human drama and its shifting scenes, and have known some of those who have played significant roles in the general community and especially in the church. To remember them is to realize how varied and fascinating human nature and human effort are; and to trust that as long as courage and high purpose last we may go on learning better what this life of ours is meant to be.

WALTER RUSSELL BOWIE

I. The Early Days in Richmond

The most decisive early event in my existence was the one which I cannot remember: namely, being born. According to the subsequent record of the christening in St. Paul's Church, Richmond, Virginia, it occurred on October 8, 1882; and according to the family, it was in the large old brick house, long since torn down, which then stood at the corner of First and Franklin Streets, where the Richmond Public Library now stands. It was the home of my grandmother, Mrs. James R. Branch; and apparently my mother and father had been living there with her after their marriage in 1881, before they moved into a house of their own. My mother, Elisabeth Halsted Branch, was my grandmother's third daughter; and my father, Walter Russell Bowie, who was born in Westmoreland County, had met her after he had graduated from Washington and Lee University and had come as a young man to Richmond to begin to practice law.

The first of the Bowies in Virginia was John Bowie, who came from Scotland about 1742, and built his house on a hill overlooking the Rappahannock River, near Port Royal. The first of the Branches was Christopher Branch, who came from England in the *London Merchant* in 1620, and in 1625 was recorded as settled in Henrico "att ye Colledg Land."

9

Richmond had not been part of the earliest history of Virginia. The three little ships, the *Susan Constant*, the *Godspeed*, and the *Discovery*, which brought the original colonists from England in 1607 had landed at the mouth of the river which they named the James, and it was in their precarious settlement of Jamestown that the first legislative assembly of the New World met in 1619. In 1699 Williamsburg, between the James and the York Rivers, became instead of Jamestown the capital of the colony and the seat of the royal governors. Richmond, farther up the James, had not been established as a town until the middle of the 1700's, but in 1780 it was made the capital of what had been the colony and now was to be the state. Such it has continued to be since then, but its more dramatic significance came from the fact that shortly after the outbreak of the War Between the States in 1861 it was chosen as the capital of the embattled Confederacy.

When I was born in 1882 seventeen years had gone by since the Confederate States of America had ceased to be an actuality with the surrender at Appomattox and the end of the war. But the aura of that great struggle, and all the emotional vibration of it, still pervaded the place and its people, including even the consciousness of a little child. My grandfather, Walter Bowie, had been a captain in the 40th Virginia Infantry; and the story of one special thing that happened to him brought a glint of amusement into what were for the most part the sombre recollections that a child would begin to hear. Once when he had a brief furlough, he came to see my grandmother who was staying at that moment with a relative in an old house in the open country of Louisa County. While he was there, a raiding detachment of Yankee cavalry got word that this Confederate captain had been seen. They came at a gallop to surround the house and to search it. But one of the family Negroes in the nick of time saw the cavalry coming, but still at a distance up the road, warned my grandfather, and sent him out the back door into the icehouse close behind the kitchen. There he hid in the straw. The cavalry searched the house, but could find no trace of him. Sure that he must be near, they threw a cordon around the house and bivouacked there for two days. Meanwhile the Negro cook put an empty tub on her head each day to go out as usual to get some ice and bring it in—except that this time the tub was not empty. She had put food in it for my grandfather to eat; and thus for the two days he outlasted the cavalry, until they disgustedly gave up the search and rode away. Two days in the straw of an icehouse might not have seemed a diversion to be chosen, but there was at least this advantage, that in the middle of the Virginia summer he did not have any difficulty—as other people had—in keeping cool.

That same grandfather at Gettysburg was struck by a musket ball which shattered the bones in one foot. As he lay on the battlefield when darkness came and fighting died down, a Confederate surgeon came along, knelt down beside him, and took out some instruments. "What do you mean to do?" my grandfather asked. "To cut off your foot," the surgeon said. When my grandfather demurred, the surgeon —dead-tired, no doubt, and drained of everything, including patience—answered, "If you know better what to do, I'll leave you to take care of it yourself," which he did.

The next day the Confederate Army began its withdrawal into Virginia. My grandfather, laid in a jolting wagon which passed for an ambulance, found the pain from the shattered foot so intolerable that he asked to be put out on the roadside in front of a house. Two elderly ladies who lived there found him and had him brought in. There was no doctor left in the whole neighborhood, so he had to manage for himself as best he could. But he saved his foot—including the musket ball which was still in it. All his life thereafter that foot was like a barometer, which could always tell when cold and rainy weather was about to come. It made him walk with a limp, but he had two feet to walk with.

For him and for my grandmother, his wife, there was a wistfulness always as they spoke of what had been before and during the war, but seldom any bitterness. They both were to live to old age, and they had each other.

But for my Grandmother Branch the war had ended with a sorrow so devastating that her involvement in it and in its memories was more passionate. James Read Branch, her husband, had been a colonel in the Confederate artillery—and had once saved his guns when nearly all the gunners had been killed. Although he had been wounded, he had come through the war alive. But he was to lose his life presently in another kind of service. When the war ended, Virginia was Military District Number 1, governed by alien appointees. The need was for men in Virginia to bring the state through the so-called Reconstruction, to allay the bitterness that prevented action, and to draw men of good will together to build up again an ordered political life. James Branch devoted himself to that effort. On July 3, 1869, he was organizing a rally on one of the small islands in the James River where it flows by Richmond. The crowd had been held back on the Richmond side until preparations on the island had been completed. When he walked out on the bridge from the island and gave the signal to let the people on, the sudden rush of them collapsed the bridge. He was thrown into the river, and caught under one of the fallen beams. He had left home that morning full of strength and vigor; he was brought home that evening dead.

Henceforth his memory and the memory of everything he had represented became the sovereign fact in my grandmother's life. Her emotions were the more intense because they were in tune with essentially the same emotions that a whole community felt—the community of men and women, and especially the women, who had suffered through the war and had borne its heavy consequences. To her, as to many in Richmond, the past was sacred. To question what those she loved had fought for, to act under any new conditions as though their devotion did not matter, would have seemed betrayal. To decorate the graves of the Confederate dead in Hollywood on memorial days, and to preserve inherited traditions like flames burning on an altar, was a continuing religion. Nothing must threaten that. And when anything did seem to threaten it, there could be personal tragedy, as we shall presently see.

Even if there had not been the special influences which set up resistance to alien thought or custom, Richmond would have been provincial in a way that the mid-twentieth century must find it hard to imagine. Nearly all small cities were. The larger world seemed a long way off, and did not impinge much on local consciousness. People stayed where they were, and as they were. Railroad trains, with their wooden coaches and the puffing locomotives from which clouds of smoke and coal dust drifted back, were not allurements to journeying. Automobiles were not yet dreamt of, and when in the first decade of the twentieth century the first Fords began to appear, there were few roads fit to drive on. When it had been raining or when there was snow, anybody who tried to go from Richmond to Washington was in for trouble. In the region called the Chappawamsic Swamp the potholes would be so deep that the neighboring country people used to have teams there to haul stranded automobiles out; and it was generally believed that some of the unregenerate among the population used to dig the potholes deeper every night to make sure that the drivers next day would stall and stay until they got the hired help.

Not until the eighteen-nineties did such a thing as a telephone begin to affect existence. Then there might be one in the neighborhood drugstore, and you could perhaps go there in an emergency and ask whether you could please find out whether the doctor you wanted had a telephone too. Gas jets were regarded as the latest—and perhaps the sufficient—advance over kerosene lamps, and the world of light which Thomas Edison would create had not dawned on the horizon. The wagons from the adjacent countryside came in every morning to bring chickens and vegetables to the Sixth Street Market, and that is where you went to buy your food—with the addition that in summer two-wheeled carts, with barrel-shaped canvas tops to keep off the sun would drive through town, and you could hear a familiar chant, with its long-drawn cadence, "W-a-a-ter-mel-u-u-u-ns, sweet an' fine!" In the eighteen-eighties, none of the residential streets were paved. Watering carts came through now and then to make their fleeting impression on the dust, but the water was turned off as the cart passed your particular house unless you had paid to have the watering done. Here and there in Richmond, streetcars jogged along, drawn each by two horses—except that at the foot of the steep Ninth Street hill there was a mule, and a Negro who hitched the mule onto the streetcar that came along, rode to the top of the hill, and brought the mule back to its station again. The drivers of the streetcars had been there a long time, knew most of those who were their passengers, and conversed with them familiarly. When some lady, holding up her ground-length skirts with one hand and catching hold of something in the car with the other hand to steady herself, went toward a seat before she could get her money out, the driver would announce over his shoulder, "Miss Nellie Tompkins, don't you know you ain't put in your fare?"

Whatever purposes the passengers on the streetcars had, one purpose they did not have was to be on their way to the Public Library to borrow a book, for there was no Public Library in Richmond in the 1800's, and would not be until twenty-five years of the twentieth century had gone by.

But if thus there seemed to be disadvantages in living in Richmond, the people whom I remember did not think so. It was a homogeneous community, with traditions and customs and friendly ways that were familiar to everybody. Hardly anyone had much money, for whatever wealth Virginians had once possessed before 1861 had been largely swept away by the war, at the end of which in 1865 Confederate notes and currency were worth no more than so many bundles of scrap paper. But an inherited quality of living did not have to depend on what anyone had to spend. Boys and girls met one another and grew up together, went to dances in each other's houses, or when they were older, and the girls were debutantes, to "the Richmond German" in one of the armories. The grown-ups had their dinners and their parties, the men exchanged opinions at the Westmoreland Club—and stayed too long sometimes at the card tables, and over their mint juleps at the bar, but properly would be seen with their families in the processions on Fifth and Franklin Streets on Sundays when the congregations flowed together after the services at St. James's Church and at St. Paul's. If life was not exciting, it was usually genial and contented; and there might then have been said by a Richmonder what was satirically attributed to the lady of Boston who, when asked if she traveled much, replied, "Why should I? I am here already."

II. A Child's World

When I was still a little child, my father and mother moved with me and my younger sister, Martha, from my grandmother's house to a home on South Third Street, near a small park overlooking the James River from the steep slope called Gamble's Hill. It was a pleasant residential street, and some aspects of it which would not suit an adult's ideal for city planning made it more rather than less attractive to a small boy. The Richmond, Fredericksburg and Potomac railroad tracks ran through a short tunnel under Gamble's Hill, and every now and then there was the excellent pleasure of hearing a smothered rumble, running along the street to the wall above the mouth of the tunnel, and waiting for the great explosion of smoke as the engine came through. Also, behind our house, the land dropped away, and on a hill less than a mile beyond stood the walls of the Virginia Penitentiary, the sight of which could give rise to fascinated speculation as to what a boy should do if some of the convicts got loose.

In his *Ode on Intimations of Immortality*, Wordsworth wrote of childhood that

> Trailing clouds of glory do we come
> From God, who is our home.

16

And that can be true in that the child has sensitive imagination and walks in a world that can be full of wonder. But also it is a world of uncertainties and shadows, in which his small mind gropes for a security which he does not always find; and sometimes it is the invasion of some sudden and perhaps inexplicable fear which he remembers longest. In my grandmother's house there was a curving staircase which ran from the very high-ceilinged entrance hall up to the second floor. Where the stairway turned, there was a niche in the wall, as though it were meant for some statue to stand there. So far as I can recall, nothing ever was there; but often I had a nightmare that in the niche an old witch crouched, and that if I went up that stairway in the dark she would snatch me.

And sometimes it is not fears but bewilderments that linger with strange persistence in childish recollection. When we had moved to Third Street, in a house opposite lived one of my mother's sisters, Aunt Annie Cabell, and her three sons, my cousins. One of the boys, Robert, had a bicycle: not such a one as is likely to exist anywhere on this planet now, but one of the queer old kind that had in front a big wheel almost five feet high, with a very small wheel behind, and the saddle up above the big wheel; so that if you fell off it, there was a long way to the ground. One day when John Cabell and I were playing around the house, a boy came along and called out that Robert had ridden his bicycle up to Main Street, had fallen off, and broken his arm. Still in my memory is the insoluble problem which at that moment overwhelmed my mind. I supposed that if you broke your arm, it broke in two and part came off, like a broken stick. I thought that Robert must value his arm, but I knew that he loved that bicycle. He had only one hand left; but there were the bicycle and the other arm, both lying in the street. Which would he pick up and bring home?

17

I do not know how Robert and his bicycle and his arm did get home, but any troubled concern I had had for him changed into respectful wonder at the happy lot of a boy who having broken his arm now lay comfortably in bed with a large box of candy—a round box with a red ribbon on it— lying on the table right by his bed. And there to look after him and to bring him what he wanted was his Mammy. In that decade of the life of Richmond, the Negro Mammy still represented the intimate devotion of the not-long-bygone days before the war and the Emancipation. The Mammy of the Cabell boys was Mammy Nelson, and to remember her is to remember not only an individual but one of a kind whose disappearance leads recollection into a poignant world of shadows that surrounds a vanished world. What was she like? In so far as words can bring the Virginia Mammy back to life, it so happens that Robert Cabell's brother is the one who has most nearly done so: James Branch Cabell, in his book of essays, *Let Me Lie.*

She is not comprehensible any longer except by those who have need to remember her forever. . . . She did not ever concede that in any circumstances any one of her children had been bad; at utmost, the small accused might have been, it was allowed fair- mindedly, sort of mischeevous, but then good lord, what child would not be when folks started to upset him . . . without attend- ing to their own business? Through this dashing gambit, any parentally discussed punishment, instead of figuring as the result of a misdemeanor, was left unmasked as the true cause of it.[1]

In the case of Robert, his broken arm would, of course, have stirred first in everybody only compassion and quick help, not punishment, even if it had been the fact that he had no

[1] (New York: Farrar, Straus & Co., 1947), p. 184.

18

business to be riding his bicycle up on Main Street. But if he or another one of Mammy Nelson's children on some different occasion had been conspicuously at fault, still Mammy Nelson's instant protection would have been at hand. "The child had been mischeevous because folks who were more than twice as big and who did not know how to keep their temper, had started in to spank him, and what child, what child anywhere upon this earth, would not be? That, and that alone, was just simply what the indignant dark lawyer for the defense wanted to ask Dr. Cabell and Miss Annie, and did ask, freezingly. . . . So the foiled parent, or it might be both parents, withdrew. And Mrs. Nelson, triumphant but still icily offended, began to speak of the accessibility of her own rooms on St. James Street." [2]

Many a child in Richmond in those days had reason to be grateful for the Negro nurses, and especially for his or her own. They had a kind of instinctive attachment which made them identify with the families into which they came, and hardly ever did their loyal protection of their children fail. In Ann Fairbairn's *Five Smooth Stones*, Abraham Tower, the Negro, was expressing what white people would have been bound in truth to echo, then and now. "I've knowed a lot of colored, Mr. David, but I ain't never knowed no colored what'd treat a little child bad, and I don't care what color the child is. Maybe they is some, maybe they is, but I ain't ever knowed 'em." [3]

For small boys of that time, the chief happy evidence of spring and the reward for its coming was to get rid of winter clothes, and especially of shoes, and to go barefoot. And for my sister and me the great anticipation for the summer was to go to Carysbrook. Carysbrook was the farm in Fluvanna

[2] *Ibid.*, p. 193.
[3] (New York: Crown Publishers, 1966), p. 654.

County where Cousin Charlie Jones, a widower, and his mother and his three children lived, two boys nearly my age and a girl my sister's age. In the recollection that reaches across the gap of more than seven decades, the journey to Carysbrook and life when we got there are like a slow motion picture seen in dreamy contrast to our present world. The train from Richmond puffed and whistled its smoky progress for some sixty miles along the banks of the James River, stopping at every station, until after two or three hours of growing anticipation for two small passengers it came to what, according to its high-sounding name, might have been a city— to Columbia. Columbia was no city, and most people would have seen there no resemblance to the gates of paradise, but those were the gates that *we* had come to, for Carysbrook lay not far beyond. No matter therefore that Columbia did not look like much: the Chesapeake and Ohio station close to where the Rivanna River flowed into the James, with the sun seeming all the hotter as it was reflected from the yellow paint; in the station the endless clicking of the telegraph instrument which seemed as it came through the open windows to be the only sound in the somnolent afternoon; a dusty road, and the rambling country store with horses and buggies tied to the rack outside. But there also was Cousin Charlie and the children, and the surrey with the fringed top and the two horses; and presently we would all be piled in, and on the way to what to a child was then enchantment.

It was only eight miles to Carysbrook, but the rough dirt road in some stretches was deep also in sand, and there were gates to be opened when the road cut across fenced farms. It might be almost two hours before we came to the border gate of Carysbrook, then across a hilltop pasture where the sheep were feeding, and down into the river valley where among big trees the old house stood: a square brick house with a porch at the middle of the front, a wide hall that ran straight through from the front door to the back, two big square rooms and some smaller rooms on each side of the hall, and a curving stairway leading to a gallery on the second floor from which the bedrooms opened.

A little way down the road to one side was the Rivanna River, with a dam and a mill race and a gristmill where farmers brought their corn to be ground into meal; and between the house and the river was the Carysbrook country store; shaped like a long shoe box, with two rough counters running down the sides from the front door, on the walls rolls of calico and cloth, on the floor a barrel of flour and a barrel of sugar and a keg of nails and a can of kerosene oil, and in one place or another the miscellany of simple things, all the way from a spool of thread to a shovel which people miles away from any other store would have to find. Sometimes they came with a few cents of money, more often also with chickens and eggs to trade. In the front corner of the store was the postoffice to which the mail—such of it as there might be—came from Columbia in its double leather pouch slung in front of the saddle of the mailman on his horse or mule. Once Julian and Tommy Jones and I, having read some melodramatic wild western tale, considered whether it would be a good idea to ambush the mailman, hold him up, and get the gold from California which the mailbags ought properly to be carrying, but then there seemed some doubt as to whether the gold had come that far.

What was there to do at Carysbrook?—nothing, and yet everything to keep a small boy content; the river where the water went over the dam to the pools below; the mill where you could watch the millstones grinding and get covered with the white dust of the ground-up corn; Wesley Kidd, the miller's son, who knew where Indian arrowheads could be found in the lowlands by the river; trees to climb, a dog to play with, an old horse to ride. In the years when Julian and I were old enough to be allowed to use the shotguns, we could buy powder and shot and empty shells at the store, put them together with the crimping machine in the gun room into loaded cartridges and go hunting squirrels. For a small boy there could be the wide-eyed wonder of new adventure—to wake up early in the morning, get the shotgun, slip out of the house alone, walk a mile or more through the lowlands where the air was sweet and fresh and the mists were rising from the fields of corn, pull the rope of the big old bell at the bank of the river and watch the ferryman bring the flat-bottom boat from the other side where he lived, and then go across and into the thick woods where the squirrels were.

Once, many years afterwards, my sister and I drove in a car from Richmond to Columbia. From there to Carysbrook by the paved road took hardly ten minutes, and when we came in sight of Carysbrook the house looked smaller than I thought it was; and as though the whole place, engulfed now in a world from which the old simplicities had vanished, could not have again the remoteness and the mystery which once were there. Life has to go on beyond the child's small involvements, but I realized the wistful meaning in the title of one of the gentle essays of Dr. Samuel M. Crothers, *On the Ignominy of Being Grown-Up*.

The time on Third Street, and the years immediately following in other houses, had their bright interludes, but sometimes they seemed to the small boy who lived through them like a day that inexplicably was becoming overcast and dark. My father, for whom I had a child's complete devotion, was a member of the Stuart Horse Guards, and one day, when he was riding with the troop, his horse shied and threw him forward on the pommel of his saddle. His hurt did not seem

severe at first, but there was an injury which became tuber-
culous. Not much was known then about how tuberculosis
might best be treated, and it may be that no treatment would
have availed. Doctors kept coming to the house, but it did
not seem that they did much good. All that a child's consciousness began dimly to take in was that something calamitous
had happened. My father could not play with me anymore;
my father could not go downtown to his law office; a lot of
the time my father had to stay in bed, and my mother would
be nursing him.

Because my father could not carry on his law practice, income stopped. He could do some typewriting and help in
little occasional matters for other lawyers, and for a while
he taught a small group of boys who came to him for tutoring at home. But the financial burden for the family fell upon
my mother, and with a woman's quiet gallantry she took it
up: baking cakes, making children's dresses to sell at the
Woman's Exchange, and all the while nursing him. The only
book belonging to my father which has come down to me, and
the only thing that carries words which he himself wrote, is
a worn copy of Thomas Hood's *The Song of the Shirt*. On
the cover there is a picture in color of a young woman whose
head has fallen exhausted on some sewing for the finishing
of which she had been working the whole night through—
for in the upper corner of the cover there is a cock crowing
against the sky where the dawn has begun to break. On the
flyleaf my father had written, *Russell to Bess, Dec. '92.
"There's a better time a'coming."* But it did not come.

In 1894, when I was a few days older than twelve, he died;
and as my mother and I came back in the old horse-drawn
hack that was used at funerals, after they had buried him in
Hollywood, it seemed that the hoofbeats of the carriage
horses were echoing in an empty world.

III. Conflict of Ideas

Not long before my father died, my mother had moved with him and my sister and me to a large house at Second and Franklin Streets. Her idea was that she could rent out most of the rooms and thus have some revenue coming in. Also, she fitted up the basement, which had a separate entrance from Franklin Street, into an extensive dining room where she served meals from which she thought she would make enough to meet the rest of the family needs. But the trouble was that her lavish generosity always outran her financial reckonings. The food she put before the boarders won their enthusiastic approval, but anyone with the least look at figures would have seen that what she provided cost more than the boarders paid; and therefore the more of them she had, the worse off she was at each month's end. So a day came when the sheriff appeared to impound such of the family possessions as were saleable, to satisfy the creditors at the grocery store and the markets. Her courage had been unlimited, but business caution was something that her outgoing nature had not been born with.

The problems arising from all that were to have a special consequence for me. My mother's youngest sister, Mary-

Cooke Branch, had married Beverley Bland Munford, senior partner in what was perhaps the leading law firm of Richmond, and their house was not far from where my mother was. She asked my mother to let me come and stay at least for a while with her, which might make the situation at the house on Franklin Street a little less complicated for my mother to manage. This, then, was what happened; and "Aunt Mary-Cooke" became from that time on a new and significant influence for all that would develop for me.

It was she who had been the other figure in relation to my grandmother's loyalties—the loyalties which might give rise, as was suggested in an earlier chapter, to costly collision. Mary-Cooke Branch (she was always called by that hyphenated name), her mother's youngest child, was also her pride and darling. An immense portrait of her as a beautiful little girl in party dress hung in my grandmother's house. As she grew up, she kept her beauty, which everyone admired; but she was also developing an exceptionally inquiring mind, which in some quarters might be less welcomed. Years later, when she wrote a brief personal sketch at the request of the editor of some dictionary of biography, she began with this: "As a child, I helped in the Confederate Bazaar, and went each year with my mother to decorate the soldiers' graves in Hollywood." The inherited loyalties were being passed on to her, but they were to be hers with a difference. She did not revolt from the old traditions and the mores that were bound up with them—as did a friend of hers who exclaimed: "My palate was jaded with the war and that whole period. . . . I have always wished to push it away from me, and go on to a new South, forgetting as much as might be the things that were past." Mary-Cooke Branch could not have expressed herself that way. She did not want to "forget the things that were past"; and she knew that deep down she could not, even

25

if she wanted to. But she did tremendously want "a new South." Of course she had not thought out yet what a new South might involve, but her own face was set in the direction that might lead to it—in the direction of independence, of imagination, of experiment not too easily made afraid. She felt that there was a debt which everybody had to pay to all the great tradition which the South had handed on; but a new generation was rising, and it might pay that debt by something better than decorating soldiers' graves.

New ideas, however, were not popular in Richmond among "the best people." There was much wonderment and considerable shaking of heads when it was learned that Mary-Cooke Branch, and some of the other girls of her group, had established a club for working girls in two rooms which they had rented in a little house on Main Street. She did this because of her sense of responsibility for girls who had fewer advantages than she had, and because of her spontaneous desire to widen her own sympathy and understanding through knowing them. Such books and magazines as the founders of the club could get hold of were put in the club; and the girls met there to play games and talk and discuss. The Y.W.C.A. had not come to Richmond then, and the little club on Main Street was the first venture in the city in the direction of equal contact between girls of different social ranks. "But what did these girls discuss?" the elders were asking, "and what upsetting notions might be in their heads?"

The adjectives "radical" and "socialistic" which have had such horrendous use in later times had not then come into currency; but there was another term which shocked ladies applied to girls whose ideas were considered too advanced. Berta Wellford was one of Mary-Cooke Branch's friends and admirers, and was slightly suspect by her family because she was supposed to share the older girl's unpredictable interests.

One day she came into the room of an aunt of whom she was very fond, and was astonished to find her weeping dismally. "Why, Aunt . . . ," she exclaimed, "What is the matter?" And from the midst of the tears came this ultimate reproach: "I never expected to live to see you grow up strong-minded!"

But as to Mary-Cooke Branch, the chief cause for consternation among her acquaintances was not the founding of the club for working girls, but something further. She wanted to go to college. That was being "strong-minded" to a degree that made Richmond society gasp. To go to college was something that simply was not done by southern women; ergo, it ought not to be done. There might be women's colleges somewhere, but they could be disposed of as "only a Yankee notion." Mary-Cooke did go, it was true, in her older girlhood to a school in New York City—Miss Peebles' school; this excursus outside the region of the late Confederacy was very doubtfully regarded by her mother, but was consented to for the double reason that it was a school of impeccably correct standing, and that her cousin, Effie Branch, was going there. But when the idea of going to college was suggested, Mrs. James Branch was shocked. She could not believe a daughter of hers wanted to do anything so unfeminine. If Mary-Cooke went, it would be over her shamed and indignant protest.

Here was a crisis in the girl's life which tested her character more than almost anything else she was ever called upon to face. She wanted to go to college with a consuming intellectual eagerness, and the strong will which she had already shown to be hers rebelled against an obstacle put in her way. Vassar had been opened in 1861 as the first college for women where they could get an education on a par with that which had long been available elsewhere to men, and her imagination turned toward it with great desire. She knew she could go if she determined to; from her father's will enough income had come to her to make her financially independent. But she saw that her going might make an emotional breach with her mother which perhaps could never be completely healed. She might have risked that breach. "Why not?" she could have said, "it is my own life I have to live." Or she might have tried to tell herself that perhaps her mother was right, and that going to college was somehow an unreasonable matter after all. But neither of these things could she honestly say. The dilemma could not be thus resolved.

Perhaps there is a far-off reflection of her struggle in the pages of an old notebook and scrapbook which she used to keep in a leather-backed cover which has long since dried and crumbled. In it she put all sorts of things that impressed her most—notes of lectures, memoranda of books, quotations of various kinds, and particularly poetry. On one of the earliest pages she had copied out the seven stanzas of Charlotte Perkins Stetson Gilman's *A Conservative*, that brilliant little tour de force, half playful, half sardonic, which described

> A new-fledged butterfly,
>   A-sitting on a thorn,
> A black and crimson butterfly,
>   All doleful and forlorn.

And why "doleful and forelorn"? Because it wanted so much more to stay a caterpillar than to be a butterfly.

> "I do not want to fly," said he,
>   "I only want to squirm!"
> And he drooped his wings dejectedly,
>   But still his voice was firm:
> "I do not want to be a fly!
>   I want to be a worm!" . . .

The last I saw was this,—
The creature madly climbing back
Into his chrysalis.

Mary-Cooke Branch wrote that down, thinking, it may be, as she did so, of herself trying to get free from her own chrysalis and being pushed back into it by devoted but mistaken hands.

For a while the decision hung pathetically in the balance; between reasonableness on the one side, and self-forgetting devotion on the other. At length the daughter realized that nothing she could say and no reason that she could explain would prevent her mother's being hurt if she did what she yet so desperately wanted to do. So she gave up college. It was the first deep and enduring disappointment of her life.

But it is one of the deep facts of life that what at the moment seems only calamitous may become instead creative. If Mary-Cooke Branch had allowed herself to be embittered, the frustration of her desire to go to college would have been calamitous. But her imagination went out toward others who might be deprived of what she had so intensely wanted for herself—toward all young people, and especially the girls, who might be craving the chance to learn and grow. She would help *them* to school and college. And in subsequent pages there will be told what she did.

IV. Boys, and Some Makers of Men

The public school system of Richmond in the late 1880's was only in the slow first stages of development toward an excellence which it has since attained; but even if the public schools had been better than they were, there was a somewhere-else to which many parents, including mine, wanted their boys to go. It was "to McGuire's," the private school which was unique because of the personality of the man who had started it from nothing, and who was to put his stamp on Richmond boys for forty-five years.

John Peyton McGuire was born in 1836, and having finished school and graduated at the University of Virginia, he had come back to teach at the Episcopal High School in Alexandria, where his father was the principal. In 1861 war broke out between the North and the South. When Virginia seceded from the Union and joined the other Southern States in the Confederacy, the Episcopal High School on its hill from which the city of Washington and the capitol were in plain view only six or seven miles away, became part of what must almost immediately be the battlefront. This meant the closing of the school, and the scattering of its boys and its faculty, including all the McGuire family.

Where the young John P. McGuire went first when the school was closed is not clear, but before long he was a lieutenant in the Confederate service. When the Confederacy came to an end in 1865, the gray uniform he had on was about all that he possessed—except his loyalty to the principles he thought Virginia had been fighting for. The struggle was finished, but not certain great inspirations which had come out of it. With John P. McGuire, as with many others of his time, there was a hero-worship for Robert E. Lee: Lee the commander whom his troops had gloried in when he had led them to victories, but for whom they had an even more passionate admiration when they saw how he bore defeat. After the surrender at Appomattox, Lee had accepted the presidency of what is now Washington and Lee University, but then was only little Washington College, its buildings in Lexington stripped and pillaged during the war by occupying troops, its material resources next to nothing, with only four professors and forty students to constitute its life. Corporations outside Virginia had offered to Lee money, land, and corporation stock if he would give his name and his endorsement to various enterprises about to be set on foot. He turned all such solicitations aside. "I have a self-imposed task which I must accomplish," he said to the trustees of the college. "I have led the young men of the South in battle; I have seen many of them die on the field. I shall devote my remaining energies to training young men to do their duty in life."

When John P. McGuire took off his uniform, no large profitable opportunities were held out to him. It might have been said that the reason he turned to teaching was that this was the only thing in sight for him to do. However that may have been, he was the kind of person who took what might have been obscure and made it into something shining, so that in what he taught and in the way he taught it he exerted an

31

influence over boys, and—as they grew up to be men—over a whole community, such as is not often equalled anywhere. And the striking part of it is that material things, and the equipment assumed in more opulent times to be necessary for a good school, had nothing to do with what he did.

At first the school was on Gamble's Hill, but when I first knew it, it had moved to Belvidere and Main Streets, and established itself there under conditions which would make the up-to-date educator not know whether to laugh or to cry. In a two-story brick building at the corner of the two streets, the ground floor was a grocery store. On the second floor was McGuire's School. What was the entrance to it, and the exit too, by which some two hundred boys came and went at Mr. McGuire's bidding? A wooden stairway at the back of the building, behind the grocery store. And what did you find when you got to the top of the stairs and went inside? One huge room with wooden desks, at one end of it a raised platform with Mr. McGuire's seat at the center of it, and in front of it, and running the width of the platform, a long curved bench, where the boys whom Mr. McGuire himself had at that hour in class sat facing him, with their backs to the rest of the room. Along one side of the big barn-like study hall were windows opening out on Main street; on the other side, three classrooms where the assistant teachers had the boys who belonged to them for the schedule of lessons and recitations that ran through the hours of the school day. That was the habitation of the school—that, and nothing more; except that on the side of the school away from Main Street there was a small open space, and on the other side an ordinary little house where Mr. and Mrs. McGuire lived. What could have happened if the incredible old firetrap had ever actually caught on fire would have been horrifying to imagine; but it never did catch on fire, and nobody seemed to bother to think that it might. Mr. McGuire's school was just not supposed to have anything untoward happen to it.

Mr. McGuire was a little, round man who appeared like a benevolent, less well-fed Santa Claus, yet who had in his eyes a look of command which no boy ever mistook. In talking to one another—not to him—the school called him "the Boss," or in later years, "Old Boss." When he had a class on the curved bench before him, none of the class nor any of the boys at their desks in the big room were unaware of his presence. If he darted at a boy a sudden question, and caught that boy in a yawn or looking sideways and beginning to stammer some vague reply, he would drop his glasses down on his nose, look at the boy over the rims, and pronounce what became a by-word in the school, "Inattention is the unpar-r-rdonable sin," and the culprit would be kept in after school to study some particular lesson and to contemplate ruefully his misdemeanor. Learning was important, and no one should be allowed to take it lightly. When a boy was really trying, the Boss could be endlessly patient and encouraging, but if a boy were lazy and trifling he was brought up short. Nobody who had been long in the school had failed to hear, nor could ever quite forget, what Mr. McGuire said that General Lee had said: "Duty is the sublimest word in the English language." To train a generation of boys to see their duty, to recognize it, and to live up to it, was the one purpose to which the Boss was dedicated with all his soul.

With a simple faith, he believed in God; and as a devout Episcopalian, at every Communion Service on Sundays in St. James's Church he would repeat the words of the Book of Common Prayer, "Therefore with Angels and Archangels, and with all the company of heaven, we laud and magnify thy glorious Name." But it can be believed that in the picture of heaven which John P. McGuire held in his mind, no angel or archangel, not even the Archangel Michael, stood closer to the Throne than Robert E. Lee. If the boys and men of Virginia could in any substantial way be brought to reflect his spirit of service, then all might be well.

Few if any of the Boss's boys fulfilled his best hopes; but still fewer were those who could be quite impervious to one impression which he gave. Here was a man who belonged to a generation which had been impoverished by the War. Many individuals would have thought that their first need, and a legitimate one, was to get out of poverty; but this man never did. It never seemed to occur to John P. McGuire that he might set the tuition rates in his school at a scale sufficient to give him even a securely comfortable living. To be sure, in the first years after the War he knew that hardly any families in Richmond had money enough to pay anything adequate for the education of their boys; but even in later years, when conditions had become different, he had become so used to spartan simplicity for himself that he was not interested in material rewards. If the suits he appeared in were worn, if the walls in his house needed repapering and the furniture needed mending, that did not matter too much—not as much as giving his whole self to the school. People who knew him might think he was very impractical to keep on being poor; but they could never forget that they had seen a man who in his absorption with the immaterial side of life which seemed to him to matter most had been "as poor, yet many rich." The boy who had been to McGuire's School had something that could lift his standards and his scale of values when he remembered that.

After McGuire's it seemed that I should go off to boarding school. First there was a year at Bellevue, in the open country looking up to the Peaks of Otter between Lynchburg and

Roanoke; and part of a year at Woodberry Forest, cut short by an illness. Then, in 1897, I found myself for the first time out of Virginia, at The Hill School, in Pottstown, Pennsylvania, where I was to feel the impress of another great schoolmaster whom those who knew him can never forget.

John Meigs had taken the school at first unwillingly. His father, Matthew Meigs, had gathered a few boys into the old stone family residence that stood at the edge of town looking out over the Schuylkill River. In 1876, when the father could no longer carry on, he called upon his son, who had just graduated from Lafayette College, taken also his Ph.D. and become an instructor on the college faculty, to come home and take his place. At the moment, it was the last thing the son would have chosen to do. The school was insignificant. Why should he tie himself to that? His abilities and his promise of success seemed to lie along another line. His own inclination was toward journalism, though his friends might have said that he belonged in the world of big business, where his driving force and his imagination could accomplish conspicuous results. But he yielded to his father's wish, and his mother's plea, and returned to take charge of the school. To distinguish him from the elder Dr. Meigs, his father, he was spoken of as "Professor" (or by the boys, when he was not around, as "the Prof"). Under whatever title, he was to bring to the school not only the practical abilities which his friends saw, but other personal qualities developing in him which neither he nor his friends knew surely that he possessed.

When first encountered, John Meigs—as most of those who met him would have been bound to admit—was not prepossessing: a thickset man with a very broad brow over deep-set eyes, and a nose so wide and flat that it looked as though he must sometime have run headlong into a wall and mashed it down. His mouth and chin had the power which his whole head and body suggested. Power he did have, and he could be passionate and hot-tempered. In the long years when he was head of the school, any boy or man might tremble if, for something he had done amiss, he were summoned into John Meigs's formidable presence.

That was one side of the man; and it was this man-of-affairs side which had to be called into action most conspicuously at the beginning. Under the different conditions and the different expectations in the North, it would have been impossible for any school to grow—or even to exist—with the meagre equipment which a community in the South accepted as the best it could expect. Therefore, John Meigs set himself to the demanding task of expanding the school physically, and strengthening it financially. He was not trying to make money for himself, and he never did, for he put back into the school and its development every amount which year by year he might be able to make it earn. And by great administrative ability and by immense energy he did expand the school's lands and buildings and magnify its resources to such a point that when at length he gave it all to the alumni, to be incorporated and controlled by them, he had built an institution which both in its physical fabric and in its academic excellence was superlative.

This matter of academic excellence meant rigorous standards both for the boys and for the men chosen to be their teachers in the school. To both boys and men John Meigs could seem relentless. Boys knew that he would not tolerate indifference or shuffling evasion in regard to what they were supposed to study and to learn; and equally the masters knew that much would be required of them. George Q. Sheppard, who taught at The Hill for nearly his entire life, once described the first

36

teachers' meeting he attended, at the end of the first week of classes after the school year had begun.

We had been told in the dining room as we were at dinner that the meeting would be held. Without a word of explanation the Professor opened the big record book and began to call the roll of the boys alphabetically, expecting us instantly to report upon each boy whom we had taught, stating whether he had made A, B, C, or D for the week, while he recorded our reports. Naturally there was hesitation in answering, since we had not been informed previously of the demand to be made upon us. Having finished the roll with some show of annoyance at our delays, he said, "Gentlemen, we shall have such a meeting directly after dinner at the end of each week, and you are to come prepared to report promptly on each one of your boys. The meeting should not occupy more than twenty minutes." Each of us, including the Professor, taught twenty-five recitations per week. Yet we were to be prepared to report on each boy directly after dinner. The noteworthy point is that we *did it*. How often have I visited schools which needed a John Meigs to wake up masters and boys and show them what they *could* do, a point on which they seemed absolutely ignorant.

It is said of certain captains in the Navy that "they run a taut ship." John Meigs ran a taut ship at The Hill; and everybody knew what was expected of him and that he had better play his part.

By all this the boys were benefited. But a Headmaster who had been a builder and an executive only would not have affected their deeper selves. The thing which made John Meigs's influence great was that he had another side. The boys might see him first as a man of action, but they came to know him as a man of deep emotions too. Along with his drive and his hot temper were the surging impulses of a big and generous heart. One of his boys wrote of him, "He was just human; got mad quickly, forgave twice as quickly; knew and recognized the boys' code of justice, and what was more, lived up to it." If there had been some explosion of his anger and he found that he had been wrong, he was filled with a humbling contrition, and he would pour himself out to make amends. He was sensitive to any suffering, and met it with a quick compassion and an instant eagerness to help; and for all little children he had a tenderness which drew them to him with instinctive trust.

Such a person, awesome yet deeply lovable, he was in his own essential nature—a nature into which the different qualities of his father and his mother both had entered. But he would not have become all that he did become without another influence which made the best part of him develop and expand. That influence came through the woman who would be his wife. Marion Butler of New York was the girl he fell in love with; and when she went abroad to study, he followed her to Germany, won her, was married to her in Berlin, and brought her back with him to The Hill. There she was to be known to generations of Hill boys as Mrs. John, and to be linked equally with the Professor in the spirit and traditions of the school. She had character and conviction as strong as his, and at the same time her woman's instinctive gentleness. She liked human beings as such, including even the unpromising ones; and when a boy looked into her eyes he knew that she was looking not only at but into him, and waking up something within him which he had not felt before. She had no official position in the organization of the school, but she was part of its whole life. If she walked in the crowd that was on its way to chapel, or if she played the piano for a dance in the gymnasium, everybody felt the kindling difference because of her being there. The influence which she had upon the group as a whole could also be particular and personal. Her own religion was a glowing thing, and she could transmit the life of it to some boy whom she would take the chance to talk to—a boy who needed to find a purpose and a strength which he had not had. Characteristic of her influence was what happened with one individual long remembered on The Hill, fullback of the school football team, and afterward one of the most noted athletes in the history of Yale, but at first a problem boy, charming but unpredictable, careless in study, undisciplined, and rebellious. Mrs. John's searching affection woke the unguessed possibilities in him; and to the astonishment of those who had first known him, he became in early middle age the headmaster of another school for boys to which in great measure he carried the spirit of The Hill.

John Meigs would have expressed in his life and work a religious dedication even if there had been no Mrs. John, for that was the sort of man he was; but in subtle ways he became a warmer and more winsome person because of her. Two disastrous fires at the school, and the death of two little daughters, tried and enlarged the courage and faith with which they met all things together. Boys in the school could not have described it, but when they watched him meet the hard tests which changing conditions brought they knew what strength and steadiness could be. Many would carry into after years the remembered sight and sound of the whole school gathering for the brief morning prayer with which the Professor always opened the school day. In the big study hall, along the side walls, were busts of great figures of history and literature, put there to make the everyday studies have more meaning; but on the wall at the head of the room was a great framed print of a painting of Christ. It was in front of this that the Professor would be standing, and this was the passage from the New Testament which he read so often that the echo of his voice still seems to sound in its words for boys who listened to him then:

Finally, brethren, whatsoever things are true, whatsoever things are honest, whatsoever things are just, whatsoever things are pure, whatsoever things are lovely, whatsoever things are of good report; if there be any virtue, and if there be any praise, *think* on these things. (KJV)

In 1900, when I graduated from the school, John Meigs was at the peak of his strength and effectiveness. But in December, 1901, in the Christmas vacation when all the boys were away, a fire started in one of the buildings and threatened all one morning to destroy the whole school. That involved an immediate and heavy problem of rearrangement and reconstruction; but far more critical than that was what came before another year was ended. There broke out an epidemic which took the lives of five boys, among them one of the leaders of the school for whom Professor and Mrs. John had deep personal devotion. What he suffered then affected him so profoundly that he slept restlessly, and would cry out sometimes at night in words that showed his dreams were tracing again the experiences which had put an indelible mark upon his spirit. Physically his heart began to trouble him, and he had moments of agonizing pain which made him sometimes irritable beyond his immediate control. He recognized this and sought continually to overcome it. Once at evening prayers in the schoolroom, in a more than usually self-revealing way he had poured out an appeal for patience and for strength. As he came down the aisle when prayers were over, his quick eye caught a boy in some petty misbehavior, and he loosed upon him a thunderbolt of indignation. "How could you have done that just after praying for patience?" one of his family asked

40

him; and he answered, "Why should I pray for it except that I need it terribly?"

His doctors put him on a rigid diet, which he hated but as to which he said to a friend who asked him whether accepting it was not very hard, "Anything is easy which you make up your mind to do." More onerous than the diet were the doctor's orders that he must increasingly take periods of rest, including trips to Bad Nauheim in Germany where the waters were supposed to do him good. It was these times of absence from the school which distressed him most, and his great longing always was to get back.

At the beginning of the school session in 1911 he was at his post, and thought he was better; but on a Sunday evening in early November he did not feel strong enough to go to the chapel service, but sat at a window looking out toward the chapel—it having been a beautiful, still autumn day—and sang the hymns with the unseen congregation as the sound of them floated across the space between. On Monday he was back at work, but that night in his room he suddenly called Mrs. John's name, and before she reached him he had gone.

The next day, as the body of the great Headmaster lay in the quiet room, there was brought to Mrs. John from one of the masters this note:

As Stanton said, when he closed the eyes of Lincoln, "Now he belongs to the ages," so in regard to Professor, there are, I am sure, some who believe that now he belongs to the school.

In the chapel porch, on the right of the entrance, with an exposure to the east, and an outlook upon all the larger buildings, is a cloistered spot where I wish he might lie. There, just a little to the Sixth's right, beyond the wall, he would still be their guide and counsellor. There, as the boys passed in to service, he would still lead them to the truth; and there at his side, at the opening of many a schoolboy's life, would be transmitted, from father to son,

41

the ideals which he praised, and the school traditions to which he gave so much.

It is late. Doubtless I intrude, and there are certain objections, but I am

Yours truly

P.S. Matthew Arnold, in his inspiring *Rugby Chapel*, adds his silent plea that even in what we call death, the school may not lose its leader. Some of us need him near. The school will rally about his grave, as he rallied the school about himself. (My personal debt to him and to the school may not be relevant, but life for me has begun again here.) It is for the boys of twenty years hence, as well as for these men of tomorrow, that I write.

That request prevailed. The body of John Meigs lies buried in the floor of the chapel cloister, with a flat stone above his grave; and on a tablet on the wall is this inscription:

JOHN MEIGS
Master of Boys
Maker of Men
Servant of Christ

⚜ ⚜

His Courage was the Foundation of this School
His Passion for Truth its Light

In the school years the final great influence which came to me was that of a man who came to The Hill only once a year. It was Professor's custom to invite to The Hill for the Sunday chapel services some of the most distinguished ministers of America, and among these was Maltbie Davenport Babcock, of Baltimore; and later, up to the time of his early and tragic death, of the Brick Church in New York City. When he was in college one of his friends asked him what he expected to do after he graduated. He answered, "I have always thought I would like to study medicine, but I think my mother may pray me into the ministry." Certainly his mother did her best; but when he had made the decision she had longed for, something had happened within him which was the shining opposite of any imaginable constraint. On the flyleaf of his pocket Bible, found after his death, he had written, "Committed myself again with Christian brothers to unreserved docility and devotion before my Master." It was that complete devotion to the service of Christ which made him what he was. Looking at him, one thought of what the first disciples may have been: of the power of a Peter, the compassion of a John. He had natural endowments such as few human beings have: quickness of mind, flashing humor, a love of music and of all beautiful things, spontaneous eagerness both in work and play. Just in his natural self he would have been magnetic, but the joyousness of his religious dedication made him incandescent. "Henceforth I live, yet not I, but Christ liveth in me," the apostle Paul had written, and in this man one felt the sudden reality of those words. It was no wonder that he woke the quick, instinctive hero-worship that is latent in the hearts of boys. Tall, handsome, vibrant, when he walked through the halls of the school, boys trailed along beside him. When he preached in chapel they listened to him with excited fascination because he could bring home to each one of them, as Thomas Arnold did to the boys at Rugby, "perhaps for the first time, the meaning of his life; that it was no fool's or sluggard's paradise into which he had wandered by chance, but a battlefield ordained from of old, where there are no spectators, but the youngest must take his side, and the stakes are life and death."

It was because of him that there first came to me the idea of the ministry as a magnet that might lay hold of me.

V. Harvard 1904

Graduating from The Hill, I went on in the fall to be a freshman at Harvard. That, fortunately, was in the beginning of the century when getting into college was a fairly simple matter. If it had been true then, as it is now, that only one in six who apply at Harvard manage to be admitted, I might never have got there. But in September, 1900, I was there—even if topographically on what seemed the outer fringe of things. Most of The Hill boys went to Yale or Princeton. Only four of us came that year to Harvard; and except for the other three out of that four, I knew nobody in the whole place. I had applied for a room in the Yard, but what I drew was a room in Conant, out on Oxford Street, a location where nobody but men in the nearby Law School particularly wanted to be.

To a lonely freshman, Harvard at first was disappointing: disappointing in its look, and in its human lack. The beautiful new Houses along the Charles River had not then been built, or even thought of. The Yard seemed almost the extent of Harvard. The old buildings had the dignity and charm of age, but the nineteenth-century ones were commonplace and crowded. Massachusetts Avenue and Harvard Square, bordering the Yard, were stark and ugly. There were no long vistas to satisfy the eye or to stir imagination. And to one who had come from the warm and close-knit life of The Hill School, college seemed impersonal and blank, as though no one cared particularly whether you were there or not. You had to wait until there were widening friendships, and until you began to feel the great academic stimulus to which you could make response.

The first affair that began to bring me into touch with a new group in the college was the call for candidates for *The Crimson*, the undergraduate daily newspaper. A convenient way to assemble news, convenient for the men already comfortably on the editorial staff, was to have the candidates go out and get it—if not to imagine and invent it, as candidates were tempted sometimes to do. The freshman, or freshmen, who brought in the largest amount of material for news and submitted it in decent written form might be elected at the end of the semester to *The Crimson* Board, after which he or they could mostly rest in peace while a succession of other candidates carried on what had been done before. It took a lot of time that first semester, but I got to know my way around the college; and by the end of that fall term I "made it," and henceforth could see my name on the more-than-needfully-numerous list of the established *Crimson* staff. It was a good group of men to be with. Joe Grew, who years afterwards was to be Ambassador to Japan, was already on the Board; and the freshman who was elected next after me was Franklin D. Roosevelt.

Chasing news, or the rumor that had to be followed toward a supposed source of news as an infatuated beagle follows a scent, kept me more engrossed in *The Crimson* enterprise through those first months than I was engrossed in History 1 or English 1, or the other college studies I was supposed to be pursuing. But later I came into contact with some of the great

45

figures on the Harvard faculty who would wake a response from almost anybody.

There was William James, who in my sophomore year gave in Edinburgh his Gifford Lectures which when published became the famous *Varieties of Religious Experience*, and to whom I listened in the junior year when he divided the periods in Philosophy 4 with Münsterberg and Josiah Royce.

There was Barrett Wendell, a Boston Bourbon, who had somehow possessed himself of an Oxford accent so foreign to everyday American talk that he might have been playing a character part on the British stage; Barrett Wendell who as you listened to him as he lectured and as he twirled the watch chain he wore across his vest you might have thought affected; but when you went to his office to hear his judgment on "the daily themes" which he made everybody regularly hand in, you found him to be so kindly in his interest and so searching in his criticism that you began to say to yourself, "Perhaps this man can teach me how to write!"

Then when the bell rang for the designated hours of English 2, the crowd would be trampling in a hurry up the stairs to the second floor of Harvard Hall, to run no chance of being like the foolish virgins who came too late and found that "the door was shut." For George Lyman Kittredge, the formidable "Kitty," when he was ready to begin his lecture on *Hamlet* or *Macbeth* or *Romeo and Juliet* or whatever else might be the subject that day in his famous course on Shakespeare, would tolerate no interruption. He strode back and forth on his platform, pouring out his erudition, looking—with his piercing blue eyes and his handsome, square white beard—as a Norse Viking might have looked, and all the while never letting his absorption in his theme make him unaware of what was going on in front of him. One day a man who arrived after a lecture had begun and did not want to miss it crept on his hands and knees up an aisle when he thought Kitty was not looking, and slipped into a vacant seat—only to be greeted by the icy proclamation, "The gentleman who has just entered the room will now go out of it in the same manner by which he came in." It was Kittredge who, when he was once asked why he had never taken a Ph.D. degree, gave the imperial answer, "Who could have examined me?"

Two other superlative figures in the Harvard of those years I never knew in a classroom, but no one could have been unaware of them or failed to feel their presence.

One was Le Baron R. Briggs, Professor of English and also Dean of the College in charge of student discipline. A man in that position had no cards stacked in his favor toward being popular, but it was of Dean Briggs that *The Lampoon* once wrote

> Of all the sprightly figures that adorn our college scene
> The most supremely genial is our own beloved Dean;
> He'll kick you out of college, and he'll never shed a tear,
> But he does it so politely that it's music to the ear.

The other, and the greatest, was the President, Charles William Eliot. One did not often come into contact with him, but the whole place seemed to have a larger dignity when you saw him as he walked across the Yard. A great red birthmark on his face which might have been a disfigurement somehow became a distinction, and in the austere carriage of his head he looked as a Roman emperor might have looked. No doubt he had warmth which those who were close to him felt, but the chief impression which he gave to the college generally was of sovereign conviction and authority. Nor was there any occasion for moral judgment from which he would flinch. He had a profound dislike for Henry Cabot Lodge, whom he believed to have destroyed the League of Nations by preventing America's entrance into it, and to have done so because of the personal feud he fomented with Woodrow Wilson. In later years, when the Harvard Corporation voted an honorary degree to Lodge, and Charles William Eliot as President was obliged, unwillingly, to confer it, it is reported that this is what he said:

Henry Cabot Lodge
Senator from the Commonwealth of
Massachusetts, from 1893 to the
present time,
With a great career of generous
Public service *still inviting him.*

After freshman year I was able to move nearer the center of things, to a room in a building not then owned by the College but on Massachusetts Avenue, opposite the Yard; and for junior and senior years I had the satisfaction of being in Holworthy, one of the oldest of the dormitories, which in the color of its old brick and in its simple lines made you conscious of the long past in which the life of Harvard rooted. Holworthy 7 was on the southwest corner of the fourth floor, the top floor. The two front windows of the large square room that was the study looked down the length of the Yard, and one side window out upon Phillips Brooks House. Back of the study were two small bedrooms, where in the wintertime my roommate Artley B. Parson and I had no impulse to linger except when each was well covered up in his bed; for both rooms faced north and neither had any heat. The only heat in the study was from the open grate where we kept a coal fire

48

burning; and the shower bath for our entry opened from the stairway between the third floor and our fourth. Dick Child, who gave the Ivy Oration in 1903, summed up the situation sardonically when he said,

> 'Tis in the yard convenience suits the price.
> They have two kinds of water, cold and ice;
> There cleanliness to godliness is nigh,
> For virtue takes a bath prepared to die.

As a matter of fact, we kept near enough to being comfortable, and entirely healthy, and it was good to know that we were linked with the long succession of men who had lived in those rooms and had given them an aura of association which no new buildings outside the Yard possessed.

A short distance back of Holworthy was Memorial Hall, in its exterior architecture a lamentable specimen of Victorian Gothic; but the great interior space had dignity in its loftiness and length, and on its walls were portraits, a few of them very fine and some of them just old and queer, of men who had been part of the history of Harvard and New England. In more recent times the Hall has been downgraded to occasional use, and for the most part is empty and unnoticed; but in the early 1900's it was one of the places where the students ate. Its bill of fare was not such as to create any glowing anticipation, but it was where men you liked sat down together three times a day. The group of us who had taken a sort of proprietorship of "Table 30" were congenial, not so much because of any identity of interests but rather because of differences and variety: some looking forward to law school, some to business; the quiet and meditative George Plimpton Adams, who would be a professor of philosophy at the University of California; the eager and warmhearted Kendall K.

Smith, who was to become widely known as an archaeologist and scholar in the history and literature of Greece; Walter Sachs, whose brother would presently be the curator of the Fogg Art Museum at Harvard, but who himself was headed toward a partnership in the powerful Wall Street financial firm of Goldman, Sachs; James P. Leake, who in the Surgeon General's Department would be an expert in the field of communicable diseases; Arthur A. Ballantine, prominent at the bar in New York City, and in Washington, Assistant Secretary of the Treasury. And most memorable of all, Francis William Bird—most memorable even though he had so little time for the material of memories to form. The poignant human fact in the early part of the twentieth century was the loss of brave young manhood in many countries through the years of the first World War; most tragically so in England, less widely, but not less pitiably when it happened, here in this country too. Billy Bird did not die on a military battlefield, but he died after having played an intense part in a battle no less real. As a young lawyer in New York, he had thrown his full energy into the recurrent struggle for social and political decency, and had played a significant part in making possible the all-too-brief administration of John Purroy Mitchel as Mayor of the City of New York. When he died of pneumonia in the influenza epidemic of 1918, the country lost a man who might have gone far and played a creative part in the possibilities for our time. Clear thinking, strong in his convictions, resolute in action, he would have brought increasingly into American politics and public life the sort of disciplined idealism which James Russell Lowell wrote of in his "Commemoration Ode."

> Unfathomed by the cynic's sneer,
> Something that gives our feeble light
> A high immunity from Night, . . .

A seed of sunshine that can leaven
Our earthly dullness with the beams of
    stars,
        And glorify our clay
With light from fountains elder than the
    Day.

In the University chapel on Sundays there usually were invited guest preachers, men who often gave reason to be remembered. Among them was Lyman Abbott, then already an old man, but a force in American thinking. Tall and thin and frail, with a long waterfall of white beard, to the supercilious he might have looked like an elderly goat; but to those who listened, he looked and sounded like a prophet.

In Trinity Church, Boston, the mighty memories of Phillips Brooks still hovered—Phillips Brooks, who according to the tablet in his memory at Harvard "brought by his life and doctrine fresh faith to a people, fresh meaning to ancient creeds"; and in Emmanuel Church on Newbury Street was the fiery Leighton Parks, who made it plain that the Christian pulpit need not be afraid of righteous controversy.

The Harvard lecture rooms, "Table 30," Phillips Brooks House—these were some of the centers of my controlling interest and companionship. The other was *The Crimson.* For two years after my period as a candidate, I did not have much to do. Then in junior year I became one of the two assistant managing editors. Our responsibility, together with the managing editor, was to have charge of the content and makeup of the paper two nights each a week. The other one of the two was Franklin Roosevelt. One of us after the assistantship experience would be elected managing editor. The Board chose Roosevelt for one semester and me for the one following. (It was perhaps the first election he won, which was to be followed by many others more important.) When we were seniors, each of us was president of *The Crimson* for half the year, which meant that we wrote the editorials and shaped the policy of the paper.

No one, I think, in those days had any premonition that Frank Roosevelt might some day be President of the United States. Gay and charming and debonair, he did not give one the impression then of special force. But there was one quality, to be conspicuous in later years, which was already evident then. He had the warm gift of making men like him and want to do what he would have them do. *The Crimson* offices were in the basement of the Harvard Union, and across the hall two rough-diamond printers, Mac and Ed, rented space for their job-printing, including *The Crimson*. Like most other human beings, their principal interest at the end of a long day was to get work finished and go home to bed. If any one of us—other than Roosevelt—had to hold up the starting of the presses, there was sure to be a stormy scene. But if Roosevelt were in charge on a particular night, he could go into the printing shop with that flashing smile of his and call out to Mac and Ed, "See here now and listen to *this!* Here's some late news that *is* news, and can make you proud to be working on this paper. Get the forms off the press till we can make room and put this in." Mac and Ed would scowl, spit tobacco juice disgustedly, pour out some quick profanity—then look at Frank Roosevelt, grin, break up the forms, and reset a column of type.

No one could foresee then the events that would make Roosevelt strong enough to become a great figure in his country's history. I think it was his infantile paralysis, and the invincible courage which grew in him as he set himself to try to overcome it; and along with that the limitless devotion of the magnificent Eleanor, the woman who was his wife.

In June of 1904 my years at Harvard were finished. Perhaps because I had been an editor of *The Crimson,* I had been elected as one of the Class Day officers. The stadium had been built that year, and it so happened that I was to be the first person ever to speak in it at a public function. It had been determined that the "Ivy Oration" should be given there, and I was the Ivy Orator. It had ceased to have anything to do with the old traditional planting of the ivy, and the Oration was supposed now to be humorous. Out in the sunlight of the June afternoon I tried to make it that, but under the jester's cap and bells there inevitably had to be also something else. No one could stand there and not be deeply aware of all that Harvard had given him: friendships that would last a long time, the provocation of great minds on the faculty for whom that one word *Veritas* on the college seal had been like a Grail which they pursued; and for four years the chance to study and learn and try to grow. It had *not* needed to be a fact, as one of the presidents of Harvard in a moment of wry humor had suggested, that "it was no wonder that Harvard is such a great reservoir of learning, because the freshmen bring so much knowledge in and the seniors take so little out."

VI. Enter, Jean

In 1904, with graduation from Harvard, the years of school and college had come to an end. They had brought me very much for which to be thankful. I did not know that in that summer there would come to me something more, and unimagined.

There were three older friends of mine to whom I owed much, and to whom I was to owe now a conjunction of events which had a quicker consequence than they could have foreseen. Two of them, Mary D. Safford, "Miss Mae," and Mary R. Sanford, "Miss Sant," whose generosity had largely made possible my years at Harvard, had been visiting in the previous summer at Wianno, on Cape Cod; and the friend in whose house they had stayed was Katherine Babcock, the widow of the beloved Maltbie D. Babcock, who had died in the winter of my freshman year. While Miss Mae and Miss Sant were in Wianno, they met a girl whose family, like the Babcocks, had been a part of the longtime summer colony on the Cape. One day they told me about her. Her name was Jean Laverack, of Buffalo, New York.

When I was leaving Cambridge that June, Mrs. Babcock invited me to come to see her, for she knew of the admiration

I had had for "the Dominie," as many who loved him called him; and once when I was at The Hill School, I had been invited to Baltimore to spend a weekend in their house. So now I was to have the chance to see her again. I did not know until I arrived that she intended also to have another visitor, the daughter of a family which in almost every summer had been in their own house in Wianno, but would not be there this year. Her name, she said, was Jean Laverack.

On the afternoon of July 4th the local liveryman, who met the trains that came to the station at West Barnstable, drove up the sandy road to Mrs. Babcock's house, bringing a girl who had come from Buffalo by way of Boston. Now for the first time the name I had heard became an actuality: slender, tall, blue-eyed, with the glowing complexion which was a heritage from her ancestors in England two generations back.

Neither of us had seen the other before; and for her part, she had never known that I existed and had no particular interest now in the fact that I did. But it appeared before long that we had some things in common. Dr. Babcock, there at Wianno, on the tennis court, in his sailboat, in the midst of all the happy outdoor activities, as well as in the readings-aloud and the discussions in which he was the spontaneous leader, had been a hero to her in the Cape Cod summers, as he had been to me when he came on Sundays to The Hill. Because we remembered him and could talk about him, and because we were both of us there in Mrs. Babcock's house, we found that we responded to the same sort of people. I discovered that she had had two brothers in Harvard, one of whom had been a senior and the captain of the hockey team the year I entered as a freshman. I had never known either one of them, but the fact that they had been there indicated that she must have the proper loyalties and was not tied up with individuals who belonged to such unacceptable places as

Yale or Princeton or what have you. I found that she had not gone to college, but had intensely wanted to. After earlier schools in Buffalo, she had gone to the Baldwin School in Bryn Mawr and had loved it. She was all ready to enter Bryn Mawr College, but had some trouble with her back which had required a severe operation, so that it seemed that for the year or two that followed she ought not to be away from home. Then she had studied kindergartening, and had taken charge of the little children in a settlement house in the Polish district of Buffalo. She was having a grand time with the children and in getting to know the immigrant parents, because she had been quick to see what was fine as well as what was funny in their foreign ways.

In front of Mrs. Babcock's house the narrow strip of lawn ended in a sandy bluff that dropped down a few feet to the shore, and to the wide expanse of Narragansett Sound. To the eye it seemed to be the unbroken ocean, for the islands that protected the Sound lay invisible beyond the outermost horizon; but though the islands thus were distant, they broke the surge of the open sea, and on the beaches of Wianno there was seldom any heavy surf, but rather a slow and tranquil rhythm of the incoming and withdrawing water that made a continual gentle murmur on the sands. It was a place in which you did not need to *do* much to be happy; it was good just to be still and to enjoy the salt air and the fragrance of the pines that fringed the shores of the Cape and to absorb the beauty of the sky and the sun and the sea. I was content with that, and seemingly this girl was too. We read aloud sometimes with Mrs. Babcock or talked and listened to her as she told us more about the Dominie; we walked along the beach or at the edge of the bluff through the pines, or went in swimming when the tide was in. And then it happened—as the romantic imaginations of Miss Mae and Miss Sant and Mrs. Babcock had foreseen that it might. Jean Laverack, who had been only a name to me, was a person now who had laid hold upon my mind and heart. In short, I was in love with her; and before the eight days in Wianno were over, she knew exactly how I felt.

No others knew then or would know soon; and that so much should have been arrived at in so short a time might have seemed to most others to be craziness. I was only one month out of college, with no "prospects" nor any certain road ahead. Who was I to ask a girl if someday she would marry me? But when two people find one another, there is something better than caution and calculation. And if telling Jean Laverack at the end of that Wianno week what I felt about her was craziness, then all a lifetime since has brought increasing gain from being crazy.

VII. Life in the Virginia Seminary

John Meigs had let me know that he would welcome me back to The Hill as an old boy who might find out now whether he could be a teacher. So in the fall of 1904 I did go back, and for that academic year I was part of the school staff, and saw the Professor from a new angle which made me admire him all the more.

Jean, of course, was not there. We would not see each other soon; and for the next months we would not even write except now and then. If the bond between us held in spite of that hard discipline, we should know that in the days at Wianno there had been no shallow emotion, but deep calling to deep.

The most decisive fact in that year at The Hill was the gradual maturing of the possibility which had dawned upon my imagination when Dr. Babcock had come there and I had seen him and listened to him as a boy. I would go into the ministry too, if I could get there; even if it meant a long time in preparation. So when I went to Richmond in one of the school vacations, I saw the Bishop of Virginia and told him what I had in mind. The result was that in the fall of 1905 I found myself getting off a train at Alexandria, and looking toward the queer old tower of the Virginia Seminary on the skyline three miles away.

I had never seen the Seminary before, and I thought I knew nobody in it. I took for granted that it must be a very holy place, inhabited probably by individuals of such unearthly eminence that I would be not much better than a naked pagan in their presence. So it was with some lonesome trepidation that I traversed the miles to the Seminary gates, and made my way among its buildings until I saw a number of men descending the steps to a basement dining room where apparently they were beginning supper. I ventured to go in, hoping that somebody would tell me that I was supposed to— when to my amazed encouragement I saw two men who had been boys when we were all growing up in Richmond, whom I had not laid eyes on since then, and of whom I had no idea that they were there: John Gravatt and "Monk" Harrison, two solid people, and—by God's mercy—not two angels from another sphere. So the Seminary was a place for human beings after all!

Thus began three years which had a quality of happiness that would be hard to duplicate. In its material aspects the Seminary was still about as far from luxurious as it had been when it was turned back to its authorities at the end of the Civil War, after it had been seized and used as a hospital for the Union army guarding Washington. Only grudgingly even then had its buildings been returned to what had been accounted "Rebel" hands. A reluctant official in Washington, facing two representatives of the Seminary and knowing that during the war years in Virginia one of the prayers in The Book of Common Prayer had been changed into a petition for God's blessing upon the President of the Confederate States, inquired: "Do you pray now for the President of the United States?" to which one of the men from Virginia replied: "Sir, we always do. In the General Confession, we pray for all sinners."

Be that as it may, the Seminary got back its land and buildings, such as the buildings were. In 1905 they had not been much changed. The central structure, Aspinwall Hall, which had been built in 1853, contained classrooms on the ground floor, and on the second and third floors rooms for students. Above its brick main walls rose an incredible looking tower of wood, painted white, with a sort of observation gallery running round the middle of it; the whole resembling a Chinese pagoda that had been blown there by some high wind and deposited upon the roof. Alongside Aspinwall, and forming part of a quadrangle were Meade and Bohlen Halls, partly dormitories and partly offices and workrooms, the dining room being in the basement of Bohlen. Another dormitory, St. George's; a beautiful but diminutive library; a newer chapel; and a structure that contained some iron bathtubs and a huge potbellied stove for hot water on Saturdays—these, except for the faculty houses—were all the buildings there were. In St. George's, where I was assigned a room, there was one hydrant in the hall from which you drew the water for your washstand. Each room had a stove, either a wood stove or a coal stove, according to what seemed inherited accident; and you kept your wood or coal in a bin downstairs and brought it up to make your fire. Everything was keyed to an existence that would be simple.

But that did not matter much. The attraction which the Seminary would prove to have did not depend on special comfort and conveniences. It satisfied something other than a possible taste for luxurious living. The place itself got hold of you. From the platform on Aspinwall Tower you could look down on great old oaks; in the distance northward, the Capitol, the Washington Monument, and the beginnings of the new

Cathedral were silhouetted against the sky; and to the east-ward on the other side of Alexandria, the wide Potomac River glistened against the background of the blue Maryland hills. The old houses where the faculty lived had an antebellum spaciousness, and the hospitality was as generous as the dimensions of the rooms. The Seminary was so small in numbers then that everybody knew everybody else: five professors, and a little less than fifty students—all of these unmarried. Berryman Green, then the youngest member of the faculty but later to be the Dean, meeting you as you walked across the grounds, was as likely as not to say, "Bowie, come over to supper to-night"; and Mrs. Green, meeting someone else or maybe two together a little later, would outdo him with "Tomorrow you two come in for breakfast." Dr. Wallis, a little man with a grey beard and twinkly eyes, by some long-standing choice not explained in New Testament Greek, which was the subject he taught, always kept a bunch of bananas in his house, and a banana would usually be part of the welcome for any student who came in to see him. And when *he* had someone in for breakfast, as he nearly always did, there might not be bananas, but there were always family prayers at the breakfast table; and everybody grew familiar with the fact that the little Doctor, who knew much of the Bible by heart, when he read the scripture lesson would be reading it with his eyes shut.

Dr. Wallis was so naïve and gentle that his good nature was continually being imposed upon. The men in the Seminary were not far enough removed from adolescent tendencies to be always impeccable in their behavior. Sometimes when there would be a momentary outbreak, the little Doctor would say: "Gen'l'men, gen'l'men, remember the dignity of the class." The trouble was that in his class there was plenty of affection, but often no dignity at all. Once, on what was discovered to be his birthday, it was announced to him that all recitations in

Greek were suspended for that day; we had something more important to carry through. So the Doctor was presented with a large candle and bidden to light it. Then the man nearest him in the front row lighted his small candle from the Doctor's candle, passed the light on to the next man, and so on to the back of the room—representing thus, of course, the Doctor's spirit communicated to all the class; and the last man lighted the candles on a birthday cake and presented it to Dr. Wallis. All very pleasant and perfect—except that as the matter came to its climax the Dean came by in the hall, and stopped to look with astonishment at what was going on. Whereat Dr. Wallis, like a small boy caught in some forgetfulness of duty, called out "Gen'l'men, gen'l'men, shut the door, please shut the door!"

Of the academic side of the Seminary not so much that would be enthusiastic could be said. It was warmhearted, like the general spirit of the place; and that could go a long way. But it did not show that much intellectual ferment had been working. There were no electives in the curriculum. With the exception of one or two older men, everybody had Hebrew, New Testament Greek, the English Bible, Church History, Theology, Homiletics, and some "Elocution." It was hopefully assumed that these content courses, with the daily worship in the Chapel and pastoral responsibility weekends and Sundays at the little mission chapels in the county, would not only feed the men in the Seminary but equip them, when they went out, to feed the people in their congregations so that they would grow into well-nourished Christians. Berryman Green could kindle men's desire to learn to preach—and "the old Dean," Angus Crawford, gave a solid grounding in Hebrew. But the more exciting questions of Biblical criticism, creedal reinterpretation, the challenge to traditional forms of worship which a new generation was presenting, and a concern lest the church might be judged irrelevant to the social and industrial problems emerging in the modern world—these seemed like sounds heard in the distance, which did not yet disturb to any great degree the serene assumptions of the Seminary.

To look back from the second half of the century upon the Seminary of those days is to begin almost to wonder whether the world it belonged to then was real—or only the dreamed-up fabric of an imagined era in a never-never land. Out in the open country, with no means generally of getting anywhere except to walk, it was like living in a cheerful monastery without monastic rules. There did not seem to be any great problems or commotions threatening the tranquil order of existence. The unprecedented reign of Queen Victoria, begun in 1837, had ended only in 1901. The British Empire was at the peak of its extent and power, and the *Pax Britannica* seemed a sure bulwark against any imaginable forces that might threaten it. Everyone began to believe in a social and moral progress by which increasing human welfare was assured. Any such portent as the coming of two world wars had not begun to appear even as a distant cloud upon the horizon of the general thinking. As late as 1910, when King Edward VII, Victoria's son and successor, died, nine kings rode in his funeral; and "the crowd waiting in hushed and black-clad awe could not keep back gasps of admiration. In scarlet and blue and green and purple, three by three the sovereigns rode through the palace gates, with plumed helmets, gold braid, crimson sashes, and jeweled orders flashing in the sun." Before long it would be seen that this had been a dying blaze of splendor, but few or none realized it then. In the last two years of the decade Europe "had enjoyed a rich fat afternoon. Nineteen-ten was peaceful and prosperous. A new book, *The Great Illusion* by Norman Angell, had just been published, which proved that war was impossible. By impressive examples and incontrovertible argument Angell showed that in the present financial and economic interdependence of nations, the victor would suffer equally with the vanquished; therefore war had become unprofitable; therefore no nation would be so foolish as to start one." [1]

Hardly anyone knew anything of Kierkegaard, or of any other seer or prophet who had recognized the passions that might be beneath the surface of the world's behavior, and the tragic forces that might darken human destiny. John R. Mott and the Student Volunteer Movement had made Christian people everywhere familiar with the hopeful slogan, "The Evangelization of the World in This Generation." Was not Western civilization essentially Christian, and might not the whole world be brought soon to both temporal and eternal salvation if men who were Christians already were faithful to their mission? That is the way it seemed; and men who went out from the Seminary went with a cheerful optimism as though the way were plain and clear ahead. On the walls of the room in Aspinwall that was the old Prayer Hall glassed cases held the photographs of the men who had gone out to establish the missions of the Episcopal Church in China and Japan and elsewhere; and each year some of the new graduates followed them. They went with confidence that the preaching of the Gospel would be enough, if they themselves were faithful. And the men who went out to little parishes and missions at home saw what was ahead of them as work that called for their clear commitment but would not be very complicated. They had few, if any, of the doubts about the church which beset so many minds today. To get to know the people who belonged to them, "to be messengers, watchmen and stewards

[1] Barbara W. Tuchman, *The Guns of August* (New York: The Macmillan Co., 1962), pp. 1, 9.

of the Lord; to teach, and to premonish, to feed and provide for the Lord's family; to seek for Christ's sheep which are dispersed abroad, and for his children who are in the midst of this naughty world"—that would be their duty and their opportunity, and they believed that by doing just that they would be helping to create little centers of Christian influence which would leaven communities. It occurred to few if any one of them that as a Christian minister he might one day have to reckon with a flood of spoken and published challenges to his assurance; such as the book, typical of many others, arriving through the mail this morning and lying on the desk as I write these words, which invites the minister and the church to consider *Design For Survival.*

The men who were to graduate from the Virginia Seminary —or perhaps likewise from other seminaries—in the class of 1908 would doubtless have been bewildered if they could have been kept exactly as they were for a half a century, and then brought out like so many startled Rip Van Winkles to confront the complications of the present world. The graduates of today are, of course, far more variously and it is to be hoped more efficiently prepared. But there was one asset which the men in the old Seminary of the first decade of the 1900's did have, and which no man aspiring to be a minister in any generation can do without; and that is *dedication.*

The relative simplicity of the times and of the life that people were familiar with helped prevent inducements for self-seeking. Few churches could offer anything but meager salaries. Nobody went into the ministry with the idea that he would make much money. The best men could have, and some of them did have, a devotion to service and a love for people which made them treat financial inconvenience as a joke. The same Monk Harrison, the sight of whose familiar face the evening I landed at the Seminary had given me the happy assurance that real human beings lived there, was sent by his Bishop when he graduated in 1907 to Northumberland County, where the Potomac River flows into Chesapeake Bay. In the previous summer he and two other men from the Seminary had hired themselves as hands on a freighter carrying cattle from Baltimore to Liverpool. The rest of the crew had no idea who they were, until one day the three of them were sitting together in a corner of the deck reading the Bible. One of the crewmen happening to come by stopped in astonishment, went below, and announced to the others, "You know them three fellas that come on the boat together? What do you suppose they is doin' up on deck? Readin' some damn Sunday school book!" There was danger that Monk and his companions would be outcasts, but as a matter of fact they got on full footing with the whole rough company before they arrived in Liverpool. And Monk would be able to adjust to the same sort of humanity in Northumberland County.

In Colonial days the Episcopal Church had been strong all through the Tidewater, but after the Revolution the Baptists and Methodists had multiplied and in many cases had taken over even the church buildings of the old parishes. But some Episcopalians were still around, and it was to these that Monk was sent to minister according to the tradition of the Book of Common Prayer. He did minister to them, but he also discovered another possible congregation. In the county were the so-called fish factories. Large hauls of menhaden were caught and brought in from Chesapeake Bay, dumped into vats, and ground up for oils and fertilizer. Nobody in the neighborhood wanted to work in the fish factories; so it was the custom to send agents up to Baltimore to round up drunks and derelicts, get them aboard the steamer which was the regular means of communication with the counties on the

Bay, and bring them down to Northumberland. Once there, there was no chance for them to get back to their haunts in Baltimore until they had worked enough to have a little money. Meanwhile, they lived in such shacks as were available.

Monk Harrison went right off to see them. He knew that he could not get them to church in the midst of a too-respectable congregation, so he took the church to them. He might or might not bring with him "them damn Sunday school books," but he brought his friendly self. His tough acquaintances saw that he really liked them, and that they could trust him; and they told him facts about themselves which if previously known to the police might have landed a number of them in the penitentiary. Instead of that, if the church be a company of sinners who are beginning to think they might want to be something different, they were discovering that they were in a sort of church themselves.

Meanwhile, the annual salary which the Bishop had assigned to the Rev. Lewis Carter Harrison was four hundred and ninety-five dollars. Out of that he had to rent a room to live in, and presumably get three meals a day, and feed his horse. Besides, there were his fish-factory friends who sometimes had to be helped out of a jam. When he had been in Northumberland for two years, he discovered that he not only had no money but that he had debts of about a hundred dollars. He had had calls to many other places, any one of which calls he would have been free to accept since he was no longer only a deacon and therefore subject to the Bishop's disposition. He had refused them all; but this day when he went to the post office he found two letters, two calls to churches, each one of them offering a salary five or six times what he was getting. "I believe I will have to go," he said to himself. "If I don't, it just means that I will be getting deeper into debt." But having said that, he looked in his post-office box again, and there was another letter. This one was from a group of young men in Richmond whom he had known. They called themselves "The Society of St. Francis"— though Monk thought that most of them had no clear idea of who St. Francis was, but thought the name suggested by somebody had a nice sound. Anyhow, they said that they had determined to send a check to the man working in the diocese who had the smallest salary, and they discovered that he was it. So they sent him a hundred dollars.

With that, Monk paid off his debts, refused the two calls, and stayed in Northumberland until doctors told him he had to leave. None of the parishes he went to afterwards were like Northumberland, but the spirit he carried to all of them was the same.

Monk Harrison graduated in the class of 1907. Our class of 1908 was larger than most classes had been, though even so it numbered only twenty. Five of the graduates would afterwards be Bishops: "Mike" Quin, who came to the Seminary with only the most meagre academic preparation but by sheer character and native ability won such quick leadership that within ten years after he was ordained he had been elected as the youngest member of the House of Bishops; John Long Jackson, friend to everybody, and possessed of such a special way with boys that the Episcopal High School adjoining the Seminary was always inviting him over there; Middleton Barnwell, mercurial and brilliant; Charlie Clingman, "The Dutchman," as steady and predictable as "Barney" was explosive; and John Gravatt, whose laugh could warm up any place and company. All of them different; but all of them destined to bring special gifts in service as Bishops in Texas, Louisiana, Idaho and Georgia, Kentucky, and South Carolina. Whatever else they may have succeeded or failed in, they did each one fulfil the affirmative promise made in answer to the question in the Consecration office, "Will you show yourself in all things an example of good works unto others, that the adversary may be ashamed, having nothing to say against you?"

After my second year at Alexandria, I began to be drawn also by another influence. A Harvard friend of mine, Charles W. Gilkey, was at Union Seminary in New York. He had told me what I might well have known anyway—of the men pre-eminent in the world of biblical and theological scholarship who were on the faculty there. I asked my Bishop of Virginia whether he would let me go to Union for part of my senior year, and—beyond what I had actually expected—he said yes. So in September, 1907, I enrolled as a temporary transfer student at Union, for courses in history under Arthur C. McGiffert, in Old Testament under Julius A. Bewer, and in theology under William Adams Brown and the inimitable George William Knox, who left us in no doubt as to what we needed to consider. "Gentlemen," he said, "remember that your profession is subject to twin vices: laziness and conceit."

Then there were two others who meant more to me even than those already named. One was James E. Frame, in New Testament, a man of immense scholarship and of humility equally as great. More than any other man I have known he kept free in his teaching from opinionated dogmatism, and seemed always to be saying instead, "Let us sit down together at the feet of truth, and listen."

The other was Henry Sloane Coffin, then a young man but already becoming one of the commanding influences in American Christianity, and for me a friend by whom life would be enlarged as the years went on.

So the experience in New York was an enrichment. But with all the stimulation of mind which Union represented, my heart was still in Alexandria and with the men whom I had known there. It had been arranged that I should come back to Virginia at the end of March and join my class again; and that is what I did.

The time moved on to the middle of June; then Class Day and Commencement. The alumni would turn up again at Commencement time: great numbers of them, to see each other, to talk about what used to be, and to see if anything was new. Thus there was plenty that was lighthearted about those days; but also of course there was the deeper undertone when after Commencement came ordination. Not in our time but only after we had left the Seminary, there came to the faculty Wilbur Cosby Bell, "a thinker who sensed the wonder of life and interpreted its fulness to a bewildered age." We had had such a happy time that we did not fully know that the age was supposed to be bewildered. We would find that out before long; and then the question would be as to whether *we* were the ones who had to be bewildered.

VIII. The Country Parish
at Greenwood

Since a bishop sends his newly ordained deacons where he chooses, we who were graduating at the Seminary in June of 1908 had waited to see what our assignments would be. They might be to posts we had never heard of. Mike Quin, the big Irishman, was sent by his Bishop of Kentucky to a place that rejoiced in the name of Peewee Valley. I was sent by my Bishop of Virginia to Greenwood. I did know where Greenwood was, because I had been there in the previous summer as a student fill-in, since there was nobody else available to hold services on Sundays.

Greenwood was a flag stop on the Chesapeake and Ohio Railroad, some seventeen miles west of Charlottesville, on the slope of the Blue Ridge Mountains, close to the opening of a tunnel which cut through a mountain spur and beyond which the trains climbed upgrade on past Afton and Waynesboro into the Shenandoah Valley. Greenwood itself consisted only of Mr. A. B. Bruce's general store, with the long hitching rack outside where the horses of buggies and wagons from all the neighborhood would be tied, the freight depot, and one house where the Dinwiddie family lived; but from it one looked

71

down on the wide green bowl of the western Piedmont, with scattered houses and many acres of apple trees. This was rolling country, with the Blue Ridge on the west and north, and the lower Ragged Mountains on the south. Two or three miles from Greenwood Depot was Emmanuel Church, set among old oak trees on the main road that ran from Charlottesville through Albemarle County to the west.

I was to live with Dr. and Mrs. M. L. McCue, whose son Purcell was a vestryman of Emmanuel. Their house, not far from Greenwood Depot, was in the midst of a large apple orchard which Purcell ran with conspicuous efficiency. Dr. McCue was a physician who had mostly retired from practice. Tall and handsome, with piercing eyes and heavy eyebrows, he could be the soul of geniality and cordial helpfulness; and the next day he would be a scowling thundercloud, either silent or breaking out into sudden and inexplicable anger against everything and everybody. When I first came as a guest boarder at "Appledore," he would generously invite me to go with him when he drove out to see some of his remaining patients, so that I as the new minister at Emmanuel might get to know them and they me; but soon I fell out of favor as he went more and more into his dark moods. But Mrs. McCue—"Miz 'Cue" to all the neighborhood—kept her quiet courage and her poise. She could manage the situation at home, and manage things outside also. She was a little round lady who had a way of tilting her head slightly to one side, which put her two eyes at different angles, and you had the sure feeling that anything she did not see about you and about the situation with one eye she would certainly see with the other. With her shrewdness went unfailing humor, and a way of dealing with people which made them want to do what she had made up her mind they ought to do. Before long she knew that I was in love with Jean. But how could I

be married and how could Jean come to Greenwood until there
should be a place where we two could live? Ergo, a rectory
there must be. So it was Miz 'Cue who began soon to stir
up the vestry and other members of Emmanuel, work out in
her mind the plan for a house, and start raising money to get
it built.

Even the Model T had not yet appeared on the dirt roads
of Albemarle. If you went anywhere about the countryside,
you rode a horse or drove a buggy.

When I was first assigned to Greenwood, I was only a
deacon, and so could not celebrate the Communion. But at
Ivy, near Charlottesville, was Archdeacon Neve, one of the
most generously helpful men in the diocese, founder of the
church's missionary work among the people who before he
had gone out to find them had been almost wholly isolated
in the coves and "hollows" of the Blue Ridge Mountains. He
was an Englishman, tall and lanky and awkward, with a
British restraint in manner and speech that made him seem
shy and remote in talkative American company but with keen
perception and quiet shrewdness underneath. He would come
up every little while to celebrate Communion for my people,
while I went down to Ivy to substitute as best I could for him.
I hope he was amused when he heard what happened to me
the first time I faced his congregation. The church building
at Ivy was small and simple, like the one at Greenwood. The
choir gathered round a small organ at the front, and I had
been instructed to come through the door of the robing room
into the chancel as the choir began the opening hymn. It
was in Advent, and the hymnal in use was the old one which
had hymns more antique than most of those included now.
But the opening hymn that day could have seemed not antique
at all, but startlingly suited to the immediate scene; for the

words with which the choir burst forth as I the neophyte and stranger first appeared were these:

> Great God, what do I see and hear!
> The end of things created!

In Greenwood the people were a very mixed group, but all of them friendly and congenial in their different ways. At the crossroads between Appledore and Emmanuel was Mr. Woodson, the blacksmith, a gnarled little man smelling of horses and of the smoke from the fire of the forge next to his anvil where he hammered out his horseshoes; in his early sixties, but with muscles that had in them the strength that might have been in all the Seven Dwarfs together. When he was still no more than a boy he had been in General Lee's army as the war drew near its end at Appomattox, and the Union forces had almost surrounded what was left of the Confederates. Being wounded one day—so he told about it —an officer said to him, "Go to the rear"; whereat Mr. Woodson, looking around and seeing the flashes of enemy guns on every side, replied, "Where in hell *is* the rear?" His two sons, Jim and Odin, were two of my boys in Emmanuel Sunday School.

Farther along the road lived Mrs. Hackett, who had in her house the switchboard for the local telephone line which had only recently been installed. Beyond Mrs. Hackett's, and close to the church, lived Mrs. Fox and her five sons, of whom the younger ones, Leonard and Dick, were still at home. It was Leonard Fox who later would be a leading member of a Junior Brotherhood of St. Andrew when that was organized. After the first meeting, at which he was elected secretary, he asked me very particularly what time it was. At the subsequent meeting I discovered why. When he was called upon as

74

recording secretary to read the minutes of the previous month, this is what he read. "The Brotherhood of St. Andrew met at the Foxes' house on October 10th. Minutes were from eight o'clock to five minutes after nine." That was all; and none of the other boys seemed to think that anything had been left out.

Besides the Woodsons and the Hacketts and the Foxes and others who worked with their hands, there were those who lived more opulently in the big houses, at "Tiverton" and "Rose Hill" and other large estates. Not far from Emmanuel, set in the midst of its trees and its box bushes and its gardens, was the beautiful old mansion of "Mirador," which had belonged to Chiswell D. Langhorne, but which he had given to his daughter, Phyllis Brooks, while he lived in another house nearby. One of his daughters was Irene, who married Charles Dana Gibson, the artist, and was the model for his drawings familiar everywhere in the early 1900's as "the Gibson girl." Another daughter was Nancy, who married Viscount Astor in England, and was the first woman ever to become a member of the British House of Commons. Every now and then Nancy Astor would come back to visit at Mirador, and would go around looking up all the people, especially the little people, whom she had known, and would give a party for the Negro servants and their children.

There was service at Emmanuel every Sunday morning at eleven, with Sunday school before that. On two Sunday afternoons I would drive down to Crozet, the next town toward Charlottesville, for service there; and then take the C & O train for Waynesboro for the third service and sermon in the evening. On the other two afternoons I would drive eight miles to the small chapel of Holy Cross, at the foot of one of the Ragged Mountains to the east. There in the Mission House for a while lived a little cockney Englishman named

75

Rickaby, brought there by Archdeacon Neve, who in his speech and his far-off ways of thinking still belonged in East-side London, and now in what must have seemed to him a mountain wilderness looked wistfully bewildered as to how he ever got there.

In the Greenwood area there was one other church, the Lebanon Presbyterian Church, but it had no resident minister, and so I had the chance to be in touch, if and when they needed me, with people quite outside the Emmanuel group. One might understand then that no stereotyped language from the inside of the church would do. A forlorn little woman from the mountains had lost her baby, and I was standing by her in the cold burying ground of Lebanon Church. I spoke as best I knew how of the love of God and of trust in the Life Beyond, and she answered: "Yes, I know. But oh, the *miss* of him now, the miss of him!" I looked at her and listened and was hushed. I resolved then, God helping me, never to forget that I must first *feel*, before I could fully minister to, the pathos and the pitifulness that can be in human life.

Meanwhile, of course, I was having to preach every Sunday. Often you think that what you may have said cannot really have amounted to anything, and so I hardly knew whether to laugh or cry at something which did happen one Sunday. Mr. Langhorne was there, as he almost always was. On account of the destruction of property in the Civil War and the poverty that followed it when he was growing up, he had never had the academic education which his background and family would naturally have brought to him. But he had great native ability and energy. Going out very young to work on the railroad and then with a railroad construction company, in a rough struggle for advancement he made his way ahead, and was a commanding figure among those who recognized a man of force. He was hot-tempered and profane, and

76

he liked to pretend that he had too tough a skin for any preachment to get through, but underneath that pretense was a soft heart, and emotions that could be very sensitive. An overseer on one of the neighboring big places had shot a beautiful dog of his, on the accusation that the dog was killing sheep. Mr. Langhorne was furious, and everybody knew it. It so happened that I had been preaching a series of sermons on the Lord's Prayer and had come to the petition, "Forgive us our trespasses as we forgive those who trespass against us." Mr. Langhorne listened, though neither I nor anyone else could know what was going on back of the listening. When the service was over, men and boys were standing around outside the door, as they usually do in country churches. When they saw Mr. Langhorne come out, they gasped—for there, standing not far from him, was Johnson, the man who had shot his dog. They held their breath as Mr. Langhorne walked toward Johnson, his face very red. Then after a moment they heard his voice, coming out like an explosion: "Johnson, *you shot my dog*. But, *damn you*, I forgive you!"

Mr. Langhorne had never been confirmed, and so he did not come to Communion. I tried to persuade him to be confirmed, but he shied away from the idea. One thing, though, worked on my side. He had a great admiration for Bishop Lloyd, and Bishop Lloyd was to come for his visitation to Emmanuel in the winter of 1911. I told Mr. Langhorne this, and his resistance melted. On the Sunday when Bishop Lloyd was there, Mr. Langhorne was one of the group prepared for confirmation. It happened that when they all knelt, he was at the end of the line, so that when Bishop Lloyd laid his hands upon him he was the last person to be received into the church during my ministry at Emmanuel. This made a considerable sensation in the community, among those who had thought of him more in reference to his language than in reference to the man himself—and especially among the Negroes, whose idea of piety was particular. Lucy Crapp, who was what she called "the section" at Emmanuel and whose responsibility was to see that the church was clean for Sunday services, cried out: "Lord, if *Mister Langhorne* is got converted, then every last sinner in Albermarle County kin jine the church!" Whether or not Lucy Crapp was right in that opinion, she did have a shrewd appraisal of people and of their ways. One day a lady for whom she worked from time to time said to her: "Lucy, I do a lot of things for you. I do more for you even than Mrs. McCue does, and yet you like Mrs. McCue better than you like me." "Yes'm," Lucy answered, "You does do a heap for me. But then you goes and does somethin' else that jest undoos it all."

I had begun at Greenwood with a salary of $800 a year, out of which I paid not as much, I am sure, as ought to have been paid for my room and board at generous Mrs. McCue's. That $800 looked to be a lot more than the $495 which Monk Harrison got, yet was not quite a fortune. But then, the next June, the vestry voted to raise the salary to $1,000, and by that time the rectory which Miz 'Cue had conjured up was finished. Somebody found for me Maggie, a blessed black saint in the form of an old Negro woman, and we moved into the rectory to set up housekeeping. My knowledge about marketing and so forth was nonexistent, and Maggie's ideas were simple. Until my mother came from Richmond to spend that first summer with me and make everything different, the one recollection I have of those first days is that I bought, not a real ham, but a salted "shoulder" at Mr. Bruce's store, and we lived on that uninterruptedly for a week.

Now at last what had been since July, 1904, the great but

distant hope on the horizon was drawing near. Jean and I could be married. In September, 1909, I went to Buffalo, and on September 29, Saint Michael and All Angels Day, we were married in the beautiful little chapel of Trinity Church.

When we came back to Greenwood, all the warmhearted people were ready to welcome the bride, from Mr. and Mrs. Bruce and Mr. Fleming and Mr. Talley, the clerks at Bruce's store, to the Foxes next door to the rectory, and everybody in the houses, little and big, between. They had liked me well enough, but now to make the rectory the warm center for the parish which it could not be before was Jean: a little shy at first but inherently happy-hearted and quick with laughter, interested in everybody, and ready to be a part of everything that was going on. Just by being what she was, something went out from her that made young and old feel better. As a young man who had been teaching school wrote of her one day: "I have been trying to sum up in my mind her many aspects. Perhaps the best description I can give of her is that she always had her feelers out making contact with humanity. She was extremely perceptive. This perceptivity would have been most disconcerting if she had not been so kind. Actually she was more than kind. She seemed to feel mankind. There was a broad understanding of our faults, but let any of us cross the line between what she accepted as human and what she condemned and you became very much aware of her moral values."

The new rectory, which was near the church, was an altogether happy outcome of Miz 'Cue's planning: attractive looking, compact and easy to take care of, and having in it everything we needed. A well had been dug back of the kitchen; and we got from Sears-Roebuck a gasoline engine, which I could hand-crank into starting, that would pump the water. Maggie was with us, under more imaginative direction now than when she and I had fed ourselves on the shoulder. Besides cooking, Maggie fed the pig—a pig which had been given us by one of the delightful young vestrymen, Armistead Shirley, who I hope realized it was just plain affection for him that made us call that prized pig *Armistead*—although the queer notion of a name she never could pronounce made Maggie shake her head. My responsibility, besides managing the pump, was to feed my little mare, Babbie, and keep her curried, and clean her stall in the small stable which had been built when the rectory was building. Thus we were prepared both for life in the rectory and for activities outside.

The rectory began to seem increasingly to be home as the people we loved came to see us there: my mother and sister, Jean's mother and sisters, Dr. and Mrs. Meigs from The Hill, John Gravatt, and many others. Then in November, 1910, our little Jean was born—born in Richmond but christened in Emmanuel after Christmas time that year.

Most important for Greenwood of those who came to stay with us was Aunt Mary-Cooke. Through the years when I was in Harvard and then at the Seminary, she had carried on a long, brave struggle against the crippling illness which had come upon her husband, "Uncle Beverley." He had contracted tuberculosis—as my father had before. Part of the time they had been in Richmond, twice she had taken him away for a winter in a better climate, once to Arizona, once to Colorado Springs. But they came back to Richmond at length, and in 1910 he had died. Now she was devoting herself increasingly to what had become with her no less than a crusade, the development of the public schools. She was the president and the inspiring force in The Cooperative Education Association of Virginia, which had been established to secure "a nine months' school term for every child, a high school within reasonable distance of every child, well-trained teachers, efficient school supervision, promotion of school libraries, citizens' educational leagues in every county and city." She saw that in the Greenwood community the school was crude and ill-equipped and only halfheartedly supported. She made me realize the concern I ought to have about it. She talked to Miz 'Cue, Mr. Langhorne, and others, and stirred their interest. She sparked a general call for a mass meeting which would present the need not only for a better school but also for better roads which would enable children to get to it and for more knowledge about the agencies for public health. The mass meeting did bring together people who had never taken joint responsibility before. Before long a new school building replaced the old one, and the whole community conception of what the school *ought* to be expanded. And she had showed me the public concern which a minister ought to have, and the responsibility of a Christian church to make its good will accomplish something for the public good.

As the time went by, numerous calls came to me from other churches, as is always likely to be the case with a young man in a small place. But neither Jean nor I had any impulse to accept them. The associations at Greenwood had already grown dear. But then, early in 1911, there came a summons that was different. The rector of St. Paul's in Richmond, the beautiful old church at the border of Capitol Square, had died, and the vestry called me to take his place. I had been baptized in St. Paul's, had been a boy in its Sunday school, and had been confirmed there. All my family belonged to it. Now they wanted me to come back. This time the only answer had to be yes.

But there was sadness in the decision, and I can still feel the emotions that stirred in me on that day in 1911 when Purcell McCue and Armistead Shirley, warmhearted and devoted

81

at the end as they had been in the beginning, brought their wagons and their teams to the rectory to haul the furniture to a freight car at Greenwood, while Jean and I, with little Jean, separated now from Emmanuel, took the train for Richmond.

IX The Beginning at St. Paul's

When the call came to me from St. Paul's, it was in Lent
I wrote the vestry that I should want to meet with them and
talk together before I could know what I ought to do. So
it was arranged that we should meet as soon as Lent was
over.

Accordingly, I went down to Richmond on Easter Monday.
At St. Paul's the Easter flowers were being taken out, the
pews cleared of the Easter leaflets and the other leftovers from
the crowded services, the carpets swept—a scene of confusion
everywhere. The only place that seemed to have been put in
order was the kindergarten room of the Sunday school, and
there the vestry assembled. Every one of the men who greeted
me was older than I was, and some of them considerably
older than my father would have been. Being only twenty-
eight, I had no ripe wisdom, but I did have a love for St. Paul's
and some real ideals for it. So I told the vestry what those
ideals were.

I said to them that they could be summed up in three
words.

First, a democratic church. St. Paul's had a particular position in the community and a tradition that was in part at

least a noble one. Many of the people and the families who had belonged to it had been linked with what was proudest in the history of Richmond. In that sense it was known as an aristocratic church. But did the vestry want it to be also something else, and in right ways something different? Did they want it to represent a real welcome and concern for human beings, whatever their backgrounds may have been? Did they want it to be the Father's house to which all his children might instinctively turn?

Second, a missionary church. St. Paul's had given—as it seemed, respectably—to work beyond its parish maintenance, the more unselfish giving which responded to the wider needs in the diocese and the general church. But it had never given in proportion to its real possibilities. Did it want to begin to move conspicuously beyond parochial involvement? Would it try to be a dynamo of power for all the church's missionary service everywhere?

Third, a working church. Did the vestry think it would be a nice idea to have a rector somehow carry out conveniently for them and for the congregation the commitments I had spoken of, or were we covenanting to try to do it all together?

When I had said that much, I said that I hoped they would understand what I was asking of them, and that I needed to be sure they did. Therefore I was not asking for someone to offer a resolution and for all of them politely to vote aye. I wanted to ask them individually whether what I had laid before them was what they really wanted and what they would stand back of. Then, beginning at one end of the line of chairs, I asked each one of them to answer.

Of course they did not actually have the chance to think out fully what might be the implications of what they would assent to, but they thought that what I had said seemed commendable; and since they had made their choice of me as rector, they were disposed to follow through. So they all said yes: that what I had outlined was what they wanted. And I said then that I would come.

It was all genuine and serious, and it remained a good picture to look back upon, even if it was bound to have in retrospect its comic side: the vestrymen, some of them grey-bearded, sitting on kindergarten chairs and speaking each one his piece like small boys in a class.

Anyway, they and the rest of the people welcomed Jean and me with warmth and with hopefulness, and we began what were to be nearly twelve years at St. Paul's—twelve years in which of course there was not always complete agreement as to what the parish did or ought to do, but years of mutual trust and of devotion which deepened more and more as life and work went on.

In their call, the vestry had specified the salary as $3,000 plus the rectory; or $3,600 if the rectory were not lived in. It was a dignified old house next to the church, on Grace Street, but larger than we needed, and hard to maintain. Besides, it seemed to me that it ought to be used as a parish house, since there were no rooms available otherwise except in the basement of the church. So we rented 105 North Fifth Street (vanished now, with the John Marshall Hotel built over the ground where it used to be); and Jean and I, with the one-year-old baby Jean, were settled there in the fall of 1911. My mother too was in Richmond, keeping house for our unmarried cousin, Effie K. Branch, but constantly in and out of 107 North Fifth Street. My sister, who two years after she had graduated at Vassar had been married to Melville C. Branch, was also in Richmond; and her happy companionship now with Jean matched the special devotion between herself and me. Around the corner on Grace Street, in one of the handsomest of the early-nineteenth-century houses that still remained, was Aunt Mary-Cooke. I was home again; and though we might tease Jean for having been born in Yankeeland, in her affections now Richmond was her home too.

Richmond being still a close-knit and homogeneous community where nearly everyone knew what was going on, there was considerable curiosity about the new rector of St. Paul's; and because he was young, and because some of the older ministers were known to have looked upon his coming dubiously, the newspapers gave him more notice than he deserved. The editorial page of the *Richmond Times-Dispatch* for Monday, October 23, 1911, began with this:

St. Paul's Church has made no mistake in the choice of its new Rector, the Rev. Walter Russell Bowie. He has preached here only a few times in his new work, and though very young, he has preached with the wisdom of the elders and with much more than their accustomed fire. He must have been at his best yesterday morning. His text was taken from the account of Christ's entry into Jerusalem and his lamentation over its unhappy estate: "And when he was come near, he beheld the city, and wept over it." There has not been a more effective plea for high Christian effort.

The generous-spirited editorial writer, whoever he may have been, had affirmed that "St. Paul's Church has made no mistake in the choice of its new Rector." There were those, however, who may have begun to incline toward another opinion. It was not long before the agreement which had seemed to be reached at the meeting with the vestry on Easter Monday faced its first test. Two members of the vestry, and the two wealthiest men in the congregation, whose interest in church matters stopped at the borders of the parish, objected to a proposed appropriation for "foreign missions"—

objected so strenuously that when the vote went against them they resigned. But the rest of the vestry, then and later, even if sometimes lugubriously, stood loyally by what had been our *Magna Carta* compact; and I had abundant reason to love them for the faithfulness they showed.

It is a wholesome thing when a parish realizes that its strength must depend upon all its people, and not upon a few who have wealth and high position. The St. Paul's congregation did learn exactly that. It developed an *esprit de corps* in work and in giving which put it in the forefront of the diocese, and set a conspicuous standard of commitment to the whole Church's missionary work. And it got thereby a new warmth of happy confidence for worship and work in its own bounds. It learned the truth of what was said by a man whose imagination went beyond the common run. "For every dollar that you give to the needy who might have seemed far off from your responsibility, God gives you ten dollars worth of purpose to deal with your responsibilities here at home."

St. Paul's had been thought of as an aristocratic church, and whatever *noblesse oblige* was involved in that belonged to it still. But if there had been any snobbishness in it, that snobbishness disappeared. It was trying to be "the Father's House" for his children generally. And one of the influences which helped to make it inclusive came about through one of those naïve contradictions in which our human nature, with its nurture of body and spirit, can get itself involved. Because it was downtown, near the Capitol and the business district, St. Paul's was in an ideal location for noonday Lenten services to which great numbers of men as well as women could come and did come, to hear the preachers from many parts of the church who came to its pulpit year by year. Lent is supposed to be marked by fasting, but by innocent chance at St. Paul's it was also marked by food. All the women of the parish combined to serve luncheons to which the crowds could come either before or after the service in the church. Girls and young women and older ones too who would never have known one another otherwise worked side by side, planning meals, cooking on the kitchen stoves, waiting on tables, washing dishes. And if the luncheons were very good, so that churchgoers rejoiced to be there, and were not conspicuous every day in fasting, it is to be hoped that in Heaven there was gentle understanding, and that the Lord looked down with favor upon the fact that so many of his children were being drawn into a comradeship that made them friends.

Although St. Paul's was the strongest church in the diocese, with the largest congregation, life as its minister in the early part of this twentieth century was almost as uncomplicated as life and work had been in Greenwood. Richmond was still a compact community, with most of the congregation living at no great distances from the church. There were very few automobiles, and movement of families to the suburbs had hardly begun. I could walk nearly everywhere I wanted to go in pastoral calling, or occasionally take a streetcar. The house in which Jean and I were settled on Fifth Street was only four blocks from St. Paul's. In the mornings I could study and work on the preparation of sermons at home. The pre-Civil War residence next door to the church where the former rectors had lived had been made into a parish house, but this meant simply that its old-fashioned rooms were available now for the meetings of the Woman's Auxiliary or for Sunday School classes or for other occasional use such as for the noonday lunches in Lent. When I remember that old parish house and contrast it with the elaborations of our present day, the gap of time and change seems almost as great as that which Rip Van Winkle experienced when he woke up in a modern world instead of the world of George the Third which was all that he remembered. The characteristic present-day parish house may look like some highly organized executive establishment, with telephone switchboard and glass partitions and the rector off somewhere giving directions as to what should go next on the mimeograph machine. None of that had been imagined in the Richmond of 1911. No previous minister of St. Paul's had had such a thing as a rector's secretary, and it was not until some years after I came that the vestry conceived the idea that perhaps there ought to be one, and to my great gain found Virginia P. Conrad for that position.

Of course, in a different age and in a crowded world that moves at a different tempo, new buildings and new equipment do undoubtedly increase efficiency, and the warmth of personal ministry may still move through the wheels. But there is sometimes the danger that it may not, and against that danger every man in the ministry must be on his guard. Something intimate and beautiful is lost if a man becomes enmeshed in the machine, if he responds to an individual's needs by saying, "Come to my office," and if he thinks he is too busy to do faithful pastoral calling and to know his people in their homes. He cannot really speak home to their hearts from the pulpit, and he cannot help them in their crises, unless through many contacts he has begun to grow so familiar that they will instinctively turn to him.

Henry Sloane Coffin expressed in one unforgettable sentence what a minister ought to be: A trusted, trained, accredited friend-at-large.

He must be *trusted*, first of all. No accident of place or prerogative by itself can make him that. He must have the personal integrity and the outreaching compassion which make people recognize that here is a man to whom they can come with their doubts and difficulties, and with the burden also of their sins and sense of guilt, and know that he will not let them down. He is to embody also something more than a personal impulse to be helpful. He must have tried—and keep on trying—to be *trained* in Christian knowledge and in all the richness of the Gospel so that he may bring to peoples' spiritual needs that which will be, in the words of Jesus, "a spring of water welling up to eternal life." And as he is trained and then *accredited*, he comes not only as an individual, but as one who mediates the proven faith of the church by which both he and those to whom he ministers can alike be fortified.

If he is thus *trusted*, *trained* and *accredited*, he can become indeed *a friend-at-large*. No genuine Christian ministry is shut within particular fences. A man's concern for human beings can be so wide and deep, and his readiness to try to be of help so evident, that a whole community may begin to feel a bond with him. Out of the pitiableness of anonymous need he may get a message such as this that came one day in a letter from a woman caught in a tragic sex entrapment for which she had not at first been responsible: "You may think that you have accomplished nothing toward changing my life, but you are wrong. . . . I have heard every sermon that you have preached since hearing of you, and I had not been inside a church in ten years. . . . I could tell you something regarding my first visit to your church that would make it plain to you how the world in general looks on a woman in my position who is really striving to do right. . . . I beg that you will not lose confidence in me, only give me a chance to prove myself the woman I wish to be and really am." *There* was evidence of the sort of pathos which may be crying out from any community, and of which a "friend-at-large" must be aware.

It was Henry Sloane Coffin, as I have written, who expressed what should be the standard which a man must try to live up to for his general ministry. It was the same Dr. Coffin who stirred me also to a more particular effort. Following the example which he had set in his church on Madison Avenue in New York, I began to have at St. Paul's a children's sermon as part of the regular Sunday morning service. The children came with the rest of the congregation and took their part in the opening hymn and the beginning of Morning Prayer, through the Psalter. Then came the very brief sermon especially to them; and while a short, extra hymn was being sung, they went directly to their classes in the Sunday School, and Morning Prayer continued to its conclusion and to the adult sermon.

This, of course, was new; and regular churchgoers are generally suspicious of what is new. Most of them could be observed at first sitting stiffly in their pews, as though preparing to endure this innovation. But the children liked it, and after a while most of the grown-ups did too. Some of them would come up to me now and then, and admit—as though they thought they oughtn't to—that maybe they got more out of the children's sermon than out of the accustomed longer one which followed. The reason was plain enough. Not only was the children's sermon shorter, and in that aspect easier to remember; it also was concrete, which—in order to catch the children's quick recognition—it had to be.

The necessity to have a children's sermon ready for the next Sunday morning kept one's observation alive all through the week. It would not do to go into the pulpit with only some generalized idea. There had to be something that would kindle the children's imagination and draw its own quick lesson: such as a sign I saw one day by a wooded roadside, "Don't let fires start, they're hot, and they run faster than you can"; or a broken bough, picked up under a tree after a windstorm which seemed to have been sound but which when looked at closely was seen to have no substance because little unseen insects had eaten the heart out of it; or a compass; or a thermometer, which only shows what the temperature *is*, as against a thermostat, which keeps the temperature what it ought to be; or any other of the innumerable familiar things which can be modern parables.

Often also sermons can come out of the unconscious meanings in some odd accident of what children say. Our little Elisabeth, reading one morning the Bible passage at family prayers, came to St. Paul's words, "Gird up your loins," and she read it, "Gird up your *lions*." Which, come to think of it, is a highly important thing to do: to take all your strength, including your temper, which might be fierce and wild, and harness it to be boldly useful.

On another day Jean (Jr.) managed to summon a sermon out of a pad of writing paper on my desk. This pad, like others, had a brand name on it, which in this instance, for some obscure reason, was *Corsican*. She read the letters slowly: C–o–r–s–i–c–a–n. "Daddy, what does that spell?" she asked. "That spells Corsican," I said. "A Corsican is a man who comes from Corsica, just as an American is a man who lives in America." "Oh," she said, with sudden disappointment on her face, "I thought that spelled 'Course I Can."

And that, when you waked up to see it, was exactly what it did spell. For the most noted person who ever came out of Corsica was Napoleon, and Napoleon, with whatever else was good or not good about him, was an example of the person who, faced with great challenge which would make most people say "I can't do it," said instead " 'Course I can!"

The gain from preaching children's sermons, and from

having to find the illustrations for them, can lead to another benefit besides the direct one of making a special bond between the minister in the pulpit and the boys and girls. It forces a man to think pictorially, and when he has done that he has gone a long way toward making all his preaching more vivid. John Bunyan—who could write *Pilgrim's Progress*—said discerningly that "the Citadel of Man-Soul can be stormed more surely through eye-gate than through ear-gate"; by which he meant that any truth becomes most convincing when the mind's eye perceives it and a listener says instinctively, "I *see* it now." The trouble with too many sermons is that there are no illustrations to let the light in; and, instead, the poor listener is carried through a tunnel of abstractions in which he sees nothing but the enclosing walls.

Illustrations for all preaching may thus come through the imposed necessity of preparing children's sermons. But the adult who thinks he is saying something to children needs to remember that by being what they are they will be continually saying something more important to him; and this is true even if at first we do not see it. It may well be that the disciples were astonished when Jesus said one day that "Whosoever shall not receive the kingdom of God as a little child, he shall not enter therein" (KJV). I think that what Jesus meant for his disciples and for us to understand is that no one can feel the nearness of God unless he can catch from the child the child's sense of the wideness and wonder that can be in common things.

All life and its meaning expanded as our own little family grew. Jean had been born when we were in Greenwood. Beverley, our sturdy little first son, named after Uncle Beverley Munford, was born in Richmond in 1914. In 1917 came Elisabeth, named after my mother—my mother whose devotion to all her grandchildren was only inadequately suggested by the dedication in a book of 52 children's sermons,

Whose love, like sunlight, falleth clear
And constant on the children's year.

Then, in 1920, last but in his exuberance far from least, came Russell, Junior.

With those four in the house, and their mother's gentleness to set their imaginations free, one could be confronted sometimes by realities of the spirit which both rebuked and illumined one's adult stodginess—the stodginess which could make one oblivious of what might be happening in a little child's fanciful and fairy world. I have never forgotten the shame I felt one day when I had spoken angrily to Beverley, then a little boy, because he had taken from the mantelpiece a vase that was supposed to be of value and had let it slip from his hands, so that it lay in shattered splinters on the floor. And when I demanded why he had done such a thing as that, he looked up at me, bewildered, "But I thought," he said, "I thought it was a horn."

So often a child may blow enchanted horns that can open the gates to wide worlds of wonderment, and our dull ears do not hear!

X. Community Activities

A man is called to be the minister of a particular congregation, and that congregation is made up of individual human beings who have their intimate personal needs. His first responsibility is toward them: to try to know them, to enter with imaginative sympathy into everything that concerns them, and to increase in them—as in himself—the consciousness of God's quickening purpose as related to all that they are and do. Therefore much of his work will be pastoral and quiet: doing his best to see that boys and girls are brought up in Christian knowledge, visiting the parish families, being quick to sense and share the joys or sorrows men and women have, going to see the sick or the dying in homes and hospitals, bringing the faith that comes through Christ to the bereaved. Thus much of what he does is within the parish boundaries. His business is to bring to those people who have made him their minister the encouragement and strength of the Christian gospel which can be to them the bread of life.

But there is something more to the ministry than the pastoral metaphor suggests. There is beauty and truth in the picture of the shepherd of souls whose duty is to guard and nurture and feed, but people are more than sheep and the church is meant to be something greater than a sheepfold. A Christian church must have to do with its people's whole selves, not only with their personal needs but with what ought to be their power. Therefore, they are not merely to be ministered to as though the gospel were something to be passively absorbed; they are to become the church militant which moves out to generous and self-forgetful service. Every Christian church is part of a larger community, and its business is to make its strength count positively for justice and mercy in the actual issues which the community's everyday life involves.

In my first year at St. Paul's I helped to create the Social Service Commission of the Diocese of Virginia, and the first thing we did was to write to all the clergy of the diocese, and especially to those in rural or small-town parishes who might have felt isolated, and ask them what facts there were in their own neighborhoods which needed the organized help of Christian people; such, for instance, as inadequate public schools, exploitation of children in labor, suffering among the sick and poor which might be worse because of their ignorance of the agencies for help which actually existed and which they could turn to if they knew. Nothing dramatic came to pass because of that Commission; but it did waken in many places a larger conception of what churches ought to be concerned with, and did lead some clergy and lay people to relate their Christian idealism in more direct and effective ways to actual human needs in the life around them.

At St. Paul's the Men's Association began to see and to follow up some demands—and therefore opportunities—for social responsibility. Liquor licenses, for example, had been granted in the city in a way that had least concern for those who would be hurt most—for the poor and disadvantaged who had no political power, which meant the Negroes. In the white sections of the city, residence areas were protected from the proximity of the saloons, but in Jackson Ward, where the Negroes lived, saloons were everywhere. A committee of the men of St. Paul's appeared before the City Council and helped to remedy that condition; and what they had seen in their own investigation of Jackson Ward led to a further awakening of conscience and conviction. It had been plain that the Negro section suffered, not only from the saloons, but from the city's relative neglect of all that section in sanitation and in other decencies. So there was organized and financed for a time an Association for the Improvement of Housing and Living Conditions, which in spite of the cumbrous name it staggered under did carry forward some improvements—and this notwithstanding the insensitiveness to human values which sometimes may be astonishingly disclosed in men who think of themselves as Christians. Once at a meeting on behalf of the Association, when it was desired to enlist a larger membership, some of us were standing at a window in a tall office building, looking out over the city. Foul black smoke was vomiting out of the chimneys of two or three industrial plants and drifting toward the sections where the poorer people lived, and especially toward Jackson Ward. Someone exclaimed at the health menace of that smoke, and one man answered impatiently, "You talk as if it might be the death of some of the people, but that smoke is the life of the city." What "the life of the city" meant to him was material enterprises whose costs must not be increased by too much regulation, bank balances, and expanding profits in the Chamber of Commerce reports. That sort of mentality does not yield easily to social concern.

But the most exciting public matter with which I had some association during the St. Paul's years had to do with a proposed Coordinate College for Women at the University of Virginia. That idea and plan had no direct connection with St. Paul's or with any other church as such, though its leading champion was a member of St. Paul's congregation, Mary-Cooke Branch Munford—the Aunt Mary-Cooke whose girlhood and womanhood have been described in an earlier chapter. Personal loyalty would have drawn me anyhow to a cause which she had made her own, but the cause itself carried its own appeal to all who saw in it the promise of enlargement of life for multitudes of young people in Virginia.

Since 1819 there had existed at Charlottesville the University of Virginia. It had drawn to itself the sons of those privileged families which had been able to provide the private tutoring which brought boys up to a point from which they could go on to college studies; but until well after the middle of the nineteenth century nothing had been done to establish a system of education available alike to rich and poor. At length in 1870 elementary schools were provided for the children of the state, and high schools were developed in 1907. Now there began to be at least a chance for every boy in Virginia who was eager for an education to get it, all the way up to the level of the University.

But what of the girls? Could they get it? The answer was flatly—no.

That stark fact stood in the face of the contrasting reality that in the public schools of the state girls were showing themselves to be more eager and more fit for what Thomas Jefferson had called "The More General Diffusion of Knowledge" than were many of the boys. A woman who signed herself "High School Teacher" wrote to one of the Richmond papers.

In my twelve years' high school experience, I have known only twice that a boy took the highest honors in his class. I have known

98

this to happen repeatedly—a boy (average 86-89 per cent) to be valedictorian and carry off the University of Virginia scholarship, while a girl (average 95 percent) and perhaps three other girls (above 90 percent) would get nothing from the state at all. . . . It seems hardly credible that a state should discriminate between these boys and girls insofar as to maintain four colleges for the former and none for the latter.

"Hardly credible" or not, that is the way it was. And the fact of it roused in Mary-Cooke Munford a recognition of injustice and a compassion for the disadvantaged that kindled in her the fire of an unlimited commitment to an unselfish cause.

As she had once written to a friend: "Education has been my deepest interest from my girlhood, beginning with an almost passionate desire for the best in education for myself, which was denied because it was not the custom for girls in my class to receive a college education at that time. This interest has grown with my growth and strengthened with each succeeding year of my life." She would turn her disappointment now into a devotion that might bring to others what she had so deeply desired and had not had. So in 1910, the last year of her husband's life, and with his strong sympathy to fortify her, she called together at their house a little group of women and a few men whose interests she knew, and suggested that they see what they could do toward the establishment of a Coordinate College for Women at the University of Virginia. The purpose upon which they agreed was not to ignore inherited patterns and traditions of the University by advocating unqualified coeducation; they believed that all that was best at the University could be preserved and enriched, and at the same time women admitted to its privileges, by the establishment of a Coordinate College, related to the University as Radcliffe was related to Harvard, Barnard to Columbia, and Pembroke to Brown. Their thought was that the College for Women should have its own individuality, its own organization and inner life, its own social, residential, and instruction halls, but that it should share the library and the laboratories of the University, and have in its faculty some at least of the same distinguished professors who were teaching the men. Thus the College for Women would be no inferior and uncertain thing, but an integral part of the University, which had been increasing in prestige through the years since Thomas Jefferson had conceived it as part of his ideal for the education of all the people.

That seemed to be a vision and a plan which might rightly appeal to thoughtful and forward-looking people all through Virginia, and to the legislators who would have the power to say yes or no. Wide response did come. When a bill for the establishment of the College had been introduced in the legislature of 1910, the State Teachers' Association endorsed it, and so did the Farmers' Union, the Federation of Mothers' Clubs, the Trade Union Council, and other state and local organizations.

Dr. Edwin A. Alderman, President of the University of Virginia, gave this testimony to the University's governing board:

My own judgment causes me to favor unreservedly the establishment by the State of a college for the education of women, and its location near the University of Virginia under its direction and control. . . . If we reject this opportunity, it seems to me that we deliberately adopt a policy of restricted effort and restricted ambition.

100

Since the idea of a College for Women at the University of Virginia was new, and since to many legislators anything new seemed to be unsafe and therefore to be treated with suspicion, it was not surprising that the bill to establish the College got nowhere in the legislative sessions of 1910 and 1912.

But Mrs. Munford and her fellow workers bent to their task with new determination. "The Coordinate College League" included women who when they had put their hands to the plough were not easily turned back. Among them were my Jean and my sister Martha; Virginia S. McKenney, a recent graduate of Bryn Mawr, young, blue-eyed, vivacious, vice-chairman of the League; and Douglas Wright Maynard, quick-witted and fearless. All of these poured into the League's work an untiring energy which was inspired by their personal devotion to Mrs. Munford. With them also were Mary Newton Stanard, wife of William G. Stanard, Secretary of the Virginia Historical Society; Katherine Hawes, President of the Richmond Y.W.C.A.; Kate Pleasants Minor, one of the first women in Virginia to rouse the public conscience against barbarities which survived in the Virginia Penitentiary and in Virginia jails; and Mrs. Norman V. Randolph, whom a group of children were once overheard to be quite innocently speaking of as Mrs. "Normous" Randolph, a superb old lady built like a full-rigged ship, who could and would speak her mind in no uncertain fashion, and whose impeccable devotion to Virginia traditions and to the United Daughters of the Confederacy, of whom she was the President, made even stubborn legislators listen with healthy respect when she added to her old interests an emphatic championship of this new cause of the Coordinate College. And many men gave the committee of women their encouragement and their active help.

It might have seemed that this weighty support, backed up

as it was by the Superintendent of Public Instruction and other school authorities of Virginia, would be sufficient to mobilize all the sentiment that was necessary for the creation of the proposed College. But now came in the opposing forces which can be roused when a new idea collides with the entrenched conservatisms of an old society. An excited group of the alumni of the University began to campaign against the College; and the arguments they used constituted an exhibit of the intellectual fixations, and sometimes the subconscious passions, which can prevent a disputed issue from being decided on the basis of clear analysis and unclouded reason.

The leaders of the alumni group were men possessed by a sentiment which to them was sovereign: a fervent conception of the University of Virginia as they had known it, and as they wanted it unchangingly to remain. They sounded the alarm that the traditions of the University were in danger. They called mass meetings of the alumni in Richmond, Norfolk, Petersburg, Lynchburg, and other cities to organize protests to the legislature. Most of these meetings promptly voted that no such thing as a College for Women ought to be established in Charlottesville. A few men, more independent and perhaps more far-seeing than the rest, tried to persuade their groups that the University was facing a creative opportunity which it would reject at its peril; but the majority were clamorous the other way. Even some of those whose own impulse would naturally have been progressive began to think that it would be a pity to antagonize so many of their friends. At a crowded meeting of alumni hastily convened in Richmond, one popular alumnus championed the new idea. But it was soon apparent that among the University of Virginia alumni the Coordinate College was not to be a winning cause. Obviously then there was something wrong with an enthusiasm which resulted in setting a man at odds with his friends. Next day the eloquent advocate regretted his eloquence, and henceforward his influence swung into line with the crowd.

The arguments which the alumni, or the majority of them, used with one another and with the Legislature were varied. Some were opposed to this idea of advanced education for women anyhow. Some said the women were entitled to more education but that they should have a separate College; let the State make one up—or why couldn't the State take one of the Normal Schools and make a college out of that? Some said that the trouble was that the State had no money for the women: think of all the money that was needed for the elementary public schools. Workers for the whole public education system of Virginia and the South, like Mrs. Munford and Dr. Alderman, had been thinking of the needs of the public schools for many years; now the alumni discovered that need as a heaven-sent rhetorical device. One of them, a columnist in a country newspaper, showed how prejudice and ignorance might be enlisted against the thing which nearly all the long-time friends of public education were espousing.

Do you pay any attention to this rot and dribble about "giving the women an equal chance with the men" when you are going to give them this uncertain chance at the expense of little children who don't even know their ABC's?

The fact, of course, was that editorials and speeches which argued the supposed desirability of a separate college, or—contradictorily—the appropriation of state money for elementary schools alone, were debating outworks set up as defenses for a central reluctance that could not well be argued—the reluctance to admit any important change whatever in the Univer-

103

sity which the alumni had come to look upon as their own possession. "After all, dear Sir," wrote one of them to the editor of the *Richmond Virginian*, "why all this discussion? Why not 'let well enough alone'? Why graft this perilous, or at least doubtful experiment upon the University of Virginia? Is not that institution—already the glory of Virginia, the admiration of the country, the pride and darling of the alumni— is it not great enough and useful enough without inviting this new departure, so foreign to its history and traditions, and so repugnant to many, if not most of its alumni?"

One newspaper, at least, saw the presumption in that. The *Danville Register* wrote:

We sometimes suspect that the alumni of a university exert far more influence in shaping its policies than they are justly or legally entitled to exercise. After all it is the people's university, supported by their funds, and not the exclusive property of the alumni. We have heard Virginia alumni speak as if the college actually belonged to and ought to be governed and controlled by them, to whom it owes nothing and to which they owe much. By what right men who have enjoyed the bounty of the State should assume to dictate the policies of the State exclusively in this matter we have never been able to see.

But from the *Montgomery Messenger* of Christiansburg came this pronouncement which might have seemed to be dug up from some previous age:

There is no special need for highly educated women; until the nineteenth century men have always taken care of women; they can continue to do it in an improved way. This higher education does not make a woman any more modest, any more charming, any more graceful, any more attractive. Her natural grace and the

104

acuteness of the female disposition will give her all she needs to make herself agreeable to men.

In 1914 the bill to establish the Coordinate College for the first time passed one of the two houses of the legislature. It came up in the Senate after its foes had tried unsuccessfully to block a roll call on it. Thus the *Richmond Times-Dispatch* of March 11, 1914, the day after the Senate action, recorded what had happened.

A packed gallery was on hand to witness the Senate's action. The crowd numbered many schoolteachers and members of the women's organizations that have taken active part in the campaign. The spectators followed the varying fortunes of the bill on the floor with intense interest, and broke out in loud applause when the chair announced that the bill was passed.

The Senate vote in favor of the bill had been decisive. There seemed good hope that it would pass the House of Delegates. But the old argument about the need of common schools and the general reluctance to take seriously the cause of higher education for women were still too strong. The bill was defeated by 47 votes to 41. Listening to some of the debates of the day, one might have remembered the words written years before by Sidney Lanier to his brother:

Our people have failed to perceive the deeper movements underrunning the times, they lie wholly out of the mainstream of thought, and whirl their poor dead leaves of recollection round and round, in a piteous eddy that has all the wear and tear of motion without any of the rewards of progress.

This disappointment meant two more years of work for Mrs. Munford and her associates. But she was not disheartened. Mrs. Norman Randolph, as stalwart and loyal as ever, wrote to her:

My dear child,

For such you are to the old woman now writing you. I just felt I must send in writing my congratulations on your splendid fight against such heavy odds, with everything against you but your *splendid cause*. Defeated? not one bit of it!

Rally your forces in time for another attack. You are the Joan of Arc that is to lead to victory this women's movement for higher education.

When the legislature of 1916 met, the women were back at their task. Again the Senate passed the bill, and again it went over to the House of Delegates. Late in the session, on the evening of March 7, after six hours of debate, the voting began. The gallery of the House of Delegates and the spaces on the floor behind the members' seats were crowded, and many people, unable to get into the chamber, watched from the corridor through the glass doors.

The voting began:

A. S. Adams	Aye
B. D. Adams	No
H. P. Baker	Aye
W. W. Baker	Aye
Beale	No
Bond	No

Thus down the list the voting went, the lead swinging by a very slight margin now this way and now that.

The roll call went on to the end: F. J. Wright, Aye; Thomas Wright, No. There was silence. Many people who had listened breathlessly were checking up their own notes. The clerk was slowly counting up his official record. He turned to the Speaker. "The vote," he said, "is 46 Aye; 48 Nay." The bill was lost again.

That night Mrs. Munford said, and the Richmond newspapers of the next morning quoted her words in display type: "We are not discouraged. In fact, we are much encouraged because of the gains we have made since 1910. At the next session we are bound to win."

But as a matter of fact they were not to win, not the main objective. In 1917, America entered the World War. When the legislature of 1918 met, all domestic issues were confused. The bill for the Coordinate College did pass the Senate again; but its foes in the House of Delegates prevented it from coming to a vote.

Meanwhile, two other important by-products of the long fight for better educational opportunities for Virginia girls had developed. The legislature took over the ancient College of William and Mary at Williamsburg, which for over two centuries had existed as a private foundation, and made it a public institution, and opened it unreservedly to women as well as to men. At the same time, it was voted that women should be admitted as graduate students at the University of Virginia, though without the privilege of admission to undergraduate instruction, and without any college foundation of their own. After that, the effort to establish the Coordinate College and to make the University of Virginia what Thomas Jefferson called the culmination of educational opportunity for all the people came to an end. In the minds of many there lingered the words which President Alderman had written:

If we reject this opportunity, it seems to me that we deliberately adopt a policy of restricted effort and restricted ambition. And the great universities of the world, and especially of a democratic world, do not grow or achieve wide usefulness along such paths.

In the long struggle to establish the Coordinate College, I

107

had been a private in the ranks, of secondary importance but at least unfailing, a sort of color guard to go wherever Mary-Cooke Munford went. I shared the disappointment and the defeat in outward fact which had come to her. But I had seen and learned from her how the spirit can conquer and life be enlarged when one human being gives complete and self-forgetting devotion to a public cause.

XI. In the First World War

In the first decade of the century there had been the almost universal assumption that we were living in an era which would naturally continue to be prosperous and peaceful. Very few Americans had any awareness of the tensions building up in Europe. Then in a vortex of national jealousies and apprehensions, beginning with the assassination of Austrian Archduke Franz Ferdinand on June 28, 1914, Germany declared war on Russia and loosed her armies on a blitzkrieg through Belgium to strike also at France; with Belgium's neutrality violated by Germany and France attacked, England also was drawn in. By August 4 what was to become a World War had begun.

In the United States, for the most part, instinctive sentiment and sympathy rallied to the side of Belgium and France and England. But this country had so long felt itself separated from the controversies and collisions of the Old World that there was no unified public opinion toward American involvement. In May of 1915 a wave of anger did sweep through the country when a German submarine torpedoed the passenger liner *Lusitania* on her way to England, and 1,153 of the passengers and crew, including 114 American citizens, were drowned when the great ship went down. Woodrow Wilson, the President, still believed that America could make its best contribution to some sort of ultimate solution by refraining from armed combat. But by the winter of 1917 the German submarine attacks on merchant shipping had become so intolerable, and the danger of defeat for England and France so desperate, that the country at large was ready for the decision to which the mind of the President now had hardened as he went before the Congress on April 2 and recommended a declaration of war.

The hopes which he voiced as to what American intervention might accomplish have had a grim rebuttal in the actualities of our world in the half century that has followed. We fight, he said, "to make the world safe for democracy" and to wage this time "a war to end war." In place of a world made safe for democracy, it may seem that we have inherited one not safe for anything, and have sown instead the dragon's teeth of danger and destruction. But in 1917 a mood of exaltation followed the President's words. The people at large began to believe that the conflict could be a crusade, and participation in it an act which could enlist the nation's ultimate ideals.

Therefore the response was swift and strong. Many now volunteered for whatever they could do. There would be need of course for doctors. In Richmond one of the most brilliant and best known surgeons was Stuart McGuire. His spine had been badly injured as a child, he had to wear a steel brace for his back, and he looked too frail for exacting service. But it was he who began to organize in Richmond a Red Cross Hospital and to recruit its personnel. He asked me if I would go as chaplain, and the vestry of St. Paul's gave their consent with the warmth which everybody then had for any part of the war effort.

It was not until the late spring of 1918 that Base Hospital

110

45—as it was to be known—was called into service and ordered to Camp Lee at Petersburg, Virginia. In July the Hospital, with its personnel split into several detachments, was shipped to France, and the doctors and the enlisted men found themselves quartered in what had been a monastery in Autun, a small city so quiet and so old—Roman ruins were still within it—and so far removed from any battlefront that there was restless questioning as to what sense there was in being there. But in August orders came for the Hospital to be moved up close to the combat area, and late in the evening of August 21 those who had been at Autun detrained in the dark at the edge of the city of Toul.

In *The History of U.S. Army Base Hospital No. 45*, Dr. Joseph F. Geisinger has described what this new environment showed itself to be.

With daylight Toul lay unfolded before us—encircled by forts, a stronghold of great strategic importance but as a city forbidding and ugly of aspect, distinguished for its lack of anything that Autun possessed. Nothing here of the serenity and charm we had left behind, but everything of what we sought. Roads stuffed with moving troops and caravans of munitions and supplies; the steady boom of cannon at the front only a dozen miles away; fleets of airplanes circling, with now and again floating puffs of smoke telling of a skirmish in the clouds; the air filled with rumors of a big push; everywhere preoccupation, hurry, the stir of war. At last our work seemed at hand.[1]

What the doctors and the enlisted men found as their base was the complex of brick and concrete buildings called Caserne La Marche, which had been the barracks for the 153rd Regiment of the French Army. The three main buildings, on

[1] (Richmond: William Byrd Press, 1924), p. 50.

three sides of a walled quadrangle which had a gate and a guardhouse at the open end, were each four stories high and three hundred feet long, and were occupied at the moment by an American evacuation hospital, a field hospital, and a small French hospital. These moved out, taking all their equipment with them, but leaving six hundred sick behind. In the barracks buildings there was no running water, no plumbing, no central heat. The hospital equipment, the surgical instruments and the medicines, and the stores of every kind, which had been provided by the Richmond Red Cross and had been shipped to France, had not arrived. The nurses, who had been sent on a different transport from the rest of the personnel, were still somewhere on their way. That was the situation faced by the doctors and the enlisted men when they first moved into the Caserne La Marche, with Dr. Stuart McGuire in command.

On September 9 the nurses arrived and on September 12 the American Army launched its first great unaided offensive at St. Mihiel. The sick in the Caserne La Marche were evacuated to hospitals farther from the front, and what had been the barracks made ready for the flood of casualties which would pour in from the battlefront. Soon after the fighting began the ambulances brought them, direct from the field dressing stations. Receiving wards, shock wards, corridors were choked with them; and in the worst hours the yards were strewn with litters upon which men lay awaiting their turn for the operating tables where the surgeons worked day and night. In the month of September, eight thousand men passed through Base Hospital 45.

In the earliest experiences of the Hospital—the group crossing of the Atlantic, the arrival at Brest, the waiting time at Autun and the first days at Toul—I had had no respectable part. When most of the unit had been ordered for embarkation at Newport News and I with them, I was a Red Cross Chaplain (all of the Hospital had been in its initial organization part of the Red Cross), but it appeared that no provision had been made for counting a chaplain in on the Army roster, and therefore I was denied shipment. Only later did I get overseas, together with some other chaplains, and after a groping progress through France and temporary attachment to another group, I reached Toul just after the nurses, who had come by way of Liverpool, had arrived.

From that time on I could try to be of some use in the superb organization which Dr. Stuart McGuire had set up, and realize with increasing admiration what unlimited service men and women can be capable of when human need demands it. To begin to create what might even look like a hospital in the stark and empty barracks could have seemed to be an impossible job, and it was accomplished only by an inventiveness and determination that requisitioned, scrounged, and put together the first meagre necessities for any life and work at all. When the lavish supplies from Richmond arrived, the doctors and surgeons had all the basic materials to work with; but the nature of the buildings and the staggering number of the wounded and the sick made demands upon strength and devotion which only extraordinary morale could have measured up to. Surgeons, physicians, and nurses had to take care somehow of desperate cases and continuous needs which a civilian hospital would have thought impossible. And the enlisted men, besides their service in the wards, had to do the work which would have been supposed to belong to a hired maintenance staff—of which there was none. They had to bring up all the water needed in the wards, the wood and coal for the stoves, the trays of food for the patients; and when the ambulances brought a new inpouring of the sick and wounded, these had to be carried on stretchers, not to any elevators but up the one, two, or three flights of stone stairs to the wards where beds were being got ready for them. Each one of those enlisted men deserved the tribute which is written in one of the chapters of the history of the hospital:

All too frequently he went to his bunk utterly worn out from his day's work, disheartened, weary of the grinding, unattractive job, but back at it again the next morning, facing with a great spirit another day which he knew would be but a dreary repetition of the one that had gone before. A fine and worthy figure it seemed to us, that ward master, that doughboy of "45," that man in the hospital trench.[2]

My business was to help when and where I could: to be on hand when the ambulances arrived, to go to the bedside of the sick and wounded, to visit in the wards, to hold services on Sunday for such of the personnel as could come and brief services of prayer and a hymn in the wards on Sundays and other days, and Communion for those who welcomed it, and to respond if I could to what individuals might need and want; and then—the sad thing—to arrange nearly every afternoon for the burial of the dead, and to try to write to the father or mother or wife of the man I had buried to tell them at least something about the spirit of the hospital which had tried to save the life of the one they loved. It was all inadequate. When you sat down by a boy dying of his wounds or—as was more likely that fall—of the virulent influenza epidemic which swept through the army, there was so little which you could say to him that he could understand. I realized how sometimes we need a symbol which can wake an emotional response which words alone cannot evoke. Henry Sherrill, who was the

[2] *Ibid.*, p. 75.

chaplain of Base Hospital 6 in that same first World War, was right when he wrote:

A friend had given me a crucifix. It does not do to underestimate outward and visible signs. What do you do when a man cannot hear or understand a prayer through weakness? The crucifix in his hand he could see and it would bring the strength and peace of the Crucified and Risen Christ. So he would die holding the Cross, and the next day the nurse would return the crucifix.[3]

The uncomplaining courage of some of the men who were brought into the Hospital said more to me than I could say to them. I was sent for one day to see a man who had been shot in the spine by a machine gun bullet. He was a sergeant, and he had been wounded while he was leading a squad in no-man's-land to mend the wire. As I looked at his face drawn with pain and asked him about himself and how he felt, this is what he said: "I certainly was proud that none of the other boys got hurt."

Now and then also in the midst of grimness and suffering there was something so ludicrous that everybody had a chance to laugh. One day a very large Negro was about to be operated on for a bad wound in one of his enormous feet.

"Doctor," he said, "you'd have to have a wound clear up to yo' waist to hurt as bad as my foot do."

Then when asked what had happened to him, he replied, "Well, we was goin' over the top. The first lieutenant was leadin' the first plutoon and the second lieutenant was leadin' the second plutoon, and the sergeant—dat's me—come behind to kind o' skeer up the stragglers. Then the shells commenced bustin' and the smoke to risin', and the company jest dis-

---

[3] *Among Friends* (Boston: Little, Brown and Co., 1962), p. 75.

115

appeared into the smoke and I didn't know where they was; and 'bout then some'n hit my foot and broke it. And then a German tank was crawlin' up towards me, and I got up and runned, sore foot or no sore foot; and the next thing I knowed, I was in the horspital."

"Well, how do you like France?" he was asked.

He kept still for a moment, as though he were seeking emphasis for one supreme utterance. Then out of his disgusted consciousness of having been brought over the ocean to a land where it seemed perpetually to be raining, he declared himself:

"Fo' Gawd, doctor, I tell you the truth, I wouldn't give one foot of Alabama for dis here whole French island!"

Sometimes one little vignette of memory may stand out from the general picture as expressive of the haunting sense of desolation which may rise out of the irrationality of war. A few of us, having a chance one day to go up to the area which only a few days before had been the fighting front, came upon what was left of what had been a sizeable town; uninhabitable not altogether because of the damage which had already been done but because the German guns still threw shells into it every night. A few houses were utterly ruined. Shells exploding through the roof had carried the upper floors and all their furniture in a great heap of tangled debris down to the ground where it lay piled up behind the broken windows. Some houses had their front walls bowed out by explosives within, so that at any moment the tottering curve might fall. Everywhere there were shell holes, ragged blinds, and doors hanging from their hinges, scars of shrapnel, smashed shop windows revealing a litter of ruined stuff within, debris in the streets, in one place a torn French flag, and in another a little broken doll. But with a few exceptions, the main outlines of the houses remained. They were wounded, but they were not so utterly mutilated as to have lost the look of human habitation. And as I stood away from the close prospect, the poignant sense of the town as claiming still its people grew the stronger. A river ran through the middle of the town, and I went and stood on the span of the old stone bridge that crossed the water. On one bank of the river was the empty building of a school for boys, and on the other side a school for girls. Some very old half-timbered houses near the end of the bridge were mirrored in the still water. Two churches, one of them with beautiful gothic towers, rose above the surrounding roofs. Somewhere, with a startling distinctness, a chime struck. With that exception, there was not a sound except the ripple of the water against the stone piers underneath and the remote echo of its falling where the river was crossed by a low dam farther down the stream. If the town had *looked* unmistakably like a ruined and abandoned thing, the stillness would not have weighed as so unnatural, but from that distance the place seemed as one that should have been alive, yet lay inexplicably dead. At that moment and at that spot, in strange and acute impression, war seemed to be a vast fatality, an uncanny dehumanizing thing before which existence might become a desert. It was as though the skeleton of the world stood there in ghastly semblance of completeness, while the life of it had gone.

Another picture. A half mile up the road from the Caserne La Marche a broken wall, and on the other side a field which the autumn rains turned into muddy bleakness. In the afternoons bodies were laid there, generally in coffins but sometimes wrapped only in blankets because no coffins were to be had. Day by day I read the burial service over boys whom those at home who had loved them thought to be still alive. The field had been the garden of some French peasant, a garden meant to grow the food by which men and women and children live. But with inexorable progression the garden disappeared before the lengthening lines of graves.

Early in November the rumor spread that the Germans were weakening. Incredible though it seemed, the end might be at hand. Then at eleven o'clock on the morning of November 11 it happened. All along the front the sound of the guns ceased. I can see again the headline sprawled across the whole width of the front page of the first French newspaper, *Fini la Guerre!*

The rest of that day and that evening, of course, there was jubilation. In the streets of Toul, doughboy and poilu, not unaffected by the freely flowing *vin rouge*, with arms about each other, marched in long lines, squawking jumbled French and English. A file of dejected German troops who had surrendered were being marched to some stockade. When dusk came, the gas lamps on the street corners sputtered dimly, being nearly choked with the dust and rust of four years of blackout; but the thing that mattered was that now at last the lights could be turned on again. Everywhere the noise of shouting and of singing. But when I went into the beautiful old cathedral, it was quiet, and empty except for one figure. There at one of the altars, with a candle which she had lighted, a woman knelt, a woman all in black; remembering someone—husband, brother, son?—whose death had been part of the price of the victory in which the crowd outside exulted.

Then as I came out I saw on the western front of the cathedral the great stone crucifix which is sculptured there. It stood then, and it stands now, as the symbol of our final faith and hope, the gospel of redemption wrought through pain; the gospel of him who lived and died not to save his own nation only but to build on earth at length a kingdom of God in which all nations might find their fulfilled life.

XII. Principles Worth Fighting For

Late in January, 1919, I was back in Richmond and at St. Paul's. Valentine Lee, who had been my assistant for two years before I went to France, had carried on the work of the church with faithful ability, and the emotions of the war had made the people respond to the Red Cross and other forms of helpfulness with a dedication that had created a new solidarity of sympathy and service in the parish. There had been losses and sorrows which all knew of and many shared: some of the finest of the young men of St. Paul's had been killed in France; others—both among the young and among men and women generally—had died in the influenza epidemic, some of them as the direct result of exhaustion from what they had done in emergency nursing at the hospitals. To come back to those who had been bereft and to try again to be their minister was to realize afresh the bond of understanding, deeper than any spoken words, which belongs to those who are trying together to be Christians.

With the war ended, it seemed to me—as it seemed to many others—that our crucial responsibility was to try to make sure that some positive good should come out of all its cost and suffering. It had been proclaimed that America was fighting

120

not for its own safety alone, and not for any narrow gain, but for a new world order of justice and of peace which could come to all nations as a benediction. Such a hope, and such a dedication, had been symbolized in St. Paul's by what we did when the United States first entered the war. We had never had a flag in the church, and one of the women's guilds came and asked me if they might give one. I answered, yes, they might—provided they gave two. When they wanted to know what I meant by that, I told them that loyalty to one's country and devotion to its cause could be a noble thing, but that it could be fully noble only if it is linked with something larger than itself. So if we were to have in St. Paul's the national flag, we should also have another flag that would symbolize God's saving purpose in which all men must be included. There had not then been devised the church flag which has since been adopted, and what I suggested was that there should be a great crimson banner with a white cross at the center of it—to remind us that God "has made of one blood all nations that dwell on the face of the earth," and that it will not be by the armies of any nation but only by the compassion of Christ that the world can be redeemed. In the semicircular chancel of St. Paul's there are six great Corinthian pillars that support the ceiling. Against one of the two of these nearest the people there would be the national flag, and against the one on the other side—the gospel side—there would be the banner with its spiritual reminder that "The Son of God goes forth to war, a kingly crown to gain," and with its continuing question, "Who follows in *His* train?"

In that same spirit I preached on successive Sundays in February of 1919 three sermons, "The Spirit of Men as Revealed in a War Hospital in France," "The Old World and the New," and "What Can We Gain from the Graves in France?" Months later there came a day when the bodies of six of the men who had gone from Richmond, one of them a young captain who belonged to St. Paul's, were brought back from France at the same time to be buried in the land that was their own. I wanted urgently to have the city find in their burial not a momentary emotion only, but a quickened sense of what they died for and of what they might say to us who did not die. "Many have been inclined to forget the war," I said. "From the unaccustomed tension of the struggle, thought dropped back, with the armistice, into the old routine. Men have said, 'Let us get back to normalcy.' Our ears have grown dull to the voice of the ideals which for a while stirred this nation, because we have turned to listen to lesser, selfish things."

But today the mighty voices call again. Today the symbols of sacrifice come home. . . .

We in this country saw the glamour and the pageantry of war. We saw the processions and the banners and the troop trains filled with laughing men, the movement and the thrill of youth going out to the great adventure. But the men who were to die saw another side of war.

A dark road, crowded with the caissons and thronged by infantry, pressing toward the front; the ugly roar of the motor of a German airplane somewhere overhead in the blackness; a bomb dropped at a crossroads—and blood, and death, and mangling—that was war, and they saw it. Regiments of men lying in the rain waiting for the dawn, stern young faces going over the parapets into machine gun fire, broken bodies on the wire—that too was war. The endless line of ambulances pouring toward the hospitals, still figures lifted out on stretchers, long wards of agony where nurses and doctors battled all night with death—that was war. Graves in the fields and in the gardens, long lines of graves dug new continually for men who would come back to them presently from the battles—that too was war, and its grim and tragic waste.

Through these things went the men who died that we might live. What then do we owe to them?

That was the question. Then there was the need to try to bring some answer as to the actual commitments which individuals and communities must make if the possible meaning from the war was not to fade into a cheap forgetfulness.

First, we are to ask ourselves whether we, in peace, can rise—as men in war did rise—above petty absorptions into loyalty to a larger thing. They died for the country. Do we, with any continuing nobility of purpose, live for it? To think generously, to vote with conscientious carefulness, to try to put the common good above the personal advantage of ourselves and of our little cliques, to make the city and the state and the nation better because of the quality of our citizenship, is not so dramatic a service as that of men who fought in a battle, but it is vital—and who can dare ignore it or deny it?

In the second place, these men were fighting for something even greater than their country—something that had to do not with America alone, but with the world. They were told that they fought "a war that was to end war." They listened to the voices of the prophets who spoke of a new leaguing of the nations to do away with the ancient curse. If that fails, havoc lies ahead. If it succeeds, we may yet begin to build that new earth of which we dreamed in the high moments of the war. To make this possible, America must discipline its own soul. We must learn self-control and patience, and a spirit that measures our own ultimate good in terms of the things which are good for all the peoples. So we may take the torch from the hands of those who died. So we may show that we who live can rise to those new determinations which may create a civilization worthy of the price they paid.

The League of Nations, which Woodrow Wilson gave his life for, failed—failed largely because America went "back to normalcy," and refused to join it. Perhaps it had to fail. But it was a great hope to fight for; and I, as one among many, did fight for it. In the pulpit of St. Paul's and elsewhere, I spoke

123

for it. I like to remember a great meeting in the Richmond Auditorium at which William Howard Taft, the ex-President, was one of the speakers. His own political party had helped to destroy the League, but with a magnanimous conviction that was too big for partisanship he championed it. Even in serious matters he had an infectious humor which made him able to laugh at himself. After four years as President, he had gone down to what might have seemed ignominious defeat. Campaigning now to get the Senate to ratify the League of Nations, he recited his own former struggles with the Senate over treaties which it rejected. "I hoped," he said, "that the Senate would change its mind. If it didn't, I hoped that the people would change the Senate." "Instead of which," he said, with that inimitable chuckle of his which no words in type can reproduce, "instead of which—a-hee!—they changed *me*." But no moment of genial whimsicality could make anyone fail to recognize the intensity of his essential belief; and one day, years later, he turned suddenly upon a Christian minister who was lamenting America's desertion of the League of Nations and the chaos of the following years, which may have been a result of that desertion, and he exclaimed, "Don't you of all men know that the best things in this world are often crucified—but that they rise again!"

When I had come back from France and was in Richmond again, I had another channel of expression besides the pulpit of St. Paul's. *The Southern Churchman*, located in Richmond, had been published with unbroken continuity since 1835, and its weekly issues had become traditional reading for a great number of families in Virginia and in the South and here and there in the country at large. Its editor had been the gentle and scholarly Edward L. Goodwin. Dr. Goodwin's strength was limited as he grew older, and he asked me to become his associate and to write some of the editorials. This I began to do in 1919, and increasingly from that time on he wanted me to write more, so that even before he retired in October, 1921, the editorial responsibility had become almost entirely mine.

New ideas, or even variations in old ideas, are not always placidly received, and it must be admitted that some of the emphases appearing in *The Southern Churchman* editorials were such as would be disturbing to those who wanted to hear only what they called the simple gospel, and were comfortably sure that they knew exactly what the simple gospel was. Conservatives would not have much fondness for an editor who might have seemed to be saying to them what Billy Sunday once said to an acquaintance who protested, "Billy, you mean well, but the trouble with you is that you are always rubbing people's fur the wrong way." And Billy Sunday replied: "No, I don't rub it the wrong way. I rub it the right way. Let the cat turn round."

There were various aspects in which it seemed to me that some of us in the church needed to turn round and look in directions which had not been sufficiently recognized already. For instance: toward a more informed understanding of the Bible in the light of the best that can be learned by those who are both reverent and unafraid; a recognition that there is a living gospel which is more important than ecclesiastical traditions and forms; and a readiness to see that Christianity belongs not only in the church's worship on Sunday but in the world's work and community decisions on Monday and all the rest of the week.

Many devoted people in Virginia and elsewhere among *The Southern Churchman* constituency had never got beyond the assumption of earlier generations that the Bible must be read as a literal and infallible whole, or else all its authority would be gone. A beloved Richmond clergyman wrote a letter to be published in the correspondence column in which he said:

"No appeal is allowed from any clear teaching of the inspired record. A pronouncement undoubtedly found in the New Testament whose meaning is unambiguous and plain, must be accepted as God's thought on the matter in hand." The trouble was, of course, that this sort of blanket treatment of the Bible, and the conviction that from any passage, read literally and without recognition of special conditions in the century when it was written, one could infallibly get "God's thought on the matter in hand," might lead to conclusions which were not God's thought at all. Therefore I tried in *The Southern Churchman* to suggest to those who were belligerently sure of what the Bible said that they remember the words of Oliver Cromwell, "I beseech you by the mercies of Christ that you consider it possible that you may be mistaken."

Not always with much success. The editor of a church paper has an enlivening experience of the astonishing ideas and emotions which can erupt in good church members when they think they are defending the ark of God. It happened that a well-known clergyman in New York said something which the newspapers distorted and made to sound like a denial of his Christian faith. It was all a misunderstanding of words that died down to nothing, but for a while those who believed they were the exponents of God's thought in the matter had exuberant satisfaction in being furious. A generally lovable layman, who was naturally so warmhearted that if an antagonist had knocked at his door he would have invited him straightway in to dinner, wrote of this clergyman whom he did *not* know, "I consider————beneath Judas Iscariot! When Judas realized what he had done, he went out and hanged himself, and I have never heard that the world was worse off on account of that act. If————can escape being deposed by some technicality of our church laws, then the true believers in the church should get a rope and administer the same law which has often been resorted to." In other words, if you don't like what the news-papers say a man's ideas are, as a good Christian you ought to go out and lynch him.

That particular Mr. Furious was certain that he knew what the infallible word of God would be. Another writer to *The Southern Churchman*, this time a lady, was not so furious, but was equally convinced that her views had divine authority. This was before the Woman Suffrage Amendment had been written into the Constitution; and she indicted *The Southern Churchman* because it published a news report of the "Wom-an's Movement for Constructive Peace," which Movement involved the belief that there might be better ultimate hope for world peace if there should be "extension of the franchise to women." But that, wrote the secretary of the "Virginia Association Opposed to Woman Suffrage," would be "at variance with God's will as reiterated in His Word and inter-preted both by the law and the church, and to which in tradi-tion, in womanly instinct, in judgment and in religious con-viction we are unalterably opposed."

It may be that the unhappy lady who wrote her protesting letter has changed her mind. At any rate, there have been changes in other matters with which *The Southern Church-man* had to do. Between *The Southern Churchman* and *The Living Church*, which was more likely to stand for the ecclesi-astical *status quo*, there was recurrent dueling, not less resolute for being always friendly. On one occasion *The Living Church* expressed its sense of outrage because of a preacher who had been invited to the pulpit of Durham Cathedral. His presence there was an intrusion, "which will be vigorously resented and opposed." And who was the preacher? Some scoffer? Some non-Christian? Some person without any spiritual credentials? No. But let those ready to be shocked hold their breath. It was —a Presbyterian! It was John Henry Jowett, loved and honored and widely known in the Christian world. Yet for him to be invited to preach in the Cathedral was accounted "a plain violation of the fundamental distinction between the ministry of the Church and ministers not of the Church." As to which *The Southern Churchman* answered: "This Church of ours has too many great things to do to spend time trying not to listen to a man who might tell us news about the Master. Let us be glad to welcome any messenger who, through his coming and our reception of him, can make us more generous in thought and more swift in service for our common Lord."

Of course, the invitation to other Christian ministers to preach in Episcopal pulpits is so frequent and familiar now that it may be difficult to believe that it was once "vigorously resented and opposed." *The Southern Churchman* used its full influence to overcome the blockade that in the earlier years was set up against such welcome. It urged the entrance of the Episcopal Church into the Federal Council of the Churches (now the National Council), which also was long resisted. It believed that the great trust committed to this Church could most surely be fulfilled by humility of spirit and not by self-assertion, by Christian comradeship and not by exclusive claims, by men among its bishops and in all its ministry who were more concerned with service than with sacerdotal rank and recognition.

Linked with all its other loyalties, *The Southern Churchman* tried to bear continual witness to what, in the relation of religion to life, may rightly be called the *full* gospel. There have always been those in the Church who have wanted something less inclusive. They have insisted fervently that what the Church must preach is "the simple gospel," and "the pure gospel." By that they mean a gospel which is bound up with the individual soul's salvation, and is not put in danger of

128

being twisted by too many secular applications. There might be in that narrowed sense a "pure gospel," but it would be a gospel increasingly unrelated to the everyday world in which men have to live and work. It could have the purity of a vacuum, but not the purity of a great wind blowing across the world, that cleanses and sets free. To be true to the gospel in its wholeness one must remember the parable of the Good Samaritan, and the promise of Jesus that those who had gone out to help human beings in distress would hear him say, "As you did it to one of the least of these my brethren, you did it to me."

Consequently, *The Southern Churchman* did try to keep the gospel livingly related to secular affairs. It urged a more imaginative and immediate recognition by white people and by the white power structure, of the deprivations and the injustices to which Negroes were subjected. It denounced the Ku Klux Klan. And it dealt, as occasion seemed to require, with other social and economic actualities in which human values were being treated as of small account, and treated thus by men who had convinced themselves that they were entirely consistent Christians.

In 1921 Judge Elbert H. Gary, Chairman of the United States Steel Corporation, gave a long and fervent address at the annual meeting of the American Iron and Steel Institute, immediately after returning from a visit to the Holy Land. "There is only one way of fairly and finally settling any controversy or question," he said, "and that is in accordance with the principles of the Christian religion. . . . Gentlemen, it is in accordance with our instincts and judgments, as frequently proclaimed, to say that it pays a nation or an individual to follow a Christian course." Such was the sentiment which Judge Gary brought back from the Holy Land. But what followed as a matter of fact? An announcement by a committee, which

129

Judge Gary headed, that the United States Steel Corporation considered it neither practicable nor advisable to change its requirement that the laborers in the steel mills work seven days a week, twelve hours a day, and at the end of every two weeks twenty-four hours at a stretch, when the day and night shifts interchanged their schedules.

This twelve-hour day was already being condemned as humanly destructive by a great body of informed opinion, but the United States Steel Corporation still defended it. In *The Southern Churchman* of June 16, 1923, I wrote an editorial entitled "Shall Life Be Fed to the Furnace?" Reaction was not long in coming. A Philadelphia lawyer, and a leading layman of the Church, wrote that the editorial was "most unfortunate, especially in a religious paper." Two weeks later *The Southern Churchman* carried "A Reply to a Valued Critic." It tried again to show that comment upon such an issue as the twelve-hour day did belong in a religious paper. Referring again to Judge Gary's speech it said: "The standards which he phrases could not be improved upon. But there is a curious nonsequitur between his religious advice and his industrial conclusions. There is revealed, we think, no slightest insincerity; but there is furnished a convincing illustration of the inconsistency which is bound to result when religion is treated as something apart from practical business. There are many men of affairs today, who, like Judge Gary, perceive that the world needs religion if it is ever to be stabilized, and yet unconsciously fail to recognize the bearing of Christian values upon the industrial problems immediately at their hand. A church that should have no message men felt to be vital for their present life, no authoritative and transforming gospel for our social wrongs, no light to indicate the path of human progress, would be a Church that would die in the world through men's sheer indifference to it. The hope for the

Church today is in that growing number of men in the pulpit, and in groups of every kind, who are determined that the Church shall be taken seriously, because it takes its own gospel as a serious, commanding, and all-inclusive thing."

Sometime before Judge Gary's speech, Bishop Charles D. Williams, of Michigan, had preached in the Cathedral of St. John the Divine a sermon in which he called for a warmer concern on the part of the Church for better working conditions in great industries, which organized labor was struggling against heavy odds to win. Dr. Manning, then Bishop-elect, from the same pulpit on the next Sunday repudiated Bishop Williams' message, "It is," he said, "our duty to meddle as little as possible, as a Church, with definite political or economic issues, as to which few representatives of the Church are qualified to speak wisely. We must not take sides in industrial conflict," he said. But as a news report quoted a layman who was present as having said, "Dr. Manning did take sides, and the side he took will not interfere with the building of the cathedral." And *The New Republic*, weekly journal of general opinion, referring to Dr. Manning's pronouncement that "few representatives of the Church are qualified to speak wisely" on industrial matters, made the acid comment that if indeed the Church cannot learn to speak and to speak wisely, then it would seem that "the function of the clergy, as Dr. Manning sees it, is to bathe in the odor of sanctity institutions and enterprises whose nature laymen have determined on wholly secular grounds."

At any rate, *The Southern Churchman* did not think that the function of the clergy is so tame a thing as that. It sought continually to advance the social gospel of the Kingdom of God, and to interpret Christianity as the leaven which must enter into all life.

131

XIII. The Final Years in Richmond

The Southern Churchman office was on the third floor of the old former rectory which was serving as the parish house of St. Paul's. All I had to do to get there was to go up one flight of stairs from the rector's office where I would be every morning anyway. Of course the contacts there and the writing of the editorials took some little time, but never enough to draw me away from my central absorption in the life and work of the parish. Always St. Paul's was the magnet to which my special affection and nearly all my thought were drawn. When a man has been the minister of a congregation for eight or ten years, the bond with its people can have become very deep and dear. Boys and girls whom he prepared for confirmation will have become the young men and women whom he knows and can rely on. Those who were just grown up when he first came may be among the leaders now; and with those who were the leaders at the beginning he has had the comradeship of an increasing mutual trust. He has had the chance to come very close to some of them in times of joy or sorrow; and the memory of older men and women who have gone ahead has helped him know the meaning of "the communion of saints."

That is the way I felt about the people of St. Paul's. I had everything to be thankful for in the way they had responded to expanding plans and programs for the parish; and "they" meant the vestry, the Men's Association, the organizations of the women, and the boys and girls too. In 1919 there had been the so-called Nationwide Campaign, an effort of the whole church, in which I had a considerable part, to lift the whole level of the people's commitment of service, and to increase missionary giving in the parishes. Loyal to the promise which the vestry had made in 1911 that St. Paul's should be "a missionary church," the congregation entered into the Campaign with quick understanding and determined purpose. The amount subscribed to the parish budget was far greater than it had ever been before; and of the total amount received only 40 percent was kept for the parish's own expenses, and 60 percent was given for missionary work beyond the parish bounds—a proportion which I think was equalled that year by no other Episcopal congregation anywhere. And with a friendly inclusiveness which made it in some genuine degree "a democratic church," St. Paul's lived up also to the third point in our commitment, that it be "a working church." Its spirit had its best expression in what one of the vestrymen told me. He was the head of a business which required his close attention, but he was conspicuous in his readiness to help in whatever the parish needed. One day when I wondered how he could, he gave me the answer. He said that every morning when he said his prayers he asked that he might be shown how he could manage to have that day some time and some clear thought for any service in the church that he could render.

Then, of course, as in every happy parish, there were those special gifts from God—the women: women who could be like Mary of Bethany and like Martha too, sensitive to all

133

spiritual realities and yet ready equally for the homely things that needed to be done, whether it was cooking in the kitchen and waiting on the tables at the Lenten luncheons, or going out to see the sick and the poor, or making out of next-to-nothing royal costumes for Magi and kings, and wings for angels at the Christmas pageants. The combination of the mothers and the children gave me the chance to work out something which the congregation may have regarded skeptically in the beginning but which they came to regard as one of the lovely features of the year. On the Sunday morning before Christmas we used to have at the regular eleven o'clock hour not the conventional service, but a special story which I wrote and then read from the pulpit as the children whom I had trained to do it acted it out in the chancel where all the choir stalls had been moved back to make room. The pageants which we worked out together then were afterwards published and have been widely used, especially the final one, *The Christmas Pageant of the Holy Grail.*

Besides the comradeships at St. Paul's, there were associations to be glad of in the city and the diocese. The annual Diocesan Council, which was held in the month of May, brought together the clergy and the lay delegates not only from the city parishes but from all the little country churches too. In that period, the early 1900's, the number of those assembling was not too large for small towns to take them in, and to welcome them as houseguests in the people's homes. That made the Council not only a church business session but an occasion of such generous hospitality that everybody felt himself part of a unity of spirit which lifted his own consciousness of belonging to the church into something warmer and happier than it might have seemed the day before. There was an atmosphere so genial that differences of opinion seemed not to matter much. Everybody recognized that the old guard would want the Council not to make any disturbing changes about anything, and that "the young turks" would be advocating something or other that could be denounced as ridiculous. Some of us, for example, were always trying to change the canons so as to admit women to membership on vestries and to the Diocesan Council itself and to General Convention. It would take nearly fifty years for that to happen; but if everything that might have been progress moved slowly, it did move some, and with a good-humored friendliness which perhaps was more important than speed.

Attendance at three General Conventions was another pleasant aspect of the St. Paul's years. In 1916 I was one of the deputies when the Convention met in St. Louis and again in 1919 when it met at Detroit. In 1922 the Convention was to meet in Portland, Oregon, "the Rose City," and on the journey to which, and on the return from there, we Virginians were to see the almost incredible grandeur of the Canadian Rockies and the Grand Canyon of the Colorado, as prelude and postlude to the Convention itself.

At Portland much of the time was spent in listening to, and voting upon, the recommendations of the Commission which had been working for years on revision and enrichment of the Prayer Book. There could be all sorts of opinions about any particular proposed change, and many of the laymen were disinclined to changes anyhow. But in the give and take of discussion there did go forward a revision which kept the essential dignity and beauty of the Prayer Book as it was, and yet accomplished also changes and enlargements which made it more sensitively responsive to the need for worship than it had been before. As for myself, like most of us in the Convention who were not members of the preparatory Commission, I added nothing to the book's enrichment; all I did was to help get out some cattle which had anciently got in.

The Penitential Office in the old Prayer Book included the whole of the fifty-first Psalm which, in its words written some twenty-five centuries ago when animal sacrifice was a part of worship, seemed to be urging twentieth-century Christians to be bringing "their burnt offerings and oblations" still. I moved—and the motion was adopted—that the Psalm as printed in the Prayer Book office end with the beautiful verse "The sacrifice of God is a troubled spirit; a broken and contrite heart, O God, shalt thou not despise"; and thus, by leaving off the last two verses which formerly were printed, we would no longer tell the Lord that in order to please him greatly we will "offer young bullocks upon thine altar."

In a General Convention some of the discussions grow inevitably long and tedious, but often also they may be surprisingly enlivened. In one of the Conventions the subject for debate and decision was whether suffragan bishops, an order in the episcopate which had just been created, should or should not be given votes in the House of Bishops. A layman from Pennsylvania was convinced that they should not. With impish reference to II Samuel 10:5, which describes how certain servants of David were caught by some of their detractors and had half their beards cut off, to their great discomfiture, this layman said of suffragan bishops, "Let them tarry at Jericho a while till their beards be grown. We don't know yet what these suffragans may look like." And then he continued: "As to our uncertainty, I am reminded of what is reported to have happened when General Sherman's army was marching through Georgia. A young lieutenant went up to the porch of an old Southern mansion where a girl was sitting with a dog on her lap. 'Lady,' he said, 'I am very sorry, but I have to kill your dog.'

" 'Why should you kill my dog?' " she demanded.

" 'Because I have an order from General Sherman that all bloodhounds in this region must be killed.'

" 'But this is no bloodhound. It is a harmless little poodle.'

" 'Madam,' he said, 'I know it *is* a poodle. But you can never tell what those things may grow up to be.' "

With which thrust, so far as that Convention was concerned, any prospect of votes for suffragan bishops was drowned in a wave of laughter. Thus wit and humor could play their part—and sometimes a deadly part—in an assembly, but also there could be moments of sudden and positive inspiration. Such moments might come when a missionary bishop pleaded for his field, when at a Christian Social Service mass meeting some passionate crusader took up the cause of the disadvantaged and distressed, or when a clergyman or layman lifted up some new and unexpected standard for the Convention to adopt and follow. The high point of the Portland Convention was the opening sermon by Bishop Edwin S. Lines of Newark—growing old then in years, but superbly young in vision and in spirit. He took for his text Deuteronomy 1:6-7, "Ye have dwelt long enough in this mount: Turn you, and take your journey" (KJV); and a fresh impulse for forward movement came to the Convention from the buoyancy of what he said. One of the crucial issues at the Convention to which some of us were committed was the entrance of the Church, after too long and timid hesitation, into the Federal Council of Churches. Because of Bishop Lines there was new strength in the advocacy of it. In the final vote it failed by a hairsbreadth, but the way was paved for the entrance which did come later.

In Portland, among men from New York and among many others who knew the Church at large, there was much general talk as to who might succeed to the rectorship of Grace Church in New York City, from which Charles Lewis Slattery had just been elected to be Bishop Coadjutor of Massachusetts.

One Sunday in December, when I was back in St. Paul's, there appeared Mr. J. Frederic Kernochan, the senior warden, and Mr. Howard Townsend, one of the vestrymen, to bring me the vestry's call to Grace.

Then I faced the decision which more than any other I had ever known involved every element of mind and heart. I had been called before, to Baltimore, to Minneapolis, and also to New York, but none of those calls could overcome my feeling that St. Paul's was where I belonged. Now there was something different. Grace Church represented the great tradition which rectors such as Henry Codman Potter and William R. Huntington had created. It had the liberal evangelical spirit which had been the heart also of Virginia churchmanship. New York was the city where the strongest influences in the life of America were centering. It came upon me compellingly that perhaps I ought to make the wider venture of a ministry there.

I wrote to the Grace Church vestry accepting their call. Then the thought of separating from the city and the parish and the people I loved most came upon me as so intolerable that I telegraphed the Grace Church vestry to destroy the letter unread.

But the decision I had first arrived at pressed upon me again as the one that I somehow had to make; and I wrote again to Grace Church a letter of acceptance similar to the one which had been destroyed.

The vestry and the congregation of St. Paul's poured the warmth of their generous affection into the expression of what they thought my ministry had been to them; but what meant most of all to me was the crucial thing the vestry did. When I gave them my resignation, they asked me what they should do next. I told them that in my thought there was one man above all others in the whole Church whom we should most want to be the rector of St. Paul's. He was Beverley D. Tucker, Jr., then a professor at the Theological Seminary in Virginia. With almost no discussion, and with no mention of any other possibility, the vestry voted then and there to call him, and asked me to go to Alexandria with the two wardens to carry him the call. That is what we did. Not many days later he accepted; and on January 25, 1923, he came to Richmond, and he and I were together at the annual meeting of the parish on the evening of St. Paul's Day.

So began his superb ministry in Richmond, through the fifteen years of which the life and work of St. Paul's went on from strength to strength. In spirit and in purpose for the Church, he and I were in absolute accord; and between the two of us there has been, and is, devoted friendship.

XIV. At Grace Church: Ideals and Aims

When Dr. Charles Lewis Slattery, the seventh rector of Grace Church, accepted his election in 1922 to be Bishop Coadjutor of Massachusetts, he had lived in the rectory as a bachelor for twelve years. Now with a new rector and a family coming, the vestry determined upon extensive changes and renovations in the house, and these would require many weeks. So when I came to the parish in March, 1923, Jean and the children stayed in Richmond until the end of the school year. Two of the generous-hearted members of Grace, Richard T. Stevens and his wife, invited me to live in their apartment at The Berkeley, on Fifth Avenue at Ninth Street, while they would be away for the rest of that winter in Florida; but I had already said yes to another suggestion. The Rev. Harry P. Nichols, who had just retired from the rectorship of Holy Trinity Church, New York, was living at a little hotel on Eighth Street called The Marlton, and he had suggested that I come there too. That is what I did; and as a result, my first days in New York brought the beginning of a warm new friendship with an extraordinary man: seventy-

three years old, and officially "retired," but still full of exhaust-
less energy. He had two enthusiasms, which went well together: one was witnessing to the gospel, and the other was
climbing mountains. His witnessing to the gospel was not
merely a matter of continuing to preach in pulpits when
invitations came to him, but more importantly of being so
companionable with people, and so responsive everyday to
what was going on in them, that he was himself a sort of
gospel of good news. It was the future that interested him
most, and he could make quick contact with all young men.
When an acquaintance of his was lamenting his lonesome-
ness because he belonged to a vanishing generation and so
many of his old friends had died, Dr. Nichols answered, "Then
make new ones." And the new friendships *he* made brought
continual stimulation to his own virile energies. His summer
home was in Intervale, New Hampshire, and up to the time
when he was in his late eighties he would spend many of
his days leading groups of friends up the trails to the top
of Mount Washington or the other heights in the Presidential
Range. In New York he was the president of the American
Alpine Club; and on the bookplate which he put as frontis-
piece in all his books was an etching of a mountain peak and
underneath it these words: *Not to climb is not to conquer.* He
had an exuberant voice which moved up to its maximum
volume as his interest in any subject grew. I would be having
lunch with him at The Marlton, and he might lean over con-
fidentially toward me and begin in a hoarse undertone which
he mistakenly imagined to be a whisper. Then as the people
at other tables in the dining room stopped their forks in mid-
career at amused attention to what he was about to pronounce,
he would say to me, "Do you see that lady over there? **She
has just CLIMBED THE MATTERHORN!**"

It was only a short walk from The Marlton to Grace Church and its surrounding buildings, and I was there each morning to meet with the parish staff—and to go out from there in the afternoons to call on members of the parish. I had inherited from Dr. Slattery a vital and varied organization: at the church two clergy assistants and an organist and assistant organist, with secretarial and maintenance staff of twelve; a choristers' school with a headmaster and four other teachers and some twenty to thirty boys in residence; a day nursery and a men's lunch club. Then at Grace Chapel on East Fourteenth Street were three other clergy, a home for old people, a medical dispensary, and lay workers to the number of fourteen.

My first Sunday in Grace Church was on March 4. I had been thinking of one particular verse in the Gospel of Luke which expressed the spirit which I hoped might somehow touch for all of us the ministry which was beginning then. It was the verse from the story of the two disciples walking to Emmaus: "Jesus himself drew near, and went with them." What I said I should not be fully able to remember, but it comes back to mind through a report in the *New York Times* of Monday, March 5, which has turned up in a hitherto forgotten file.

I have taken these words for us to think of this morning because they seem to me to symbolize what ought to be the spirit of that comradeship in Christian experience which we now begin. "While the two disciples communed and reasoned together, Jesus himself drew near, and went with them." Is it not plain that this must be what we should desire and seek? We begin today a relationship in which we who look into one another's faces share. We start out on a road together. There will be much that together we must try to do. Here is this great parish with all its noble traditions wrought out of the service of men and women who have gone before; here is all the beauty of this visible shrine; here are all these buildings adapted for human service; here is the machinery of an elaborate organization in which the energies of a modern parish seek expression. But it is possible to have all these things and yet in the end to lose the one thing that would be eternally significant. We might be busy in many restless ways and have much talk and planning as to what we thought it well to do. We might bring here into our work and into our counsel our own shrewd estimates of practicality, our own prepossessions as to duty and truth, our own opinions which reflect the views of the not always Christian civilization in which we live.

If upon the basis of these things we should reason together, it is certain that our utmost efforts would be both shallow and brief. One thing only can put into our life and comradeship an element of spiritual immortality. Among the figures of our visible company there must come another figure to whom the eyes of eager souls are lifted up. As we go along the road that leads before us, Jesus himself must draw near and walk with us.

On that Sunday when I preached for the first time as rector of Grace, James Sheerin, a clergyman of the New York diocese, was in the congregation. He wrote an article which he entitled "A New Voice in New York," and sent it to Richmond, where it was printed that month in *The Southern Churchman*. What he wrote about was enlarged by his own generous spirit, but he showed that at least one listener had caught the message which I tried to give that day. "There seems to be always a crowd in Grace Church, New York," the article began, "but March 4 it was more than usually difficult to get a seat. Its new rector, Dr. Bowie, was to preach his first sermon, and members of the parish, as well as general admirers of the young Virginian, were eager to be there and hear him. . . . I was one of the polite outsiders who took positions at the rear of the aisles. . . . But when the rector went to the pulpit for the sermon, I was able to get standing room inside the middle-aisle swinging doors, whence I could hear and see perfectly. . . . What interested me most was the youthfulness of Dr. Bowie's aspect."

Then the lengthy article went on:

There was nothing in the manner of Dr. Bowie that indicated nervousness, though he is probably one of those strong-willed ones who can look cool when inwardly excited. . . . It was not, however, merely the looks that marked his youth. There was that in his tone that revealed it. There was a note of joyous energy in every word, except in occasional half-sentences, when his voice dropped to a bass undertone, as though he was afraid he had been just a little too exuberant and natural for the moment. There is a seeming indifference in the eager utterer of a message to mere externals. But this indifference is but further testimony to that note of youthful enthusiasm which ever has been the peculiar quality of the great preacher. Phillips Brooks had it to the extreme, with his husky voice, his tremendous speed in delivery, and his rugged gestures. . . . The two dominant things in this great Grace Church service were the voices of the boy soloist and the new rector. In both was an insistent note of irresistible, never-dying youth, which carried older and staider people along into a world of renewed hope. "Jerusalem, Jerusalem, O Turn Thee to God," was the message of the singer. "And Jesus himself drew near and went with them," was the theme of the preacher. Both had the notes of reality.

To me the significant thing was that the young man in the pulpit, even though not so young as he looked, has willingly become a member of the Church League for Industrial Democracy, and the Modern Churchman's Union, meaning thus that he is in sympathy with social yearnings for better things, and that he believes in welcoming deeper and broader thinking in problems of theology, and yet he has not lost the enthusiasm for old-fashioned Christian religion. It is necessary to say this because there are ministers now in the public view whose ideas have become so democratized, or whatever they may call it, that they speak and act as if it did not matter whether Jesus draws near or not. The day is coming when to be a modernist will not mean a denier of the faith, and to be a social reformer will not oblige a man to forget Jesus Christ and Him crucified. Some of our present-day radicals seem to think that they are only radical when they can throw out of the Church windows every theological tenet the older people loved. It is comforting to such to perceive in younger men, like Dr. Bowie, a new power to unite a fervent personal gospel with an ardent faith in social progress and a fair respect for intellectual advances.

All this is inferred because the new Grace Church rector unconsciously revealed that he is a modernist who unqualifiedly believes that there is nowhere so much certainty of individual and social progress as when Jesus Himself draws near and goes with us. The churchman who has lost sight of this is surely not preaching the gospel, no matter how true his sociology or how helpful. We need modern interpretations of ancient and holy things, but they are only weakened for the Christian if set forth without Jesus Himself drawing nigh. The non-Jesus type of preacher has had his say in the last decade or two. His days are numbered by the prophets who build their social hopes about the person and the teachings of Jesus Christ.

Anything that Grace Church and its ministry actually did fell far short, of course, of bringing the meaning of the Lord Jesus Christ to the present needs of men. But it was good to know that some of those who came there realized at least that this was an ideal that had not been forgotten. One day the mail brought a letter from the rector of one of the parishes of the diocese outside the city in which he said:

There is a friend of ours living at 44 Washington Square, Miss———, an author, who goes to your church but has not yet become a member of it. I wish you might call upon her. She is a woman of rare gifts and Christian life. Here is what she writes to me this morning. "At Grace Church the service is built around the Lord Jesus; one feels that His service is first there."

During the years at St. Paul's, I had had abundant reason to know that parts of the South were still fenced in by the rigid conservatism which made H. L. Mencken describe them sardonically as "the Bible belt," and that even in Virginia and Richmond there were many men and women who would be disturbed by questioning of accepted ideas. I had taken it for granted that in New York the facts would be altogether different. Here, where the winds of thought from all the world were blowing, surely the people in such a parish as Grace would have become familiar with the exciting new interpretations of the Bible which modern scholarship had set in motion—would have breathed these in already, and found their religious faith made more vital in this new atmosphere. But that assumption of mine was to be quickly jolted. In October, 1923, Bishop William Lawrence of Massachusetts, on the thirtieth anniversary of his consecration, gave to a great congregation an address in which he told how his thought had moved from old literalisms to new—and to him more inspiring—conceptions of the Bible and the creeds. Some of what he said shocked traditionalists, and protests were made to the House of Bishops. In Grace Church in November, in a sermon entitled "Liberty in Faith" I expressed my allegiance to all that Bishop Lawrence had thought and expressed. "In such words as Bishop Lawrence has lately spoken, let the church rejoice today," I said. "There are many men in her pulpits, and I am one, who will not stand before the men and women of this age, with the inevitable reinterpretation through which their intellects must pass, and say that the kind of dogmatic affirmations concerning Christ which once were considered binding are really the necessary way to living faith in him."

To my surprise, Grace Church was startled, and some of its devoted people were offended. In one instance, especially, there was revealed the conflict which can occur in minds which have to face new ideas and for a while may try to understand them, but then are driven back to their old fixations when some angry reactionary persuades them that the new ideas should be considered as an outrage. A very wealthy old lady in Grace Church wrote me that she was shocked by the "Liberty-in-Faith" sermon. She had longtime loyalty to the parish and had been welcoming to me, and so I sent her a book of published sermons of mine which might give her a better perspective on what had been said in the one sermon she had heard. Her gentle self found expression in her first letter of reply. She wrote:

The book has come into my home, bringing light and inspiration. . . . I never before fully realized that, as you say, a single sermon gives of necessity an incomplete angle on the full meaning of the preacher's message. I realize too, in learning more and more of the messages of our own rector, we gain fuller insight into the train of suggestive thought that he would have me understand.

Believe me always, gratefully and affectionately yours.

So she wrote on the last day of November. But some other influence laid hold upon her. Early in the following January she sent a different message: "I request that I be given a letter of transfer to the Church of ——— in this city. I am moved to make this request for reasons that I consider good and sufficient. My understanding is that with my transfer from the parish of Grace Church all pledges made by me auto-

147

matically cease." And after the letter of transfer which she requested had been sent, she wrote that in the parish where she was now enrolled, she found "the conservative teachings which through long years have been my support and inspiration. Under guidance that stands firm as a rock in these days of stress within our beloved church, I now find peace."

It is saddening, of course, for any minister when he fails in what he wants to do: namely, to interpret the Bible and the creeds in a way that will satisfy honest and inquiring minds, and at the same time not shake but rather strengthen the faith of those who have believed in old-fashioned ways. Yet he must be true to what he sees as truth, even if disappointments come. Meanwhile he must try all the harder to widen and deepen the personal relationships with his people so that the trust which gradually they may begin to have in him will be enough to overcome the unwelcome they may feel toward something they may hear him say. One recollection which I treasure, as against the message from the lady who had to go elsewhere to "find peace," is linked with one of the aristocrats of old New York, J. Frederic Kernochan, the senior warden of the parish, who was one of the two who had come to Richmond to bring me the call to Grace Church and for whom I came to have a great affection. Some years later when he died and I was standing by his grave, his daughter said to me: "When you first came to be our rector, my father used to be disturbed at what you preached. It was not what he had been accustomed to think and believe. But one day he said to me, 'I still don't know whether I understand some of the things Dr. Bowie is saying, and once I might not have liked them. But now I am not troubled any more. I have decided that if he says them, they must be so.' "

One of the supreme privileges which can come to a man in the ministry is the chance for friendships, on the highest

148

and the deepest levels, with other men: with laymen in his congregation, like my senior warden, or with other laymen in the community quite outside the church's ranks. In a city such as New York there were, of course, men in many professions of such eminence, and of such wide-ranging knowledge, that any contact with them would be a stimulus. Moreover, as soon as I found myself in Grace Church, I realized the excitement that could come from association with other ministers whom now I could increasingly know: first of all with Henry Sloane Coffin, whom I had first seen and heard when I studied at Union Seminary in 1908 and who now, as the minister of the Madison Avenue Presbyterian Church, was the shining example in his pulpit and in his pastoral relationships of what one would want to try to be. So was Harry Fosdick, beginning then his electrifying preaching at the old First Church on Fifth Avenue, only a few blocks from Grace, that was to lead to "the Fundamentalist controversy," and to his subsequent world-famous ministry at the newly built Riverside Church. Then there were the companionships that I owed to *Kilin*—which symbolically at least was to a Chinese idol! At St. Mark's-in-the-Bouwerie the rector was William Norman Guthrie, as brilliant as he was unpredictable, restless and wide-ranging in his intellectual interests, warmhearted and impulsive and always getting himself into trouble with ecclesiastical conservatives, but with a mind that was like a rocket that sent up explosive balls of fire that burst into a shower of stars. Herbert Shipman, the beloved rector of the Church of the Heavenly Rest, had been elected a suffragan bishop in the Diocese of New York, which meant that he would be a subordinate to William T. Manning, not a hopeful prospect. Guthrie decided that he must devise something "to save Herbert Shipman's brains." He had got somewhere a carving of a legendary beast which represented a Chinese nature-god of curiosity and wisdom; so with the idol as a centerpiece he gathered fourteen men who were to meet one evening in each month for seven months in the fall and winter, to read and discuss the most important of new books. In one year seven of the men were to be the hosts at dinner, and the other seven the essayists; the next year, the roles were reversed. Each essayist was to make a thoughtful study of the assigned book, and to read his analysis of it. But that was not all. Every other man was to have read the book for himself, and at the meeting every man was called upon for his ideas.

That was *Kilin*, and from 1922 it has continued in existence to this day. Leighton Parks (who had been rector of Emmanuel Church, Boston, when I was at Harvard and then had come to St. Bartholomew's in New York) retired from the rectorship and left New York in 1923. He had been one of the original members of *Kilin*, and when he resigned, I was elected in his place; and so it was that I came quickly to know and to delight in the group that Guthrie had brought together. Among those who were in it then, besides Guthrie and Shipman, were Hughell Fosbroke, the Dean, and Burton S. Easton and L. W. Batten of the General Seminary; Foakes Jackson of Union; Caleb Stetson, the rector of Trinity Parish; John Howard Melish of Holy Trinity, Brooklyn; Roland Cotton Smith, who until his retirement had been rector of St. John's in Washington; Malcolm Douglas of Short Hills, New Jersey; Theodore Sedgwick, the rector of Calvary; and Wilbur Caswell of Yonkers. Nearly all those original members are long since dead; but the spirit, the organization and the program of *Kilin* continue as Kuthrie imagined them, now almost half a century ago.

Jean also found happy new friendships: with the wives of some of the vestrymen, particularly Mrs. Howard Townsend, Mrs. Augustus T. Hand, whose husband was a distinguished federal judge, and Mrs. Francis C. Huntington, the daughter-in-law of Dr. Huntington, the sixth rector of Grace Church; with Deaconess Garvin, the rector's secretary, who was as lovely to look at as she was lovely in herself; and with other members of the Grace Church and Grace Chapel staffs. Living in New York also were "Miss Sant," the beloved "Miss Mae," and her close friend and companion, Miss Julia C. Wilde, who was one of the executives of the Chapin School to which Jean (Jr.) and Elisabeth were to go. The contribution which a rector's wife can make to the spirit of a parish by her welcome in the rectory was already familiar to Jean at St. Paul's. The rectory at Grace next to the church, bordering directly on Broadway but separated from the busy street by a little oasis of grass and flowers and a fountain, was an extraordinarily beautiful old house, and one of the few left from the period when the city was still mostly south of Union Square; and Jean used it with warm imagination to draw many people to it: members of the general congregation to teas in afternoons, students from the General Seminary who would come in on Sunday evenings after having been in church for evensong, the boys of the Choir School and the whole church staff at Christmas and other special times. Some of the formal old ladies who came in the afternoons might try her patience and she might laugh afterwards about their pompous ways, but she could keep the whole occasion keyed to her gay spirit. It was through the Sunday evenings in the rectory that we first knew Ted Ferris, then a student at General Seminary, now rector of Trinity Church, Boston, and began a devoted friendship which has grown closer with the lengthening years.

The whole complex of buildings at Grace Church, as Henry C. Potter and William R. Huntington had created it, made an extraordinary little enclave of related life in what could be for so many the detached and impersonal existence of an indifferent city. Facing Broadway, between the church and the rectory, was Grace House. Back of the church on Fourth Avenue, was the Choristers' School. Next to that was the Clergy House, where the clergy assistants had their apartments; next to that a Day Nursery, afterwards changed, as Huntington House, into a boarding home for a lively household of girls who had come to New York for business jobs; and in the fourth building, apartments in one of which lived the engineer, who kept the whole establishment going from its furnace rooms and dynamos. All these buildings were connected with Grace House and with one another in what was a self-contained and almost a self-sufficient community in the midst of downtown New York. So there was the chance for constant contact and for friendliness among those most closely linked with the church's work such as would not often be found in the modern city.

The one drawback in relation to the congregation lay in that word *downtown*. The original Grace Church had stood at Broadway and Rector Street, not far from Trinity. When in 1843 it was decided to build a new church "uptown," the vestry bought land at Broadway and 10th Street, from Henry Brevoort, a descendant of one of the old Dutch families of New Amsterdam. When I came as rector of Grace Church there was in the congregation Mr. Theophylact B. Bleecker, then nearly ninety years of age, who lived in the neighborhood before Grace Church was built. In 1922 he had written down some of his recollections. "At the time of the laying of the cornerstone," he wrote, "I was a boy of nine or ten and living on the southwest corner of Broadway and Tenth Street, diagonally opposite the Brevoort apple orchard. My attention was first called to men engaged in cutting down the trees which

I considered a piece of vandalism, being at that period very fond of apples. A short time after I noticed they were digging the foundations of a building; and then a number of people, some clergymen, gathered around the hole. Although I had not received any invitation, boylike I joined the throng to find out what was going on, from the front row." Then he describes how the ropes that held the cornerstone slipped, so that the stone fell into a large bed of mortar, scattering it over everybody, including himself; after which "the subsequent proceedings interested me no more." But then he adds these details about the neighborhood:

At that period the old Brevoort farm house was standing directly opposite Eleventh Street. The block on the west side of Broadway between Tenth and Eleventh Streets was a florist's garden and green-house. Judge Roosevelt lived on the east side of Broadway between Twelfth and Thirteenth Streets (I think) and Weir Roosevelt on the northwest corner of Broadway and Fourteenth Street.

So in 1843 when the cornerstone of Grace Church was laid, distinguished families of New York lived close to its doors. In the decades following, residences were all about it. A nostalgic picture of what its neighborhood was like rises from the pages of a diary kept by a little girl named Catherine Elizabeth Havens. She wrote in 1849:

I am ten years old today, and I am going to begin to keep a diary. My sister says it is a good plan, and when I am old and in a remembering mood, I can take out my diary and read about what I did when I was a little girl. . . . My father bought a house in Ninth Street in 1844. He bought it of a gentleman who lived next door to us and who had but one lung and he lived on raw turnips and sugar. Perhaps that is why he had only one lung, I don't know. I am still living in our Ninth Street house. It is a beautiful house and has glass sliding doors with birds of paradise sitting on palm trees painted on them. And back of our dining room is a piazza, and a grape vine, and we have lots of Isabella grapes every fall. . . . New York is getting very big and building up. I walk some mornings with my nurse before breakfast from our house on Ninth Street up Fifth Avenue. Fifth Avenue is very muddy above Eighteenth Street, and there are no blocks of houses as there are down town, but only two or three on a block. . . . On Irving Place, between Fourteenth and Fifteenth Street, there is a rope walk, and we like to watch the men walk back and forth making the rope. It is very interesting. . . . stages run through Bleecker Street and Eighth Street and Ninth Street right past our house, and it puts me right to sleep when I come home from the country to hear them rumble along over the cobble-stones. There is a line on Fourteenth Street too, and that is the highest up town. . . . I roll my hoop and jump the rope in the afternoon, sometimes in the Parade Ground on Washington Square and sometimes in Union Square. Union Square has a high iron railing around it and a fountain in the middle. My brother says he remembers when it was a pond and the farmers used to water their horses in it.

In the second half of the nineteenth century and the opening years of the twentieth, in all the area around Grace Church were handsome houses where single families lived. During Dr. Slattery's rectorship conditions began to change. The center of the city's life was moving farther north. The old houses began to fall before the hammers and chisels of the wreckers. Hotels and commercial structures of all sorts rose on the ground where they had been. This disintegration of the area residentially went on more rapidly in the early 1900's. When I came to Grace Church some of the members still lived near, and they and others who were held by longtime loyalty were in their pews on Sunday mornings. But they belonged to a vanishing generation. Their children and grandchildren were living either outside Manhattan altogether, or on the streets and avenues around Central Park. It was not easy for them to keep their ties at Tenth Street and Broadway.

Nevertheless, Grace Church was for me an inspiring place for service to be attempted, and my heart was in the parish ministry; so I could not feel that I should go to Pennsylvania when in December, 1928, I was elected Bishop-Coadjutor of that diocese.

XV. In the Rectory and the Rector's Study

The rectory at 804 Broadway, next to the church, where the family took up residence in the fall of 1923, belonged in its handsome spaciousness to the old New York of which little Catherine Havens had written in her diary. The other residences which once had been around it had mostly disappeared, and Broadway was altogether a business and shopping street. But the rectory kept its distinctiveness and its untroubled charm. Over the basement where were the kitchen and serving rooms, the first floor had a very large dining room and a breakfast room on one side, and on the other side a reception room and the walnut-paneled rector's study. From the front hall a broad staircase led up to a balcony which encircled the second floor. From this opened on the uptown side two beautiful great living rooms, each with a fireplace and a marble mantel; the front room with a bow window looking out across the rectory garden to Broadway, and the back room with two windows facing to the east. Across the hall were two bedrooms of dimensions like the living rooms; on the third floor four more bedrooms; and on the fourth floor rooms for the servants. There had come with us from Richmond our beloved mother's-helper, Mrs. N. E. Armstrong, daughter of an Episcopal clergyman, to whom the children were devoted, and who to them and to the family and the family's friends was "Miss Arm." There was plenty of space for everybody, and what might have been the difficulty of living downtown was largely overcome by the fact that the vestry gave us, as it had given to Dr. Slattery, a car and a chauffeur. So Jean (Jr.) and Elisabeth could be driven to the Chapin School, which at first was on 57th Street and soon moved much farther off to 84th Street and East End Avenue. Beverley also began in an uptown school, but soon entered the Choir School instead, where Rusty followed him when he was big enough to go to school at all.

It was the first time in many years that there had been any children in Grace Church rectory, and their presence added to the affectionate interest which the parishioners took in the new family. They could smile at the infantile reflection of the city, if not of the rectory, which they got from small Rusty, then three years old, who when asked how he liked New York replied that he did not like it much "because it was too dirty and had too many people in it." And perhaps they could think it was good to be *very* young when Rusty was heard one day to say to Elisabeth, "Wouldn't it be nice to go to heaven and play with the little Lord Jesus?" and she from her advanced age of six replied, "Oh, Rusty, you ought to know better than that. He's grown up long ago!"

With their mother and Miss Arm, the rectory was a happy place for them; and generally I was at least not far away. The rector's study opened directly into Grace House, and it was there that I would go at the beginning of the morning to confer with the staff and to learn from Deaconess Garvin what I might most usefully be doing in and for the parish.

She had been the rector's secretary both for Dr. Slattery and for Dr. Huntington, his predecessor. She knew all the people, and with her gentle wisdom she could help the new rector know whom he should go to see, and where and when. Every morning I would find on my desk the memoranda she had already made of the matters that might be of prime concern that day. She would take my dictated replies to the morning mail, and through the day she could be depended upon to handle with a gracious wisdom any matters that did not need to be referred to me, especially in the afternoons when I would usually be out calling in the parish. Dr. Slattery in his pastoral faithfulness, and in the way he kept in touch with his people, in hospitals or in their homes, the sick and the well, set a standard which few men could attain to. I could not equal him, but I could follow his example.

Miss Garvin had also a special part in the preparation of sermons. From the time when I was at the Seminary, I had determined that I would not be dependent upon a manuscript in the pulpit. But equally I wanted to avoid the discreditable business of bringing to a congregation a sermon scanty in substance and slapdash in form. So the sermon must be thought through completely and then put into complete expression before it should be preached. Therefore, I wrote it out in full; and having done that, I trusted that it would be so engraven in my mind that I could leave the manuscript behind and preach the sermon not in memorized words but yet substantially as it had been written. Then later I found that better than writing was dictating. After I had thought and meditated long enough to feel warmly what I wanted to say, and then had made an outline of a coherent structure— like the blueprint for a building—I would go with Miss Garvin into the beautiful rector's study which I had inherited, and speak the sermon to her as she took it down. In that way the sermon might be delivered from the danger of sounding like an essay, which sometimes happens with the written word. The *spoken* word could have the intonation and the directness of expression which becomes instinctive when one is thinking of listening people and not of the paper on one's desk. I tried to do the preliminary thinking and outlining for a sermon on Monday and Tuesday, and regularly to have our session for dictation on Wednesday morning. Then I would have the manuscript in abundant time to read it, to change it possibly here and there, and most of all to absorb the thought of it again so fully that on Sunday morning I could hope to transmit it, without any paper in between, directly to those into whose faces I looked as I stood up to preach.

In some seminaries there is insistence that the students form the fixed habit of preaching on every Sunday from some part of the collect, epistle and gospel which appear in the Book of Common Prayer for that particular day. That always seemed to me a dreary and destructive notion. Of course, one will preach at the given times on the great cardinal themes which the church year makes luminous: Advent, Christmas, Epiphany, Lent, Good Friday, Easter, Pentecost, the major Saints' Days; but it can be stupid and deadening to suppose that a man must force himself to preach on what was printed on a particular page of the Prayer Book for—say—Septuagesima, or the Seventeenth Sunday after Trinity, whether there was anything in what was given for that day which stirred his mind and heart or not. If one did find anything that kindled him in the material that came according to the calendar, well and good, and he would do well to study it and see. But the church year is meant to help him, not to cramp him into a procrustean bed. In addition to following the great stages in the sequence of the church year with faithfulness, one may well train himself to disciplined regularity of thinking by work-

ing out and announcing series of sermons on related subjects
—such as are richly suggested in Charles R. Brown's *The
Art of Preaching;* but the preaching on Sundays must not be
bound by such compulsory commitments that spontaneity is
destroyed. There may be stirrings of the spirit which are more
sovereign than rules which homiletic formalists may lay down.
A sailor on the Boston waterfront, who had listened to a man
who preached to men like himself with an irresistible conviction, spoke the living truth when he exclaimed, "What I calls
preaching is when a man takes something hot out of his heart
and shoves it into mine."

Harry Fosdick expressed a crucial truth about preaching
when he wrote that the man who is to preach should have
above all in his mind not the subject of a sermon but the object of it. What is he preaching *for?* What is it that he wants
to do? It is not to develop—even though he might develop
truly—some general theme. It is to bring to the men and wom-
en there before him a word so vital and immediate that something real will happen in them. *That* is the object, and everything else must be keyed to that. Father Bull, the British
evangelist, has told what that purpose meant with him. He
would go into the church where he was to preach, into the
church when it was empty, and sitting in one of the pews or
kneeling down he would imagine and try to visualize the people who would be there the next day, with their human long-
ings and their human needs, and try to let what would be
his sermon shape itself in relationship to them. That sort of
personalizing of a sermon, and the importance of it, was
stamped upon my thought by one memorable experience.
After I had gone to Grace Church, I went back one Sunday
to preach again in St. Paul's. I had brought with me the
material of a sermon which I planned to use. But when I
woke up in Richmond on that morning it was as though that

sermon had gone dead. No spark seemed to be in it anymore. There was a moment of near panic. What should I do? I had to preach; but nothing except the sermon I had brought with me was in my mind. Then I began to see in my mind's eye some of the actual people who would be there that day: that father whom I had been with when the news came that his splendid son at college had been killed in an automobile wreck; that younger man whom I had been able to help in a time of special temptation; that older woman who had in her life so little that the world calls good fortune but who in her daily faithfulness was "as poor, yet making many rich"; that girl and her young husband whose marriage I had celebrated and whose baby I had baptized. What would they want me to say now that I was again in the place which we all loved and around which so many associations gathered? What good news from the gospel could I bring that would come home to them? As I asked myself that, the answer seemed to kindle. What I preached that day I cannot in the least remember. All that I know is that it was not what I had planned to preach, but that it had life in it where without the consciousness of the people no life would have been. Help came perhaps because as my imagination looked into their re-membered faces I was hearing the cry of the human heart that was echoed in Thornton Wilder's *Our Town,* when the spirit of the girl who had died goes home and, among those she had loved who do not know that she is there, cries out, "Oh, look at me one moment as though you really saw *me!*"

A man who is trying to preach the gospel will have his times of happy freedom, but also times when his spirits sink. There are periods when it seems that there is *not* something hot in his own heart for him to put into the hearts of others. And his *mind* also may go dry. Ideas that in his best days may

161

have flooded in upon him will not come. In all the area of his thought the tide is out, and the possibilities for sermons which he wishes might float free into the deep waters are stranded on the flats. Then he may become frightened, and ask himself whether he ought to have tried to be a preacher at all. Perhaps his religion was not real. Has he lost his eagerness for preaching and even for the ministry itself?

So he may wonder, but the fact is that he is going through those alternations which belong inevitably to all creative effort. He cannot prevent a dry spell from coming, but he can do something to create the climate out of which the rains from God may fall again on the parched ground. He can read his Bible, and read it perhaps in a new translation which may give to some familiar passage a freshness of suggestion which it did not have before. He can kneel down and not *ask* God for anything, but remember thankfully all that God has already given him in his own life and in the life of those he loves. And turning from himself he can go out and see somebody who is in trouble, some person in his parish who is carrying a heavy load that he might help in at least some little way to lift, some man or woman whose gallantry in the face of hardship makes him know that human spirits do not have to be cast down. From them he may find the quickening which his own soul needs.

That quickening may come also not from some contact which is immediate and visible, but from the remembered certainty that on any Sunday there may be in the congregation some person he has never heard of who needs that day the help from God which he, and he alone, right then must mediate. Every preacher can recall—if he stops to think—some evidence he has had of the anonymous man or woman out there in one of the pews whose heart was like an empty cup that craved a draught of living water, and to whom by God's grace he did bring help that day. Every preacher will have had sometime a letter such as this unsigned one which came one day to me:

Who of us does not bear a cross? Mine is often heavy, and it is sometimes hard to realize that strength does come if we can believe it will. . . . It matters not if I am a stranger, or if my name is John or James Doe. I have a right to thank you for the message you gave last evening.

The pathos of human life was speaking there, as was a new hopefulness from this other letter: "Thank you for all you do for me. I don't know exactly what it is or how you do it and I have long since ceased to ask, but I do know you send me on my way with direction and completely free." For the preacher thus to know that God has used him once will help him in even what may seem to be his dryest time to trust that he may be used again. The human need will certainly be there, and if he thinks of it tenderly enough an answering word of God may become for him "a spring of water welling up to eternal life."

Because I had Miss Garvin, and also quick and skillful Myra Baker on the secretarial staff, I had the possibility of writing more than the weekly sermons only. The same thought and study and meditation which had to be devoted to preparation for preaching could widen into other, and perhaps more permanent, expression. So in 1928 I wrote *The Master: A Life of Jesus Christ*, which when it was published became the Religious Book Club's "Book-of-the-Month." That was followed by *On Being Alive*, written to be given as the Reinecker Lectures at the Virginia Seminary, and dedicated "To Berryman Green, by whom religion has been made to many men a clear light shining on a hill"; and in 1935, responding to an invitation from Dean Luther A. Weigle to give the Lyman Beecher Lectures at the Yale Divinity School, I wrote *The Renewing Gospel.*

The book which was to prove most useful, in the sense at least of being most read in its many reprintings since it was published in 1934, came into existence not through an idea that originated with me but because of a message which was brought to me one day from John A. Langdale, the editor in New York for the Abingdon Press. He asked me to come to lunch with him at his office on Fifth Avenue; and when I got there, he and Arthur Stevens, the manager of that division of the Press, said to me, "We want you to write for us a Story of the Bible." "What do you mean?" I asked. "More than one Story of the Bible has been written and is in existence already." "Yes," said John Langdale, "but none of them is exactly what we want. We want a book which will give the whole Bible story from Genesis to Revelation, not just some stories *from* the Bible. We want it written—as some of the older books have not been—in the light of the best knowledge we now have as to the times and circumstances in which the different parts of the Bible came into being, and the relationship between them. We want it in that best sense to reflect what could be called a critical scholarship, and at the same time to be reverent and devotional, as any right treatment of the Bible ought naturally to be. And will you do it?"

I answered that what he was suggesting was a brand new idea so far as my attempting it was concerned. I didn't know, I would go home and think about it.

So I did think about it; and the more I thought, the more it seemed to me an alluring thing to try to do. Consequently I began. The work went on at odd hours through weeks and months of the more commanding schedule of the parish responsibilities; and when it was finished, it was dedicated "To

Bertha Maud Garvin, Edward Felix Kloman, Myra Stetson Baker: Comrades in happy endeavor, without whose cooperation much which has been completed might never have been begun." Bertha Garvin and Myra Baker have been spoken of already. Felix Kloman had come to me at Grace when he returned from missionary service in Liberia. First at Grace Chapel and then transferred to the staff of the Church, he was for eleven years such an associate as few men have ever had: full of happy energy and unselfish devotion to the parish work, in friendship warmhearted and unfailing.

The Story of the Bible was due, as I have said, to a suggestion which came from someone else. The same sort of prompting from another editor led to the writing of *The Story of the Church*. Other men, like myself, may have had reason to be grateful because they were launched upon efforts which they themselves might not have imagined, but afterwards were glad of, by the encouragement of friends who said, "Here is something that needs to be done. Why don't you try to do it?"

XVI. Some Not Unwelcome Combats

The Christian preacher looks out from the pulpit on men and women who have their own particular and private needs: for light and hope when the routine of life grows heavy and discouraging, for strength against some secret temptation, for a message of the love of God that can give meaning to existence even in the midst of human loneliness. It is with sensitive awareness of inner needs like these that the preacher must try to interpret and bring home the Christian gospel. But at the same time he must remember that he and those to whom he preaches belong to a world which has not only its individual but also its social realities, and that what happens in "the secular city" cannot be held apart from what may be happening in people's souls. Therefore, if he is to be faithful to his full commission, he must preach sometimes not on personal but on public issues, and dare the risk—as the prophets did—of controversy.

Some persons in the church, and many outside it, will resent this. They like to think of the church as the place for a kind of sequestered piety which is not to be disturbed by the conflicts of the larger world. They will echo the sentiment expressed in a letter I received one day after a sermon in which

166

I had referred to a matter that might concern all citizens. The writer said: "As a parishioner whose family has been closely associated with Grace Church from the time of its foundation in 1806 to the present day. . . I want to let you know that I consider international and interracial questions of this character outside the province of the rector of our parish." He represented what has aptly been called "the indoor mind." He did not want the thought of the congregation to be led toward any provocative challenge outside the conventicle walls.

I did not make the mistake—I hope—of failing to remember that any public issue must be subsidiary to the proclamation of the essential Christian gospel, and must never be made into a separated diatribe. Its proper relevance was and is by way of specific illustration of some larger truth. But in the measure that it *is* specific, any reference which brings some entrenched interest into question can certainly cause commotion—commotion so extreme as to verge upon hysterical comedy. Once when I called attention to what seemed to me signs that the American Legion, which began with an imaginative ideal of service to the whole country, was in danger of becoming instead a legislative lobby bent upon grabbing benefits for its enlarging membership, there came not only a flood of denunciatory letters but a solemn threat from one indignant Legion Post that I would be sued for $100,000 libel—a threat which of course was no more than a verbal pop-cracker which exploded in momentary noise. On another occasion, reflecting upon the pompous fussiness of a D.A.R. annual convention and the dull insularity of the resolutions the convention passed, I said that the D.A.R. might have to be recognized as "Daughters of yesterday's revolutionaries, sisters of today's Tories, and mothers of tomorrow's reactionaries." Whereat one lady sent me a communication in which at the beginning her offended spirit held itself in icy restraint, but as she went on her indignation overcame her, and she ended with this magnificent outburst: "What you said was abominable, and even ridiculous, you old crow!"

It is not strange that any particular vested interest which is brought into unfavorable light should be offended, but that is only the fringe of what can occur. Any positive preaching which touches upon contemporary realities may provoke a reaction so widespread and irrational as to go beyond the bounds of what would have seemed to be common sense. In the two decades which began about 1930 new and critical tensions were rising in American thought and life. The slogan which many had wanted to follow at the end of the first World War was "back to normalcy," but life does not go backwards and "normalcy" cannot be allowed to mean suppression of the new thought and purpose which might lead to human betterment. The overthrow of the Czarist regime in Russia and the rise of communism had been accompanied by violence and disruption which were terrible, but the danger was that our Western world might see only the violence and disruption and fail to acknowledge that there might be social evils everywhere that needed to be corrected lest new collisions come. Now in these late 1960's, with international and interracial passions threatening an ordered civilization, it is plain enough that there had been need for more imaginative and creative thinking than we have had. But this human nature of ours will often resent being prodded by inconvenient ideas. As in the words of *Pilgrim's Progress*, "Simple said, 'I see no danger,' and Sloth said, 'Yet a little more sleep,' " so whenever any voice within the church tries to direct religious consciousness toward what is happening in the world of public affairs, the response may be, "Forget it. Let us alone."

Furthermore, there are forces which if not let alone will

go to fanatical extremes in denouncing what they do not want to hear. Anyone who invites new interpretations of religious truths—interpretations which rightly understood could bring back the fire to convictions over which the dust of old indifference has drifted—must be "a destroyer of the faith." Anyone who in the practical application of religious truth disturbs the privileged and the comfortable must be "a radical."

Like all my friends and all the thoughtful people whom I have known best, I have always abominated the cruelty of communism and its suppression of freedom in thought and speech, and have looked upon it as a contradiction to our highest American heritage. Consequently it was a matter of ironic amusement when—on account of what ought to have seemed some quite obvious and ordinary efforts to make the living Gospel relevant to public issues—I found myself accounted as "subversive" in *The Red Network*, and in the malicious innuendoes of *None Dare Call It Treason*. But to be listed there was to be in goodly company, for in these and other rabid right-wing publications those who were denounced as dangerous included such names as Eleanor Roosevelt, Bishop G. Bromley Oxnam, John A. Mackay, the president of Princeton Theological Seminary, and—believe it or not—Dwight D. Eisenhower. As in the years when Joseph McCarthy was riding high in the United States Senate and many people were frightened at his influence, whoever challenged the herd ideas was likely to be labelled as "communist inspired."

Even the plainest word or act of instinctive human decency could rouse a feverish reaction if the human beings who needed to be defended happened to be hated by the privileged and powerful—as were, for instance, the Negroes in some parts of the South. One Lent when I was preaching for a week in Birmingham, Alabama, I came into contact, through

169

some of the finest citizens of that state, with evidence which made me believe, as they did, that a group of Negro boys, in what was to become the notorious "Scottsboro case," had been arrested, tried, and condemned to death through the framed-up false testimony of a disreputable woman, in proceedings which were little different from lynch law. I joined with others who believed the boys were innocent to try to have the whole truth brought to light. When that was done in appeal to higher courts, the falsehood of the charges was made manifest, and Negroes who by themselves had been helpless and who might have been executed were set free. But in an inflamed community, passions had run so high that prejudice took the place of reason. Any person who had run counter to the crowd opinion must be an agitator and a "Red."

It was true that some actual communists did espouse for their own devious purpose causes of human justice which men of a higher loyalty had championed through the simple compulsion of a Christian conscience. Thus the communists might create the impression that *they* were the ones who cared most for social righteousness. Some of the reactionaries were stupid enough to help them seem so, by opposing any generous social programs themselves and denouncing as "communist sympathizers" anybody responsible for the disturbing suggestion that things as they are might possibly be made better.

People otherwise unlike but alike in clinging fanatically to what they think they know, and what they possess already, find ready allies in one another. So the ultraconservatives both in the church and in the general community turn their joint enmity against whoever seems to be a representative of change. Some of the comfortable and the prosperous have had no use for preachers who raised any question about the *status quo*. The so-called fundamentalists have no use for thinkers who hold that the truth might be larger than their supposed in-fallibilities. Therefore, those who are looked upon as "liberals" may arouse the fury of both camps, and the amount of miscellaneous evil attributed to each liberal could give him a highly diverting picture of what a demon he must be. By the twisted logic of the stupid or the malicious, he can be called a communist sympathizer and a fellow traveller if he advocates anything progressive which communists claim they favor too; and in matters of religion, such as translating the Bible, it can be asserted that his purpose is somehow atheistic since that is what communists are supposed to be!

Why then not keep silent on public issues in which the stand one takes may be misrepresented and belied? Because no man of decent spirit can be guilty of that contemptible timidity. With humility concerning himself but with confidence in his commission, let him try to speak the truth of God which the ignorance or the recklessness of men may contravene but cannot overthrow.

Inside the church itself, of course, there are differences of opinion; and though these differences may be about less crucial matters and ought not to lead to any discourteous division, they also have to be faced and dealt with.

The Diocese of New York in earlier years, under Bishop Henry Codman Potter and David Hummel Greer, had for the most part represented the spirit of liberal evangelicalism which had long been familiar in Virginia. Bishop William T. Manning brought to his episcopate a mood and a purpose more conservatively Anglo-Catholic. He had a courage and a resoluteness which could be admirable, but it seemed to some of us that he was often resolute about mistaken things. He was not a member of the House of Bishops when in a Pastoral

171

Letter at nearly the end of the last century they had declared that "fixedness of interpretation is of the essence of the creeds," but his mind appeared not to have moved much beyond that antique opinion. Temperamentally he liked "fixedness": the fixedness of formulas which were supposed to be able to contain the faith, fixedness in canon law, fixedness in the claimed status of the Episcopal Church as distinguished from the communions considered to be outside the grace of Apostolic Succession. Consequently his tendency was to repress, if he could, opinions and practices which seemed to him to violate the rigid literalisms of creed or canon that he thought to be essential. William Norman Guthrie, at St. Mark's-in-the-Bouwerie, on Second Avenue, in a neighborhood of people who had no faintest interest in Episcopal formalities, tried to present the beauty of the church's message in experimental dramatic forms on Sunday afternoons, but Bishop Manning would have none of it. Howard Chandler Robbins, Dean of the Cathedral of St. John the Divine, trying to make the type of the Cathedral's worship and the message from its pulpit such that all simple Christian folk would feel at home, found the Bishop so unsympathetic that he resigned. The rector of St. George's invited Henry Sloane Coffin to be the preacher at a communion service for a special gathering, and Bishop Manning inhibited it as something not to be allowed. In all these things the Bishop was completely conscientious, and wholly convinced that he was defending the integrity of the Church. But equally it seemed to some of us who were rectors of churches in New York that a lack of sensitive imagination, and an insistence by the Bishop on nonessentials, were diminishing the appeal which the Church's message, if generously interpreted, might have to all the people of the city.

172

In 1933 a group of men, representative of a number of parishes in the city and the surrounding region, met in the rector's study at Grace Church and organized the Liberal Evangelicals; "as communicants of the Protestant Episcopal Church who desire fellowship for the purposes of prayer, study, and conference on the basis of these convictions:

That revelation through the Holy Spirit is progressive, and that God reveals in every age new aspects of His purpose by which both the theology and the practice of the Church must be enlarged.

That the authority of ancient creeds and conciliar definitions consists in illumination, not in inhibition; and should be treated therefore not as setting limitations to thought but as expressing insights into the meaning of God which are valid in so far as they can be continually reproduced in the language and life of every time.

That dogmatism concerning "faith" or "order" endangers the pursuit of truth, and that the need of the Church is not for propaganda of exclusive claims but rather for an open-minded search of all Christian reality within which whatever is divine in its own inheritance, as also in the inheritance of other communions, may be trusted to survive.

That the test of the Church in this time will be its power to carry the gospel of Christ not only to the life of the individual but to all the spheres of men's social, economic, national and international relationships, and that to fulfill this purpose Episcopalians should seek a progressive cooperation in worship and work with all Christians of kindred spirit.

At a later time, something that began as a controversy but turned into a prelude to something quite different was sparked by a letter which came from Lawrence E. Spivak, who was then the editor of *The American Mercury*, asking me to write for the magazine an article under the title of *Protestant Concern over Catholicism.*

The title was inadequate, and could be misleading, for those who share the liberating spirit of the Protestant Reformation can still possess the great heritage of Catholicism rightly understood—the heritage of the agelong life and devotion of the universal church that goes back to Christ. So in what I set out to write I was careful to make clear that Protestant concern has to do with *Roman* Catholicism, as meaning the exaggerated claims of the Church of Rome, and the questionable influence which it may seek to exert on social and educational policies in public affairs.

The statement which I sent then to Mr. Spivak was a lengthy one, specifically documented, but to the best of my ability irenic in tone. "Why should there be any concern about Roman Catholicism?" it began; and then the introductory paragraph went on:

Ideally there ought to be none. Protestantism and Roman Catholicism are both in their own conception interpreters of one and the same gospel—the gospel of God as revealed in Jesus Christ. Furthermore, Protestants can sincerely admire much that Roman Catholicism specifically represents. We can admire the steadfastness with which, in the midst of contemporary secularism and shallow thinking, Roman Catholicism bears its constant witness to a higher world of which every man must also be a citizen if his soul is not to shrivel. We can recognize the massive dignity of an organized life and worship rich with the tradition of many centuries, and the width of a fellowship which reaches round the world and includes communicants of every nation and race. We can honor the heroic devotion of many priests and missionaries, the life-long and unreserved dedication to God's service in religious orders both of monks and nuns, and ideals of saintliness to which the greater souls in generation after generation have aspired. What, therefore, are Protestants concerned about?

Then followed the answer, made up of cited facts concerning some aspects of Roman teaching and practice which seemed to me to be close to superstition, and—more crucially —certain instances in which organized Roman Catholic forces had been used to advance particular interests, even to the point of threats of boycott against newspapers or other organs of opinion which opposed them.

The American Mercury gave my article to the Rev. John Courtney Murray, S.J., for a Roman Catholic reply. His answer appeared in the same issue of the magazine which carried what I had sent, and he had had in hand all that I had written, while I had had no knowledge beforehand of what he might wish to say. But notwithstanding this advantage he made the mistake of evading the substantial issues and adopting instead a tone that was almost supercilious.

It occurred to me—a wry thought, he wrote, that I could very well sit down and myself write the Protestant article. The formula has become entirely familiar; some introductory pious platitudes, a superficial advertence to the Catholic doctrine of the Church, the stock tags from a few Catholic documents on church and state, the allegation of the 'horrible example' (the 'Catholic State' on the Spanish model), . . . a rhetorical flight on the unparalleled contribution of Protestantism to the growth of democracy, and the final concluding plea that Catholic and Protestant leaders should sit down together and discuss their differences.

In a succeeding issue, *The American Mercury* gave the entire space of its "Open Forum" exclusively to letters concerning Father Murray's article and mine. Many of the writers wrote scathingly of what they felt to have been

Father Murray's evasiveness, so much so that he sent to the editor "A Statement," which began:

Sir: In reply to your request for an over-all comment on the 52 letters you have sent me, let me make four points:

First, controversy is a dreary business and (as several correspondents remarked) largely a profitless one; I had thought to maintain a certain lightness of tone. It was therefore disconcerting to learn that I had been supercilious, sarcastic, arrogant, slippery, disparaging, cavalier, haughty, disdainful, glib, cocksure, tricky, contemptuous, smug, (these are some of the epithets with which your correspondents adorn me). Apparently my attempt at lightness misfired rather badly.

What the two articles contained is of course too long for any copying now, and the whole argument might be accounted as among "old, unhappy things, and battles long ago" which now can be forgotten. And that is exactly what in one important sense they are. For in the years since that magazine debate there has been the near miracle in interchurch relations wrought by the astonishing Pope John XXIII. In the 1949 exchange my chief suggestion was that serious differences and growing possibilities of collision and hostility between religious forces in this country could best be resolved if the leaders from both sides should come together in Christian comradeship to consider face to face what the differences were. "Always the leaders of Protestantism will be ready to do that," I wrote. "The Roman Catholic hierarchy refuses." In 1949 Father Murray defended that refusal, and considered any suggestion of mutual discussion to be only one of Protestantism's "stock tags."

But the whole sky has brightened since that time, and a Pope in Rome was largely responsible for it. Roman Catholics and Protestants do meet now to think and pray together, do join at least on the fringes of united worship, do join in constantly enlarging cooperation to bring their joint spiritual influence to bear upon the problems of our contemporary world. And it may be that John XXIII will be included in a Protestant calendar of saints even before he has been canonized by the Vatican!

XVII. Friends

The gracious old rectory of Grace Church is linked always with the thought of those who in the years from 1923 to 1939 broke bread with us there, or stayed for a longer time under its roof. A near neighbor was Karl Reiland, the rector of St. George's, with a great warm heart as he was also large and strong of frame, a preacher of courageous righteousness who in what he said and did had no timid concern for ecclesiastical consequences. Also, only a few blocks away at St.-Marks-in-the-Bouwerie, not only the neighborhood but the church in general was enlivened by Guthrie, to whom was owing the creative stimulus of *Kilin* which has already been described.

In Brooklyn was S. Parkes Cadman, who had grown up in England as a Methodist and was now the pastor of the Central Congregational Church and at the height of his unbounded ministry as the first of the men who were heard by the thousands who had begun to listen to sermons on the radio. He would sometimes walk home with me from the bi-weekly luncheons of the clergy club of Sigma Chi, and in his warmth of comradeship make all supposed denominational difference disappear as though it never could have been.

Two other men of spiritual power were in Brooklyn: John Howard Melish, rector of Holy Trinity, crusader for all beleaguered good causes that needed championing; and his immediate neighbor and friend, who was as close to him in sympathy as he was parallel in name, John Howland Lathrop of the Unitarian Church of the Saviour. It was through Jean that I first knew John Lathrop, for she and he were associated in interest and in leadership in the New York Consumers' League. The children brought home some of their friends from school and college, among them one who became like a member of the family—Raymond Walsh, then an instructor at Harvard, whose warmheartedness woke affection and whose intellectual exuberance was a stimulus to everybody.

For two or three years there came down to us from Boston for one day and night each week Dr. Elwood Worcester, the rector of Emmanuel Church. He had created what was widely known as the Emmanuel Movement, a joint ministry of religion and medicine. Physicians and the clergy of Emmanuel worked together to help those whose ills might be both physical and psychical. Dr. Worcester had had a life of varied and vivid service and adventure, and in the latter years of it he began to write his autobiography, *Life's Adventure,* which recounted some of the extraordinary things which had happened to him, and had happened in the Emmanuel Movement. When he showed to his two sons what he had written and asked them whether they had any suggestion for a title, one of them answered, with an impish paraphrase of the promise of healing recorded in the fourth chapter of the Gospel of Luke, "Yes, Dad, I can give you a good title. Call it, 'How I healed the dead, cast out the sick, and raised the devil.' "

179

As a matter of fact, Dr. Worcester by his own faith and encouragement did help to bring healing, and that is why he came to us at Grace Church for special appointments with troubled people. A large, calm figure, who seemed to embody both gentleness and strength, he would sit in an armchair with his hands folded, like a benevolent Buddha, and people would feel better after they had poured out their perplexities and listened to the quiet words that came from him. Besides that, he was the nonprofessional friend whose coming all the rectory family, including the children, looked forward to because of the serene enjoyment of life in general which he had himself and could make everybody feel.

The most frequent, and one of the most welcome, visitors to the rectory was the retired Bishop of Arizona, Julius W. Atwood. The fact that he was linked with Arizona had not been due to any original choice of his own. He had been born in Vermont, of a long line of New England ancestry. All the associations which were most naturally congenial to him were in the East. His going to Arizona came about through what seemed at first to be only a calamity; but out of which, in the strange unpredictableness which is part of human destiny, enlargement of life would also come. When Julius Atwood was at the high point of a satisfying ministry as rector of Trinity Church in Columbus, Ohio, in 1906, his wife was stricken with tuberculosis. She must go to a completely different climate, the doctors said. So the two of them, with their young children, moved to Arizona—to Arizona which then was only a territory, and which to an Easterner sounded like a far-off, half-empty desert. In 1907 Mrs. Atwood died, so that the new country might have seemed all the more a place of lonely exile. But in his ministry at his church in Phoenix, and then when in 1911 he was made Bishop of Arizona, Julius Atwood let his loss become an incitement for larger service. More and more people with tuberculosis were coming to Arizona, some of them not only ill but financially desperate, and he brought about the establishment at Phoenix and Tucson of the St. Luke's Homes, where they could have the shelter and treatment that might bring about recovery.

When he was sixty-eight, he retired as Bishop, and freed then from responsibilities, he could follow up the friendships which he had always had a gift for making. He had a quick recognition of what was important both in the church and in public affairs, and a shrewd judgment which men of consequence respected. Above all he had a constant zest for life: for talking with adults, making friends with children, responding to what was funny as quickly as to what was serious. Also he was the more rather than the less lovable because sometimes he could be laughed at. I called him Caesar, and then Jean and the children called him that too. He told somebody once with much pleasure that I called him so because I had such a high opinion of his dignity as a bishop. I did have a high regard for him, but I called him Caesar just because I thought it was a nice convenient nickname for anyone whose name was Julius; and meanwhile I could smile at the innocent little vanities he sometimes had in *being* a bishop, such as wearing a rosette on his hat.

Life at the rectory was further enlarged by those who came to us from places more distant than Arizona. Events and programs of one kind or another were continually bringing to New York men of distinction from England, and what at first were accidental contacts with some of them led to associations through which they became no longer strangers but friends. Among these were the Bishop of Winchester and his wife, whom we would afterwards visit in England; and Lord William Cecil, Bishop of Exeter, who looked like the pictures of his Victorian kinsman, Lord Salisbury, and who with his Bishop's gaiters and the pleasure which he and Mrs. Cecil had in endless cups of tea was looked upon with awed wonder by the servants.

In 1925 F. W. Dwelly, Canon of Liverpool but afterwards to be the Dean, came to New York at the invitation of some group to tell of the plans and experiments being worked out in the great new cathedral. After I had heard him speak one day, I persuaded him to leave the loneliness of his hotel and come to stay with us in the rectory. I wanted to talk with him about his leadership in generous broad churchmanship in the Church of England, and in the imaginative new special services which he was developing in Liverpool. But Jean, with her woman's intuition and her instinctive sympathy which reached to people's inner selves, soon knew him on a deeper level. She learned that he had lost all of his four children in a diphtheria epidemic, and her understanding won his heart. Also he was drawn affectionately to our daughter Jean, who reminded him of one of the children he had lost; and the bond between him and all the family was to be continued and strengthened later when we should see him again in England.

It was Dwelly who asked me during that visit to write for him a hymn for the Church of England's *Songs of Praise,* which he was then helping to compile; and I wrote the hymn which begins "Lord Christ, when first thou cam'st to men," and in its final stanza ends with the words

> O love that triumphs over loss
> We bring our hearts before thy cross
> To finish thy salvation.

Another visitor from England was Guy Rogers, the rector of Birmingham. He had been born in Ireland and educated at Trinity College, Dublin. Of an Anglo-Irish family and nurtured in the Anglican traditions and loyalties of the Church of Ireland in that Roman Catholic country, he was all the more a Protestant on that account. After he had been ordained, his first ministry was in Dublin; then he went to England. In 1914 England was drawn into what was to be the first World War, and from October 1915 to early 1917, as chaplain in the Grenadier Guards, he was involved in the most gallant as well as the most costly ordeals of the British Army in the defense of Ypres and in the first battle of the Somme. Back in England he served for eight years in the East End of London, and then went to become for the rest of his ministry the rector of Birmingham, with his center at the old Church of St. Martin's-in-the-Bullring.

Guy Rogers carried with him everywhere the warmth of heart and the strong manliness which had made him admired and loved in the Grenadier Guards at the front in France, and the concern for people and especially for the disadvantaged which had grown in him as he ministered among the poor in London's East End. He had been in many controversies on behalf of more militant involvement by the Church of England in the social and industrial problems which followed the war. When he was persuaded to write his autobiography, he entitled it A *Rebel at Heart* [1]; and in it he said:

It is the ministry on its human side which has brought me the greatest happiness and the greatest spiritual assurance. I have never been especially interested in myself as a priest offering any particular kind of sacrifice at any particular altar, though I often thrill to the preaching of the Gospel. But to try to be a good pastor and friend to the individual seemed to me to be the true glory of the ministry.

[1] (London: Longmans, Green & Co., 1956) pp. ix, 309.

And at the end of the book he wrote:

Though I cannot claim to have reached a condition of complete serenity in old age, neither have I succumbed in the least to cynicism or disillusionment. I hope this may encourage many of my fellows on their way. I like to think of myself as one of Bunyan's pilgrims still on his way to the Eternal City, apt to make a mess of it at times, but still pushing on. I amuse myself asking what sort of name Bunyan would have invented for me if he had had me on his hands. I reject Mr. Ready-to-Halt; Mr. Scape-grace would be nearer the mark. If I were allowed to choose I would prefer something between Mr. Hothead and Mr. Warmheart!

To know a man like Guy Rogers was to realize afresh how virile a thing the Christian ministry ought to be.

After Dwelly and Guy Rogers there came from England another one whom we met first in New York, and who was to be linked thereafter with our deepest affections. This was Hugh Laurie Richard Sheppard, to give him his full name, but no one bothered to know what his full name was. To innumerable people who had been touched by his wide-reaching humanity he was just Dick Sheppard, the man who seemed to belong to everybody.

As Vicar of St. Martin-in-the-Fields, which stood no longer in any field but in the thronged center of London at Trafalgar Square, he had made what had been the old and nearly empty church come alive with a ministry so devoted and so imaginative that multitudes thronged to it: to its services on Sundays, to all sorts of activities through the days of the week, to the crypt at night into which friendless and forlorn people came to find a haven and someone there to listen to their need. When he was first appointed by the Bishop of London to be Vicar of St. Martin's, he spent a whole night going about its neighborhood to see what it was like: through

Carlton House Terrace and the circle of clubs nearby, into the shabby side streets and public houses, to coffee-stalls on Charing Cross; and then he decided that "no square mile could provide a more thrilling and adventurous pitch for a parson's job." The vision that came to him, at the end of that night, of what St. Martin's might become was expressed in his own words:

I stood on the west steps, and saw what this Church would be to the life of the people. There passed me, into its warm inside, hundreds and hundreds of all sorts of people, going up to the temple of their Lord, with all their difficulties, trials and sorrows. I saw it full of people, dropping in at all hours of the day and night. It was never dark, it was lighted all night and all day, and often tired bits of humanity swept in. And I said to them as they passed, "Where are you going?" And they said only one thing: "This is our home. This is where we are going to learn of the love of Jesus Christ. This is the altar of our Lord, where all peace lies."

Nothing that was stuffy and conventional could last where Dick Sheppard was. When, during the first World War, St. Martin's was being used in ways that no one had ever heard of before, a disgruntled old lady wrote to him, "What with the air raids outside the church and you inside, there's nothing but explosions." And that is exactly what one could be sure of with Dick Sheppard: explosions of generous affection for his friends, and—more important—explosions of vital concern for all poor and forgotten people and eager determination that the church should get real things done to make their lives and all life better.

As a happy and satisfying house in which to live, nowhere else in New York seemed to us to equal Grace Church Rectory; but when the summer came one had to recognize that

Broadway was not much of a place for children's play or for adult recreation either. So a part of the privilege of the Grace Church years belonged to the weeks when we were out of the city altogether. In some summers we were in Castine, that beautiful old village at the head of Penobscot Bay, which we got to by the Bar Harbor express from New York to Rockland (now, alas, a nostalgic thing of the past, like so much of railroad travel) with the fascination for the children of sleeping in Pullman berths, and then the wide-eyed wonderment of going the next morning on board the little white steamer *Pemaquid,* and seeing as they ran about its decks the blue water and the rocky coast of Maine. In more numerous summers we went to Hancock Pond, not far from Portland, where we lived in and mostly out of a diminutive red cottage which in its bare simplicity seemed the other end of the world from the marble rectory on Broadway: with pine trees round it, and a few steps from its sleeping porch the placid waters of the Pond which stretched away some two miles to the hills that bordered it. Jean (Jr.) was in the girls' *Camp Wabunaki,* on "the island," which was a promontory connected by a narrow causeway with the shore, but Bev and Elisabeth and Rusty and Miss Arm, and Buddy the black spaniel, had enough to keep them happy in the pine trees or on the sandy beach or in the water and in the canoe. As the children grew older there was more scattering, according to where the different ones might happen to want for a while to be. But there by Camp Wabunaki was the haven to which the general desire turned—except for the summers when the whole troup, or a large part of it, went abroad, to renew the friendships with some of those who had come to us in New York.

The first of these excursions was in 1926. The personnel that time was made up of Jean and me, Jean (Jr.), Elisabeth, and the daughter of my sister Martha, whose name officially was Mary but who actually to everybody was Mate. I wrote for the parish paper, *The Grace Church Bells*, an account of that journey and all the grand time we had, but like everything else that happened in the family it was not complete until Jean put her touch upon it. This is the way her account began:

My maternal instinct has been aroused. . . . When I read the last issue of *The Bells*, I realized that no one who read it, unless he had previous information on the subject, would ever know that there were other Bowies; the Bowie boys, who, though they did not go abroad, are of equal importance with the Bowie girls who did. The fact that they do not favor European travel is nothing against them. On the contrary, I was frequently impressed as the summer wore on, with the singular wisdom beyond their years which made them choose emphatically to spend the summer in the woods of Maine rather than take any chance with English Cathedrals. You see Beverley, who is eleven, goes to Choir School. Cathedrals smacked too much of rehearsals and long services and anthems, and he could see no reason for crossing the ocean to hear his father preach in Westminster Abbey, Salisbury and York Cathedrals and elsewhere, when that, to him, doubtful privilege was accorded to him twice every Sunday all winter. As for Russell, Jr., aged six, when I consulted him as to whether he would like to go with us, he considered the matter solemnly for a few minutes and then rendered his decision: "There's reasons why I would, and there's reasons why I wouldn't. I'd like to stay here so I could go to Camp, but I'd like to go to England, so I could see the King and Queen." Feeling that if this were his only objective, his chances of a happy summer were rather slim, I felt constrained to discourage his going, so both boys went to Maine, where the restrictions of civilization are at a minimum, and thrived accordingly.

Doubtless they chose right; but what they missed was a leisurely progress in a rented early-model automobile that looked as big as a stagecoach, with a London driver, up through Oxford and Warwick and Stratford and Lichfield to Liverpool and the north of England and then down through the country and towns of the east coast to London again; and then to Paris and Chartres and the Châteaux country of France.

The next time we went, in 1930, the boys did go; and also Dick Winslow, a nephew of Jean's, and Ted Evans, who after he had graduated from the Virginia Seminary had spent a year studying at Union Seminary in New York, and was helping part-time on the staff of Grace Church. We crossed on the *American Farmer*, which carried mostly freight but also took good care of its small group of passengers; and on which Rusty, then aged ten, found to his excited satisfaction, when he was handed the long printed menu for breakfast, lunch, or dinner, that he could order unconstrained from top to bottom of the list, since all the food was included in the steamship ticket.

It was on this trip that we saw again the Bishop of Winchester and Mrs. Woods. They invited the whole eight of us to come to spend two days with them in the Bishop's Palace, so spacious that it could take in everybody, in rooms which each had on its door the name of some one of the Bishops who had been part of the centuries-old succession at Winchester. Elisabeth and Rusty were a little awed by that, but a happy sense of the immediate life that was more vivid than history could come to them, as it did to the rest of us, when in the evenings Bishop Woods sat down at the piano in the living room that looked out toward the noble old cathedral and the fragment of a ruined wall and we all sang together the hymn from *Songs of Praise* that begins:

> Glad that I live am I;
> That the sky is blue;

Friends

Glad for the country lanes,
And the fall of dew.

After the sun the rain,
After the rain the sun;
This is the way of life,
Till the work be done.[2]

Not long after the visit in Winchester we were to see
Dwelly again, and with some comic touches to the scene, even
if it was on Sunday. Perhaps because of some miscarriage of
a letter, he did not know that we were near. We arrived at
the Cathedral after the morning service had begun and went
inconspicuously into the congregation. When the service
was over, we went back of the chancel toward the robing
rooms, to be met and stopped by a grumpy verger. "Where
can I find Dean Dwelly?" I asked. I had on no clerical collar
or any other ecclesiastical badge, and he looked at me and
at those behind me as though he were regarding another
cluster of annoying tourists. The Dean would be tired after
preaching and oughtn't to see nobody, he informed me. "Well,
I think he might like to see us," I said. "Will you give him this
card?" He looked at the card disgustedly, hesitated as to
whether he would take it, then turned reluctantly, and went
and knocked at a door. When he handed in the card he said,
as we afterwards learned, "Shall I get rid of these people?"
But the door was flung open, and out rushed Dwelly. He
lifted "little" Jean up off the floor in his happiness, threw
his arms around big Jean; then to me, "You will preach here
this afternoon," and to the thunderstruck verger, "Go and
find what robes will fit." Next he sent the verger for his secretary who was to telephone somebody who was listed to

preach that afternoon and inform him that he was *not* to preach, but that I was and that Ted Evans was to read the lessons. Then to complete the discomfiture of the now deflated verger, he sent him off to get some money for a festive dinner in a nearby hotel to which the Dean insisted that the whole contingent should go.

Other visits and preaching in Cathedrals which were less unceremonious are also happy memories, and the summer included a Sunday morning sermon in London at St. Paul's. There I encountered a custom which was typical of the faithfulness to tradition which leads the British people to bring the long historic past right down into the present day. In St. Paul's, before the preacher goes out of the robing room, the verger solemnly brings to him a bottle of sherry which has come from the cellars of the Lord Mayor of London. Back in earlier times sermons used to be preached outdoors at St. Paul's Cross, and the sherry was on hand in case the preacher might have preached so long that he needed some refreshment to continue. So far as I know, the preachers do not now partake in the Cathedral, but the handsome bottle of sherry is handed to each one all the same.

In that summer of 1930 we came in touch also with something older than the traditions at St. Paul's. We went to the Passion Play at Oberammergau. The dark spell of Adolf Hitler had not then fallen completely on Germany and Austria, and the little town and all the life of it was still tuned to the devotion which made it the desire of every boy and girl, and of those grown up, to have some role in the Passion story. Anton Lang, who had played the Christus with strength and beauty twice before, had now become too old for the part, and his successor did not have his greatness; but the cast as a whole gave to the play an immense and reverent reality. They had not been "taught acting" in a theatrical and artificial

190

sense; instead, the power of the thing they were doing had mastered them. It had uncovered in them native resources which were amazing to watch. They were not merely playing parts. They were *being* the persons whose names they bore. The village blacksmith played Caiaphas; but on that great stage of the Passion Play the village blacksmith had vanished, and Caiaphas himself was there, vivid, passionate, masterful, magnificent in his ability to command and to rally the Sanhedrin and the mob of Jerusalem round him, the living center of the dramatic movement of the Play whenever he was on the stage. Judas was a woodcarver who kept a little shop behind his house on the bank of the river. On the Sunday afternoon when the Passion Play was finished, I was walking along the stream, and here in knickerbockers came a man with long brown hair streaked with grey, and with the most lovely smile, leading a little boy who appeared to be his grandson. I looked at him, and it was Judas. To be chosen for the part of Judas is always esteemed a high honor, not only because dramatically it is a great part, but because it is said that only a good man could play Judas since only a good man could rise to the climax of his remorse. And on the stage this gentle woodcarver was Judas, not perhaps as one had imagined him, but, better, as one will always imagine him after that—Judas with his mixed motives, Judas with his passionate revulsion of disappointment from the Master whom he believed to have involved his disciples in his own illusion and failure, Judas who told the priests where they could lay hold of Jesus, but Judas at length with terrible repentance for the thing which he had done.

But the most important and exciting fact in that summer of 1930 had nothing directly to do with Oberammergau or with any other place or event in the planned schedule. It had to do with a new romance. Ted Evans, in the year when

191

he was taking some courses at Union Seminary and assisting on the Grace Church staff, had known Jean (Jr.) then as a schoolgirl. Now he was with us in our group of eight, and Jean was a Vassar sophomore. The next thing we knew, they had fallen in love. With mature judgment, they decided that they should not be married until Jean had finished her college course. So back to Vassar that fall she went, and Ted back to his parish in Tuscaloosa, Alabama. Then, in June, 1932, immediately after Jean had graduated with Phi Beta Kappa standing (as Beverley had done at Harvard, and as Elisabeth was later to do at Vassar), they were married in Grace Church; and the old rectory, which had seen the generations come and go, was the scene—for the first time, so far as I know—of the wedding reception of a rector's daughter.

Twice more before the second World War broke the life of the continents apart, Jean and I were to go to England, and see again some of the people who meant most to us.

Two memories stand out as vignettes from a larger whole.

We are at Birmingham in the pleasant big rectory of Guy Rogers, out beyond the crowded center of the city. His small boy Martin has climbed partway up the stairs. Then he turns toward his father who is standing on the floor, shuts his eyes, and flings himself out and down—to be caught in his father's arms. Tomorrow he may go up higher on the stairs and jump from there. They called it "the faith game," because the little boy had to trust that his father's arms waiting for him would not fail. Better than by any words it taught that it is love we can be most sure of, and that human love can become to us the assurance also that "underneath are the Everlasting Arms."

The other memory, from an evening and a morning afterwards in London.

We had been to dinner with Dick Sheppard in the house

where he was living then in Amen Court, in the shadow of St. Paul's. He came out with us to Fleet Street by the Cathedral where we were to take a bus back to Whitehall Court. As we got on the bus, Dick Sheppard was calling out "Good-night." On the front seat of the bus were two British laboring men, cloth caps pulled down over their eyes, slumped in the seat as though from a long day's work and weariness. As the voice from the street reached one of the two, he straightened like a shot, caught hold of the shoulders of his companion, turned him round, and cried excitedly, "Dick Sheppard!" All over London people of every rank and class knew him and recognized him like that.

Again: it is on the platform of Paddington Station, with the boat train for Southampton on the point of pulling out. Along the platform, hurrying and breathless, comes Dick Sheppard, to tell us again goodbye. "Dick," I said, *"where* have you been and *what* have you been doing to look so tired as you are?" "It doesn't matter," he said, "it's just that I spent the night in St. Martin's crypt." Years before, when he was Vicar of St. Martin's, he had opened the crypt as a refuge for anyone who might be in trouble. He had no official connection with St. Martin's anymore, but his compassion still drew him back to where the homelesss and the troubled were.

It was the last time that we should see him. A few weeks later, his heart exhausted, he died as he was writing at his desk.

XVIII. A Hurdle Not Surmounted

In the years at Grace Church one lengthening shadow began to fall upon what was otherwise a happy and might have been an increasingly helpful ministry. This was trouble with my voice which made many people find difficulty in hearing clearly and therefore in understanding what I said from the chancel and the pulpit.

The cause of it is still too obscure for any full explanation of it to be possible, but it is worth considering because it involved not only some clinical facts but the much more significant question of what may happen within one's own self when a conflict arises between confidence and confusion.

When I was at The Hill School, I had keen pleasure in whatever involved public speaking: in declamation contests and on the debating team. In senior year at Harvard when I was elected to be the Ivy Orator for Class Day, I felt no trepidation when it was decided that the oration should be given outdoors in the large and presumably difficult space of the Harvard Stadium. That was where I did give it; and in a Harvard scrapbook I have found two letters which until

I came across them I had forgotten so completely that I had no consciousness that they had existed. One of them was written in the evening of the day when the Ivy Oration had been spoken, June 24, 1904, and the second on the next day.

The first letter was from Ned Krumbhaar, chairman of the 1904 Class Day Committee—afterward to be Dr. Edward B. Krumbhaar of the Medical School of the University of Pennsylvania. He wrote:

In the rush of events, I did not have a chance to thank you on behalf of the Committee, as well as on the part of the spectators at the Stadium, for your very successful speech. . . . I have heard nothing but praise about it, and during it I myself went to all the different parts of the stadium where it would have been hardest to hear. You could not only hear everything that was said, but could hear it without any effort; in fact, it would not have been necessary to speak as loudly as you did.

The second was this note from Professor George P. Baker, then at Harvard but later to be the head of the Drama Deparment at Yale, whom I did not know.

I must congratulate you on the Ivy Oration. . . . You delivered it in masterly way. I did not miss a syllable, and I know how hard it is to so control one's delivery as to make every syllable tell in so huge a space.

Such seemed to be the fact and the promise in 1904. But in a summer vacation not long after that year there happened something which appeared at first to be no more than a small cloud "like a man's hand," but which was destined to grow larger and to become part of a complication that would be menacing. I took singing lessons for a while from a teacher

195

who was excited at what she thought were the possibilities in my voice. In her eagerness she gave me exercises which were probably mistaken. They strained one of the vocal chords. As a physical fact, that might not have been unduly serious; but the need to overcome it could produce an anxious effort that would be accentuated by any special stress in circumstances or in the subconscious self. In St. Paul's, an easy church to speak in, the difficulty sometimes showed itself, though not acutely. Among the gothic arches of Grace Church it was more manifest.

Before long the word began to spread that the new rector at Grace could not be heard.

One most baffling fact was that different people had contradictory impressions, and the same person might have completely different impressions at different times. The vestry, of course, were eager to remedy whatever conditions in the church might be in part responsible for poor acoustics. An old-fashioned shell sounding board which had for many years been over the pulpit was removed, and amplifiers installed. One of the vestrymen wrote to me,

Two Sundays ago neither my wife nor I were able to understand enough of your sermon to get anything out of it. Three of our friends who had sat in different parts of the church went uptown with us. They were in equal despair, saying that they had hardly understood a word. Last Sunday morning when the sounding board was removed and the amplifiers were in use I heard you better than I had ever heard you before. Two friends who went uptown with me had the same experience. We were all thrilled by the sermon itself and by the satisfaction we had enjoyed in really hearing it. On Sunday evening when the amplifiers were not used I heard only fairly well while you were in the pulpit, but while you were reading the prayers I strained to listen intently, but from the beginning to end I was not able to understand a single sentence.

It sounded then as though the amplifiers would be the happy answer to all the difficulty; but amplifiers or no amplifiers, there continued to come out of the congregation distressed word of those who again were "in despair."

Meanwhile there was the inexplicable contrast of what some others felt and thought. In the same year in which the letter from the vestryman just referred to was written, I preached for a week in Lent in Richmond at St. Paul's, where there were no amplifiers; and a member of the parish who was also a singer wrote to me: "Did I make it plain to you what I thought of your preaching? Truly there is a new fire and authority in you. *What* you said was always high and extraordinary, but now *how* you say it is newly inspired. Are you conscious of this, or is it a slow blossoming? I'd like to know. Whatever it is, it is splendid and thrilling."

And in Grace Church, the year before—again when there were no amplifiers and after a service when most particularly the voice might have grown tired—a parishioner of another New York church wrote: "I wish to express my gratitude for the beautiful 3-hour Good Friday service yesterday. It was satisfying from every standpoint. . . . You never spoke better or with more power; each address so different, so original, and inspired, were a refreshment to our hungry souls. To say a three-hour service was a delight may seem strange, but it was so to me. . . . Your message cannot fail to be heard when it comes through so unhindered a channel."

In that same year a member of Grace Church who had moved to Washington to be a Presidential Aide in the White House wrote for *The Churchman* a long article which was printed under the title of *Looking Back at Grace Church*. In it he wrote:

When Dr. Bowie first became rector of Grace Church, nearly a decade ago, the combination of a marked southern accent, a little tendency to tension under stress of interest in his subject, and the reverberations common to large Gothic edifices, was said to make it difficult for some of his auditors to hear him clearly. The difficulty is seldom heard of anymore. We do not experience it ourselves. On the contrary, his voice seems to us particularly clear, rich, warm and pleasant. We would even welcome the return of the vanishing Southern accent.

"The difficulty is seldom heard of anymore." He was sorely wrong as to that! "A tendency to tension under stress"—that, as will appear later, may have been truer than he knew.

But there was another letter which was most acutely memorable. Nine years after the message from the vestryman who had been "in despair," I was preaching again in Richmond, in 1942, at noonday Lenten services which were broadcast; and a Presbyterian minister in one of the Richmond suburbs wrote to me:

During the past week, I have been sick abed, and thus had the opportunity to listen to all your Lenten addresses, on the radio. I should like to thank you, for you have helped me, and I needed help. Everyone knows that you are a great preacher, and your material was excellent. However, there are many good preachers. The unique thing about your addresses and the thing which impressed me most was your voice. I hardly know how to express the impression which it made on me. I was heart-sore and weak and weary and greatly troubled about world conditions, and your voice seemed to express compassion and sympathy and love; and as I listened, it was as balm to a wounded soul. It was almost as though there was a restrained sob in your voice (though not weakly sen-

198

timental). If God were to speak audibly today, there would be such a sound in His voice, or so it seems to me. How could it be otherwise, as He broods over his warring children?

But the voice that had brought something helpful to the minister in Richmond had not been registering in Grace Church. Perhaps the "tension under stress" had been increasing. Yet sometimes when in preaching there had been the most joyous sense of freedom, even then the chilling comments would come back: "We could not hear," "You go too fast," "You must take time to be more distinct." So the inhibiting consciousness of "*how* must I say it?" could block the spontaneity of the spirit that needed to get loose. It was as though there existed now some dark contradiction that could not be escaped—as irrational and yet as menacing as the nightmare of the witch coming out of the shadowed niche on the wall which I had had long ago as a small boy in my grandmother's house.

What was the reason of it all?—a reason deeper than any matter of Gothic church acoustics, or sounding board or no sounding board, of amplifiers or no amplifiers. Had the beloved "Jack" Horner been right in a letter which has come to light in what might have been a forgotten file? Clarence H. Horner had been on the Grace Church staff, and a tie of great affection had been woven between us two. He had left New York to be the rector of St. Clement's Church, El Paso, Texas, but he came back one summer during the great depression of the early 1930's to take the services and to preach at Grace—and to see the signs of the tragic unemployment and poverty that marked the great cities then. In nearby Union Square men were selling apples in a desperate effort to earn a few cents with which to buy their next meal. At

Grace Church, with Felix Kloman's devoted planning, there was set up a shop in which men could get some employment in repairing furniture and in other extemporized work, but that of course was only a drop in the bucket of help as against the crucial human need.

Toward the conclusion of a long letter at the summer's end Jack Horner wrote:

You have much to say in the best place in all the world to say it. If any man ever had the vision and the words with which to frame it you have. . . . For three years I sat under your pulpit and looked up to you, as I still do, and I know that the Master has often spoken through you. I have heard Him. And because I have, I know that He has something to say and do in this pending struggle. And I want you to say it for Him. . . . I have not said a word about your voice. Your people have talked to me about it this summer and I usually remained quiet. They told me that when you were inspired no one had the least difficulty in hearing you, for then the sermon lifted you, and your voice was but the medium to show a heart afire and all saw it. . . . I know that your voice will take care of itself if you will undertake the most difficult job in all the world and let the Master speak through you to industrial America. . . . You have had a prophet's training for seven years in old Grace. You have eaten bitterness and been a man through it all. . . . The Church cannot stand for a civilization of "class against class" as I often saw in Union Square this summer: nor ought it to be necessary for men to fight to keep from starving. . . . Our industrial leadership has weakened and in places it has failed. Take up that charred torch of failure, relight it in your hands, carry it for the Church into readjustment and understanding. You can. . . . An economic readjustment, an understanding of "liberalism" and labour, the Kingdom of God in industry, a sanity and justice in life, and Christ in all. These things a dream? No, not under your leadership, Chief.

If I had been able to fulfil his vision! That could have meant a great new day for me and for Grace Church. It ought to have been possible to breathe deeply enough of what comes from God to be unaffected by another atmosphere, but the long frustration of "not being heard" took its toll. Utterance was inhibited by the increasing subconscious question as to whether anything I had to say was "inspired" enough to reach those who did not want to listen.

There *were* those who did not want to listen or respond to anything that cut across old ways. In New York there was a Negro musician whose great desire and devotion was to gather and preserve, before they should be forgotten, the "spirituals" and their poignant music which were the precious heritage of his people. I invited a quartet which he led to sing at a Good Friday service in Grace Church. When the announcement of this had been printed in the previous Sunday's bulletin, a member of one of the old families wrote to me:

It is with regret that I write to you that I shall not attend the three-hour service in Grace Church on Good Friday. The Negro spirituals are melodious and appealing in a way—but surely they are an expression of an illiterate and superstitious people and are below the intelligence and need of the more educated and privileged. To have an unusual activity in our church on Good Friday would do away for me with the solemnity and spirit of the day.

At the same time there was on the vestry a younger man who was courteous and pleasant and in many ways most likable, but representative of some others like him for whom the church seemed to have not much more than the formal interest of an inherited association. He wrote to a succeeding rector that he was leaving Grace Parish. He said that he did not like the class of people who were being drawn into it.

They were not the sort that he was congenial with, and therefore he wished to leave. He said he knew that what he was writing might sound like a snob; but if what he felt made him a snob, he was quite content to be one.

After I had left Grace, one of the young assistants on the then rector's staff whom I have never met grew interested in the history of the parish, and wrote some brief sketches of the various rectors as these appeared to his interpretation. He described my ministry as beginning with bright prospects.

There was a building boom on lower Fifth Avenue, which was supplementing a hitherto dwindling neighborhood population. Plans formed in the young rector's mind: he wanted to build on the corner of Fourth Avenue and Tenth Street so that the church might have more space (for a parish house). Architects were called: the future glittered with possibilities. And then the heavens fell. The depression came. It ended the architects' plans; it ended the building boom; and it was the beginning of the end of the old aristocracy. The war to end all wars had not ended trouble. The decline in power of the families in the Social Register had many causes, and the new rector preached about them, relevantly and forthrightly. Many of the fine old families were upset by the things that the rector was saying. They almost came to think that *he* had brought their new troubles on them. They began to think that they could not hear and he began to feel that he could not speak. The prophet had much to say, but the pressure of the new situation wore down both the preacher and the congregation. . . . The days of quiet felicity were ending. Many people blamed the rector because Grace Church was changing. The old elegance had given way either to bitter nostalgia for days that would never return or to eager anticipation of new forms of Christian vitality. And the battleground on which the changes were fought was the heart of the rector. He was a man of human proportions, but looking back one must admire his courage in speaking out clearly, in refusing to compromise with those who wanted Grace Church

202

to be as it was in the nineteenth century. Much that was good in Grace Church today was bought by the pain of that man.

So wrote the warmhearted young clergyman about a rector of whom he knew only by hearsay, and of whom he gave a better picture than was deserved. Nor did he do full justice to the congregation's reason for unrest if they "could not hear." And as for myself, had I been too conscious of the difficulties to trust and to find instead a releasing power of God? Had I failed to be so greatly caught up in some self-transcending message, such as Jack Horner envisioned, that all little disappointments and resistances would have seemed insignificant and therefore not have been subconsciously frustrating? That is the searching question which one's own inner self could not silence.

It had become evident that my ministry at Grace Church could no longer be as fruitful as it ought to be. Accordingly, in April of 1939, I sent out to all the members a letter printed as a leaflet:

My dear friends of Grace Church:

Today I am making the announcement of my resignation of the rectorship of the parish. . . . I have been asked to come to Union Theological Seminary, New York City, to take a position on its faculty. It is a great post of opportunity. At the same time I cannot refrain from letting those among you who have been my dear friends know that I should not instinctively want to leave the associations here for any other position whatever. I know, however, that there has been real difficulty in Grace Church, or at any rate in some parts of it, in regard to hearing me easily. Individuals have said to me this winter that so far as they are concerned this difficulty has largely vanished. Nevertheless, there are many others among whom the difficulty, and the tradition of it, continue as a serious handicap to co-operation in building up the parish. This being so, and in the light of the call to Union, it seems to me right for the brightest and fullest future of the parish and for my own maximum service to the Church at large that I should accept the position at Union which has been extended to me.

So I have submitted my resignation to take effect as of October first. In the meantime we shall all do our utmost to make the parish strong and ready for my successor, whoever he may be. Nor will there be any break in those mutual friendships and affections which I am deeply conscious of as I write these words. There are many of you who have given to Mrs. Bowie and me a kind of devotion which nothing that I may have been able to do in and for the parish could have been by itself sufficient to win; and for that you have not only our gratitude but our unfailing comradeship in spirit always.

XIX. At Union Seminary

It was by that incomparable friend, Henry Coffin, that the call to Union was brought to me, in the name of the Board of Directors and the faculty. I had been called to Union once before. When I was at St. Paul's, Dr. Francis Brown, then President of Union, had come to Richmond to invite me to the newly created professorship of Christian Institutions. I told him at once that I had no specialized learning in the field indicated by that chair. He replied that he had anticipated that, but I was desired; and the Seminary was ready to make it possible for me to go for a year of concentrated study abroad before taking up teaching in the autumn of the following year. I let him know, I hope, how greatly I appreciated his confidence, but I knew that I could not bring myself then to leave St. Paul's and the parish ministry.

Now conditions were different; and in the fall of 1939 Jean and I took up residence where we were to spend our next eleven years, at the Seminary. Of the children, Jean and Ted Evans were in Cleveland, Ohio, where Ted was the rector of St. Paul's Church; Beverley was working in Washington for Senator Downey of California; Elisabeth was on the secretarial staff at Vassar, and Rusty was in his junior year at Harvard. The beloved "Miss Arm" had gone for a year's visit with her sister on the Pacific Coast, so Jean and I were alone in a small apartment. The next year we moved to a larger one in the Seminary's McGiffert Hall, where there was more room for the children when they came home. And "Miss Arm" rejoined us and continued living with us until she went into nearby St. Luke's Home, which she had chosen and begun to arrange for some years before.

Because of the spirit that radiated from Henry and Dorothy Coffin in the President's house, Union Seminary was a warm and companionable place. All the faculty and their families lived either in Knox Hall, at one end of the great quadrangle on Broadway, or in McGiffert Hall, on Claremont Avenue directly across the street. Everybody was less than a hundred yards from everybody else. The apartments had their own complete privacy when that was what was wanted, but there was much going back and forth and informal sociability. I already knew the Seminary well; for besides having studied there for a term in 1908, I had taught a course in the history and polity of the Episcopal Church in two of the Grace Church years, and I had been a member of the Board of Directors of the Seminary. Now I was to be a colleague of the group that included such men as William Adams Brown, James Moffatt, Ernest F. Scott, F. J. Foakes Jackson, Julius A. Bewer, Reinhold Niebuhr, Frederick C. Grant, Hugh Black, Eugene W. Lyman, Cyril C. Richardson, and Samuel Terrien; and Harry Fosdick, though he had ceased to teach full time at Union since he had become the minister of the Riverside Church across the street, was still living in Knox Hall. The faculty was further enriched by the coming, from Hitler's Germany, of Paul Tillich and Richard J. Kroner; and later of James Muilenburg, John T. McNeill, John Knox, and Paul Scherer.

Jean, who had her own special gift for friendship, found at once her place in a circle of congenial friends. The apartment in McGiffert Hall was not as spacious as the beautiful old rectory at Grace Church, but she made it a place of happy welcome for faculty and faculty wives and students. That friendliness of hers led to an incident which in its comic unexpectedness became a longtime recollection for her and for the rest of us. Everybody in the seminary had warm liking for Dr. Richard Kroner, who like Paul Tillich had come to Union only a little while before, and had just begun to know what went on in the Seminary life. It was the custom to have on an evening at the beginning of each session the so-called Round Robin, in which a committee of seniors guided groups of all the new students through the buildings for a ten-minute welcome in each of the faculty apartments. It occurred to Jean to ask Dr. Kroner to come and be with us, so she telephoned him.

"Dr. Kroner," she said, "this is the evening of the Round Robin, and I want you to come and share it with us in this apartment."

"Who iss zat, and vat did you say?" came the reply.

Jean repeated what she had just said.

"But I do not know about 'Round Robins,' and zis iss not Mrs. Bowie."

"Yes, Dr. Kroner, this *is* Mrs. Bowie. I have a cold, and so it may not sound like me, but it *is*."

"No, I know Mrs. Bowie's voice. Zis iss *not* Mrs. Bowie. Somebody iss trying to fool me. Somebody iss trying to se-dooce me." And the telephone receiver was hung up with horrified finality.

My chief responsibility was to teach courses in "homiletics," which meant to have men preach sermons in Chapel to me and to a small group of fellow students and through the general discussion which followed to help the preacher to discover whether what he had tried to say had registered with those who heard him. This was not a new experience. Back in 1929, at about the midpoint of my ministry at Grace Church, Dean Fosbroke had invited me to come over to General Seminary one morning a week in the fall semester to give a special preaching course. For ten years I went from Broadway and Tenth Street to the Seminary on Ninth Avenue to carry out that schedule, and from Union on Morningside Heights I continued going for ten years more. Also for two or three years I responded to an urging from the Divinity School in Philadelphia to come for the same sort of one-time-a-week teaching there, all of which meant a warm contact with those two seminaries and a chance to have some part in their life and work.

To listen thus to sermons from seminary students who are trying for the first time to learn to preach, and to reflect discerningly on what each man who has preached has tried to do and then to help him see the ways in which he may have been right and other ways in which he has fallen short, can be—and ought to be—an exacting business. It would be comparatively easy if all that the instructor needs to do is to give *his* idea of what might best have been said about the text and theme, as though to say, "This is what *I* would have preached, and you would do well to follow that pattern." But his real responsibility is to discover what the man himself was seeking to express, to reach through what may have been the groping utterance to the genuine purpose, and then to try to show the preacher how his sermon might have been better worked out in order to be a straight and clear channel for his own thought to come through. The criticism—to use a word which had to be turned into something so evidently friendly and construc-

tive as therefore not be resented—must help the man to fulfill what *he* essentially had in mind. Even if the particular
sermon he had preached was poor, he needed to be encouraged
to believe in the possibilities that might be in him.

God's message for the world, with the note of a man's own
personal conviction: that was the purpose which ought to
be in heart and mind. I used to suggest that any one who was
about to preach his first sermon might well ponder the words
of the blind man healed by Jesus at the pool of Siloam. After
he had been healed, the Pharisees got hold of him and tried
to tangle him in quibbling questions. "Who healed you, how
did he do it, what explanation of your healing can you give?"
The man refused to be caught in the trap of trivial arguing.
"One thing I know," he said, "that whereas I was blind, now
I see." (KJV) Let the man who is to preach begin with what
he knows, not with some theological book he thinks he ought
to show that he is familiar with, not with secondhand ideas he
has caught from some professor—but with what he knows.
Let him ask himself what reality of God and Christ has come
home to him, what fact about life and faith which once he
did not see he does see now; let him begin with *that*, no matter
how limited and inadequate it might seem to be, and he is
on solid ground where he can stand sure and from which he
can speak with power.

Then, besides the work in the Seminary itself, there were
two other large interests which developed while I was at
Union.

One was the creation of *The Interpreter's Bible*. Pat Beaird,
the business manager of the Abingdon Press, had been talking
one day with George A. Buttrick, and he had asked Buttrick
what he thought might be the most significant new religious
publication that could be thought of and developed for the
time in which we live. Buttrick said, a new commentary on the

Bible which would enlist the work of the best scholars and preachers of the English-speaking world. Out of that conversation *The Interpreter's Bible* was to grow.

Buttrick was the head of the editorial board, and the other editors appointed were Samuel Terrien, John Knox, Paul Scherer, and myself, all from Union Seminary, and Nolan B. Harmon, of the Abingdon-Cokesbury Press. The Press established a secretarial office on Broadway directly opposite the Seminary, where the editors were to meet to shape the overall plan and begin to assemble the materials which would make up the commentary. First there had to be a determination of what was to be covered, and a reckoning of the relative length of treatment to be assigned for the several books of the Old Testament and the New. Then a list was made of the scholars of most authority in America and abroad who should be invited to write, and a larger list of those to be asked to be consultants. Each of the five editors was to be one of the writers; and each editor was also to be in special contact with a certain number of the invited contributors, to try to make sure that what they wrote should fit into the general plan, and to suggest revisions if or when these seemed required.

Obviously, it was a large and lengthy piece of work. Its accomplishment was due, not only to the editors and to those others whose names would publicly appear, but also to the secretaries in the office who examined and filed the material as it came in and put it together in the form that was needed for what would be the intricate printed pages in the commentary, with their parallel divisions of the King James and the Revised Standard Version texts of the whole Bible, and the related exegesis and exposition. Under George Buttrick's leadership there was smooth and happy functioning of the whole group, and unbounded cooperation by Pat Beaird and all the Abingdon Press officials. For the Press the venture of a publication on so great a scale was a daring risk, involving very large expense before any possible return could come in, and necessary uncertainty as to how well the work when finished would be received. But the outcome justified the best hopes which had been held. What made bold to be announced as "Christendom's Most Comprehensive Commentary" has proved itself to be widely helpful and by the end of 1968 over 1,670,000 copies of its twelve volumes had been sold.

The other chief interest and activity outside the Seminary had to do with the new translation—the Revised Standard Version—of the Bible. In 1928 the International Council of Religious Education, with which the educational boards of forty-four of the major Protestant denominations of the United States and Canada were associated, appointed a committee of scholars to undertake such a study as might result in a translation embodying "the best results of modern scholarship as to the meaning of the scriptures in language native to our time, that yet might preserve those qualities which have given to the King James Version a supreme place in English literature." For a while the projected work was at a standstill. Then in 1937 sufficient money was advanced to cover the travel expenses of members of the committee and for living expenses during the days when they should be together in their work. (Other than this, the members of the committee served through the years without compensation, except for the happy satisfaction of companionship in the work itself.)

The committee, with its original personnel somewhat enlarged and, in a few instances, changed, was divided into two sections, one for the Old Testament and one for the New. The members of the committee to deal with the New Testament were:

Millar Burrows of Yale Divinity School

211

Henry J. Cadbury of Harvard Divinity School

Clarence T. Craig of Oberlin Divinity School

Edgar J. Goodspeed of the University of Chicago

Frederick C. Grant of Union Theological Seminary in New York

Abdel R. Wentz, President of the Lutheran Theological Seminary at Gettysburg

W. Russell Bowie of Union Theological Seminary in New York

The chairman of the whole committee and of both of its sections has been Dean Luther A. Weigle of the Yale Divinity School, and the secretary until his death in 1944 was the beloved James Moffatt.

Here, then, was the task, and here was a group of men assigned to try to do it. How was the work organized and pursued?

Each book of the New Testament was assigned originally to one or two members of the committee for a preliminary translation. This draft was then typewritten and a copy sent to all the other members of the New Testament group to be read and studied before the meeting in which it would be reviewed. At that meeting, with all the men sitting around a table, it would be discussed word by word, verse by verse. A new draft prepared by Dr. Moffatt and embodying whatever changes the whole group had agreed upon was then mimeographed and distributed for further study. This revision was again studied and amended at a subsequent meeting.

When all the books of the New Testament had thus been translated into preliminary form, then twice reviewed by the entire membership of the session, copies were sent to the committee's colleagues of the Old Testament section and their opinions were invited. Other scholars not on the committee, widely representative of different churches, were also invited to read the manuscript and submit their criticisms and suggestions. With these in hand the entire work was reviewed for the third time at a two-week session in Northfield, Massachusetts, in August, 1943; and after that, still further editorial examination and correction was carried out by individual members and subcommittees of the New Testament group.

These are the bare facts. The recollection of those who were privileged to have part in the translation is more pleasant and more picturesque. The meetings were in various places at different times of the year. They amounted to thirty-one separate sessions, ranging from three days to more than two weeks and covering 145 days. Some of the meetings were at Union Theological Seminary in New York, among the crowded bookshelves of Frederick Grant's study. Many of them were in New Haven in the delightful buildings of the Yale Divinity School. In two successive summers the committee met as guests of Dr. and Mrs. Edgar J. Goodspeed on Paradise Island, Plum Lake, Wisconsin. And the final meeting of the whole group was held in the ample spaces of that extraordinary structure known as the Chateau, which is part of the Inn at East Northfield, Massachusetts.

In these meetings of the committee, for most of the time, there was just plain hard labor. Ordinarily, the first session began at nine o'clock in the morning and lasted until lunch. Then came an afternoon session which continued until about an hour before dinnertime, and after dinner there was a third session until it was time to go to bed. For a total of about nine hours every day the men sat about the long table, in front of them the typewritten manuscript of the particular New Testament book which was being studied. In the middle of the table or somewhere else near at hand were the lexicons, reference books, and other translations, old and new, which from time to time someone would pick up to consult.

213

At the head of the table, presiding, was Luther Weigle, round-faced, hearty, and genial, endowed with what seemed to be an inexhaustible and unflagging energy, holding the committee to its work. Dead in earnest, he transmitted his sense of compelling responsibility to all the others. Along with that, he had a quick sense of the ridiculous that would break out every little while in a delighted laugh. The only times that he grew vexed were when the proceedings seemed to him to drag unreasonably. Then the harvest moon of his usual countenance would cloud and he would explode, "Come on, fellows, *can't* we quit this discussion and begin to get ahead?"

At his side would be James Moffatt, sucking his pipe with a serene obliviousness to the rank smoke which puffed from its ancient bowl, or else, if his pipe were laid aside, rolling a pencil abstractedly between his palms. All his life he had been a person of prodigious industry. He knew everything there was to be known about the Bible, and his mind had ranged over wide areas of history and general literature. In spite of a critical heart ailment, which he inflexibly ignored, he took more than one man's share in the labor of every meeting of the committee; and in addition to that, he would carry an armful of books, including detective stories, to his room every evening and read late into the night. Tall and frail and soft-spoken, he embodied always an Old-World courtesy. Sometimes in the discussion of a suggested translation he would urge his own long-considered judgment with animation and force, but at other times he would fall completely silent, and no urging from the chairman could get a word of opinion from his lips. Then somebody would reach for a familiar book on the table, open it, and say, "I observe that a certain unnamed reviser has translated it as follows," thus disclosing that Moffatt himself in his own New Testament version had anticipated the choice of a word at which our committee had now arrived.

There he would sit, however, like a gentle sphinx, refusing to throw his weight toward a particular decision lest it might seem that he was trying to introduce his own personal rendering too much into the verdict of us all.

At the table would be Henry Cadbury, a scholar of the most implacable patience, never content to let any decision be reached until every imaginable point of doubt as to the exact text to be preferred among variant manuscripts and the exact shade of meaning to be attributed to each Greek word or phrase had been pursued to the ultimate. Frequently a point would seem to have been settled, when Cadbury, getting up from the table and searching in some book, would raise a new query which would stop the whole proceeding and turn the discussion back to its starting point. "Where is Cadbury?" somebody asked one day when he had gone for a moment out of the room. "Oh," came the answer, "he is out relining his brakes."

More than most members of the committee, he moved in an eternal world of knowledge where time meant nothing, and to him conspicuously and to his placid Quaker resolution may be attributed the fact that nothing the committee ever did was casual or careless or in haste. Nearly always next to him at work, as they were also roommates in some of the places where we met, was Clarence Craig, and the two were well matched in thorough scholarship, in exact knowledge, and in clear expression of what they thought.

Millar Burrows of Yale was taken away from the New Testament committee late in the period of its work and transferred to the Old Testament section, for his knowledge not only of Greek but of Hebrew made him equally valuable in both. Another authoritative Greek scholar in the company was Frederick Grant, ranking with Moffatt and Cadbury and Craig in his mastery not only of the language of the New Testament, but also of its background of Greek and Aramaic influences, a large man, quiet and unruffled, with exact opinions always advanced with considerate courtesy, and with the fine literary sense native to one accustomed to the liturgy of the Anglican Church.

Off a little to one side usually, because the lights directly over the table bothered his eyes, would be Goodspeed, a scholar of wide learning and confident mastery, a ready fighter in linguistic battles, with a razor-like incisiveness of thought and speech, an aroused and formidable protagonist for a particular view, especially when this fell within the area of evidence drawn from the recently discovered papyri, to which he attached immense importance.

When Weigle was not present, his place as presiding officer came to be taken by Abdel Wentz, the member most recently added to the committee, but one of the most energetic and helpful, who had opinions of his own which he defended with great tenacity, yet who, as chairman, could be as impartial as he was prompt. As a member of the committee he had one pet aversion. He hated what he called "backing into an idea." By that phrase he was expressing a general dislike for any kind of sentence that did not follow the most obvious and straightforward order of subject, predicate, and object. In many of his objections he was outvoted, but he would come up to the next contest fresh and undismayed on behalf of what he thought was the needed terseness and simplicity. That was important. Something else also was important, and it was this something else that concerned me most in our discussions and our conclusions. It was to achieve if we could in modern language some comparable parallel to the rhythm and beauty of sound which have given to the King James Version its enduring greatness in English literature.

Altogether, it was a happy and memorable fellowship.

216

Whatever may be the result of our joint work, the process was its own reward. Long hours around conference tables, with eyes shifting between the typewritten English manuscript and the Greek New Testament, were often physically and mentally exhausting, but they were also immensely stimulating and informing, as the minds of different men played upon the same problems.

In two summers we met on Paradise Island, Wisconsin, in the gay and generous hospitality of Professor and Mrs. Goodspeed. Even there the unsparing routine of the appointed labor went on regardless of the surroundings and I have a snapshot of the members of the committee on their way to Dr. Goodspeed's outdoor study as somebody began to sing the refrain of the seven dwarfs in *Snow White,* "Heigh ho, heigh ho, it's back to work we go."

Whatever else the committee may have done or left undone, one thing it never failed in was the conscientious purpose to reproduce what the writers of the New Testament had actually said and had meant to say. No one had a partisan slant, or any desire other than to make a translation as accurate and right as honesty and diligence could accomplish. Most lovers of the Bible have recognized this, and have regarded with a mixture of amusement and compassion the outcries of a few belligerent Fundamentalists, angry at the change of some familiar word, who have proclaimed that the translators of the Revised Standard Version must be accounted as no better than "godless communists." And if we who produced the R.S.V. were alleged to be godless communists, we have been joined by remarkably good company; for it is not only by great numbers of Protestant churches that the new translation has been adopted. The Roman Catholic authorities in England, headed by the Cardinal Archbishop of Westminster, have asked and been granted permission to reprint the

R.S.V., with a few approved changes, and have recommended it for use by their own Roman Catholic people. So this translation has become the ground of agreement as to the form and content of the gospel on which Christians of different traditions meet as they had not met before.

XX. Changing Tides in Religious Thinking

It is curious to see and to remember the changes in theological emphasis that come and go as the years pass by. They roll in like successive tides, flooding the edges of the religious world, reaching their climax, and then slowly withdrawing to leave the sands for the next recurrent tide to cover.

When I first was in the Seminary at Alexandria in 1905, there could be an innocent acceptance of the Bible and the creeds just as they were. One did not encounter the belligerent Fundamentalism which later became familiar, because there had not begun to be differences sharp enough to cause conflict. But the literal interpretations which the Fundamentalists would afterwards defend so inflexibly pervaded the general mind; and the creeds, including "the resurrection of the body" and the "ascended into heaven" were an inherited picture of concrete reality which was slow to change. For most people in the pews the whole Bible was the Word of God, and authoritative—or at any rate properly to be regarded as authoritative—"from cover to cover." The professors in the Virginia Seminary were aware of course of "the higher criticism" and of the reexamination of traditional ideas which that criticism made necessary. They did not forget the courageous words of old Dean Sparrow who as far back as the middle of the nineteenth century had said, "Seek the truth, come whence it may, cost what it will." So their approach to the most modern scholarship was honest, but it was also cautious. Meanwhile they brought into their teaching something that was more important than academic analysis. They communicated a conviction and a feeling that was profoundly evangelical. They could approach critical questions with a central assurance, drawn from their own religious genuineness, that at the heart of everything could be the experienced fact that "God was in Christ, reconciling the world unto himself."

The searching thought which was rising in the church, and increasingly in the seminaries, with its questioning of old formulations of the truth, became the new tide of liberalism. To the conservatives that word had an invidious sound. It suggested irresponsible and unlicensed departure from old ways and old faith. But at its heart the liberal movement did not mean that. It was no irreverent casting off of what had been believed. It was instead a rediscovery of the meaning of the words of Jesus that "every scribe who has been trained for the kingdom of heaven must bring out of his treasure both what is new and what is old." It meant to adopt toward what might be our own rigidities of thought the same spirit which the Apostle Paul had urged his Christian converts in Galatia to adopt toward their inherited dogmatisms—to stand fast in the liberty wherein Christ has made us free. The man who tried to follow a reverent liberalism was set free from little inhibitions, and could enter a wider area of thought and action in which a Christian could go forward unafraid. He did not have to be apprehensive lest his gospel should be lost if he followed honestly on the ways of biblical scholarship. Neither

did he have to think that his church loyalty would be com-
promised if he had an open and generous mind toward the
truths that might come to him through other churches. A
permanent debt is owed to the liberal movement and to those
who were part of it. Anyone who should speak the word
"liberal" with glib disparagement could do so only because of
carelessness, or ignorance, or a flippant effort to sound smart.
Those who understand the richness of our inheritance know
that the liberal mind is one of the treasures that must never
be lost from the Kingdom of God.

One vital result of the wider and deeper new study of the
Bible was an excited awareness of aspects of its message which
the church had too seldom grasped. The old evangelical piety
had been beautiful; but sometimes it had been concerned more
with calculations about heaven than with consideration of
how the grace of God might come into saving contact with
the immediate life of needy people here and now. Too little
recognition had been given to the words of Jesus when in his
parable of the Judgment he said to those who had fed the
hungry and clothed the naked and welcomed the stranger and
visited the prisoners, "As you did it to one of the least of these
my brethren, you did it to me." With a kindled imagination
Christians began to see that their business as disciples of Jesus
was not only to worship within the church's walls, but to go
out into the city to help the neglected and the impoverished
and the oppressed, and to change for the better the conditions
of the actual world in which the poor and the helpless have
to live. So from men like Washington Gladden and Walter
Rauschenbusch there began to sound "the social gospel."

All this was part of the liberal movement, and its great
value was that men's minds and imaginations were moving out
rewardingly into areas wider than those in which they had
rested before. Yet the trend of thought denominated by the

221

blanket term "liberal" ran the danger of being distorted. There could be a type of so-called liberal who followed new notions wherever they might seem to go, without carrying the old convictions with him. That kind of left-wing liberal actually belonged under another classification and under another name. He was a non-Christian humanist, and no more than that. "Glory to Man in the highest! for Man is the master of things," sang the poet Swinburne in the bland confidence of a generation which thought that all it had to do was to ride to unlimited progress on the escalator of its own self-sufficiency. Man as the master could make a new earth; and as for a new heaven, perhaps man could make that too if anyone should want it.

That mood passed with the shocking dislocation of the first World War. The dark passions and ferocities which emerged from under the surface of a human life which had seemed to be secure gave its grim answer to whether man was master of things or not. Optimism vanished; and instead, as T. S. Eliot wrote in *Murder in the Cathedral*,

> Sweet and cloying through the dark air
> Falls the stifling scent of despair.[1]

Then around the borders of the religious world there rolled in another tide—the tide of neo-orthodoxy, expressed particularly in the writings of Karl Barth. The impact of neo-orthodoxy came out of a consciousness of tragedy, like an upheaval of deep waters from a dark and troubled sea.

Its force was in its reassertion of the authority of the Bible and of the Bible's central message of the sovereignty of God.

[1] From *Complete Poems and Plays*, © 1952, p. 195. Used by permission of Harcourt, Brace & World, Inc., New York, and Faber and Faber, Ltd., London.

It found the Christian world in a mood to listen to its sombre indictment of shallow human self-assertion, and to recognize the judgment which had fallen upon humanity's shortcomings and its sins. Men had forgotten God, and had thought they could live by their own devices. Now the great part of the earth which the war had wrecked testified to their need for a righteousness and a wisdom that must come from something higher than themselves. Let men stop and listen to the chastening word of God.

That message of neo-orthodoxy had immediate relevance and salutary power. It exposed the hollowness of the conceit that a world could be built of shifting expedients which took no account of eternal facts. Men must turn again to the Bible and wait for the revelation by which alone they could be saved.

In that central emphasis upon the subjection of our pride, and a readiness to hear a word from heaven that is wiser than our imagined wisdom, neo-orthodoxy had immense value. It forced men to recognize the fact and the formidableness of human sin, and to acknowledge that by themselves they could never overcome it. Neo-orthodoxy was saying again and more emphatically what had long been said in the General Confession of the Book of Common Prayer, "We have erred, and strayed from thy ways like lost sheep. We have followed too much the devices and desires of our own hearts. . . . We have left undone those things which we ought to have done; And we have done those things which we ought not to have done; And there is no health in us."

"No health in us." In the sense of wholeness, that is devastatingly true. It is also true that what broken elements of goodness there may be in us are always mixed with sins. But neo-orthodoxy committed the exaggeration of representing the human spirit as so completely corrupt that no clear reflection of what God is and what God means could be found within it.

A more balanced theology had maintained that "Man is the son of God even if a lost son; and it is his proper destiny to be partaker of the divine life." [2] But Karl Barth insisted that God is the "Wholly Other," and Emil Brunner wrote that "He reveals himself as the unheard of, unrecognized mysterious person who cannot be discovered anywhere in the world." [3] Thus in the early proclamation of neo-orthodoxy (though modified since, as in Karl Barth's *The Humanity of God*) there appeared an almost fanatical denial of any image of God still present in man, an ultimate hopelessness concerning all human activity, and such belittlement of everything in the human sphere that interest in the life and words of the actual Jesus of Nazareth disappeared in dogmatisms concerning a wholly metaphysical Christ. "How Jesus found God, how he prayed, how he lived is not divine revelation for us," [4] wrote Emil Brunner. "Jesus as an epoch-making personality is—like all other world history—dust, mortality." [5]

The consequence which had to come to ordinary people from such pronouncements of neo-orthodoxy was the chilled idea that God is not within the real life they had to lead. Neo-orthodoxy's virtue was that it brought again the awesome and purifying message of God's transcendence, but in its drastic chastening of human vanity it obscured the truth that God in his purpose of redemption may always be coming near, and that he touches man in what the best in man still knows and feels. So neo-orthodoxy could become not a Christian gospel, but a Christian heresy, in a bleak denial of the central message of the Incarnation. If God were indeed the "Wholly

[2] H. R. Mackintosh, *The Doctrine of the Person of Christ* (New York: Charles Scribner's Sons, 1912), p. 434.

[3] *The Theology of Crisis* (New York: Charles Scribner's Sons, 1935), p. 33.

[4] *Ibid.*, p. 36.

[5] *Our Faith* (New York: Charles Scribner's Sons, 1936), p. 58.

Other," then we should be turned back to a kind of Gnostic theophany in which God's communication of himself to man becomes a process unintelligible to the general mind, and paralyzing—like arctic cold—to the instinctive hope which men's everyday experiences can make them feel. When the divine is pushed off into the distance, existence is cut in two, and there is a gulf of separation between the academically religious and people who go about their ordinary work. The neo-orthodox insistence on the degradation of man and the futility of his endeavors belittled the social gospel, and tended to make people accept the deadening conclusion that all programs for social betterment were only vain illusions. So it began to be seen that uncorrected neo-orthodoxy could dim even the central Christian faith that the reality of God came near in the human life of Jesus, and make men and women lose their trust that the common place and the common occupation can be the medium through which God's purpose shines.

Because neo-orthodoxy had thus gone too far in its own direction, a surge of contrary questions was inevitable. What evidence could be given for this all-ruling sovereignty of a transcendent God which had been proclaimed? Did the facts of human life and the events of history actually suggest a heavenly power that men must believe in and be ruled by? And if there was such power, suppose it should be only what Thomas Hardy had called "the dreaming, dark, dumb thing that turns the handle of an idle show." Against the emphatic affirmations of neo-orthodoxy a mood of skepticism came in like a grey fog over part at least of what had been the area of religious thinking. Sometimes wistfully and sometimes defiantly, men here and there began to say that, so far as concerns the old patterns of faith, God is dead.

225

That sort of reaction from the religious beliefs which most people used to hold could have one of two results. One would be plain atheism—which would mean the assumption that this physical and material world in which we live, and its obvious calculations, are all the reality there is, and anything beyond it can be denied. When that denial has been blatant, then atheism has been an ugly word, because it has implied the assertion that there are no infinite dimensions to life at all. The inherited faith that there is some transcendent reality over and beyond material facts and their obvious practicalities would then be regarded as naïve illusion to be got rid of.

But the present contradiction to traditional belief is not necessarily as crass as that. Some of those who write most emphatically of "the death of God" are *not* blatant, nor careless either. In their view, most of this generation has simply ceased to live for or live by what used to be its conception of God. They say that our age is inevitably secular in the sense of starting from and being concerned with the actualities of the here-and-now; but this does not necessarily mean a secular*ism* which has no ideals beyond the obvious. That is what Bishop Robinson has recognized in *Honest To God*, and what Harvey Cox has expressed in *The Secular City*. Similarly, Paul M. van Buren in *The Secular Meaning of the Gospel*, has held on to the figure of Jesus as a supreme source of inspiration, even when he has laid aside belief in a God who is something more than a projection of our human wishful thinking. Thus it is not true that contemporary thinkers who have swung completely away from dogmatic neo-orthodoxy must represent the stark emptiness which the word atheism has been assumed to convey. The best of them are looking for "the beyond in the midst," for something in their secular commitments which can give the lift that men were looking for when they spoke more traditionally of God.

226

Reality must be experienced in fresh ways as times and occasions change. It will be learned—or lost—not in arguments but in life. The contemporary writers who still call themselves theologians although they hesitate to speak in old accustomed ways of God are right in their reminder that what is to be for us divine must move not in some distant orbit of the supernatural but in the moral forces of our secular world. They are wrong when in a misreading of what Bonhoeffer meant in his compressed phrase of "religionless Christianity" they lose the awed sense of the *mysterium tremendum* which is vaster than our little thinking and wider than our secular concerns. They are wrong if and when they disparage the function of the Church as the fellowship of the would-be faithful, by whose worship the great heritage of the Spirit is preserved, with its canon of continuing judgment, and at the same time its gift of sustaining grace.

Any human conception of God must inevitably be groping and imperfect, and it is important to be made to realize how inadequate and childish some of our conventionally accepted conceptions have been. That is what Bishop Robinson sought to accomplish in *Honest To God* when he pointed out that many of us have not got beyond the idea of God as an entity outside ourselves, "up there" or "out there," and, in the language sometimes used, "The Man Upstairs." In reaction against those crude extremes he would have us think of God not as a Being or as a Person, but—in Tillich's terms—as the "ground of being." Yet in his own deeper consciousness he recognizes that a God conceived as only a ground of being could not be the One to whom the hearts of men can turn. Asked how he could pray to a Ground of Being, he answers: "I would say at once that I do not pray to the ground of my being. I pray to God as Father. Prayer, for the Christian, is the opening of oneself to that utterly gracious personal reality

227

which Jesus could only address as Abba, Father. . . . The only God who meets my need as a Christian is 'The God of Abraham, Issac, and Jacob,' the God and Father of Our Lord Jesus Christ." [6]

But to say that God is *not* a Person, and yet is "the utterly gracious *personal* reality" which Jesus called his Father, can sound like a semantic run-around. There is need for language less involved than that. The way through the seeming contradiction may open when we think of God as the *Heart* of Being, from whom comes the pulsebeat of all life, and the warmth of whose reality flowing into us is at every moment the strength by which we live. So it would be true to say again that God is not *a* Person set over against ourselves, but with that and instead of that to say that he is *the* Person, the one Reality, creative and loving, from whom everything that is most real in ourselves proceeds. Because he is in *this* supreme sense personal, he can be for us the standard of continuing judgment and the living God from whom there does come to us sustaining grace.

Then when we ask, Where do we find God? the answer must be: *in fulness of living, deep within and wide without.*

Religion must have the profundity of the agelong faith which rests upon a divine Reality that undergirds us, and it must have the immediacy of experience that finds God most as it reaches out in service to the world.

The supreme embodiment of union between the depths of life and the wideness of life is Jesus. All the way from Galilee to Gethsemane, in the communion of his prayers, he drew from the infinite depths of God; and the power that thus belonged to him went out to meet the needs of the least and lowliest to whom his strength and compassion could minister.

[6] *The Honest to God Debate* (Philadelphia: Westminster Press), p. 261.

So should it be with souls who are seeking to know God now.

Each one needs first to be part of the continuing fellowship of worship within the Christian church, the agelong power of which only the impatient and the shallow will forget. In the church's worship there is the flame of witness to all that the many generations have believed and lived by—the flame from which may be lighted the candles of single souls whose light when the winds blow strong might otherwise flicker and go out. No man can give what he does not have; and if any man is to bring a kindling spirit to the world he is a part of he had better have tried in thought and deliberate desire to come, in the fellowship of the faithful, close enough in prayer to God for some burning coal from the heavenly altar to light a fire in him.

Then when the fire is lighted in his own religious consciousness, his business is not to stand where he is and warm himself, but to go out into the weekday world of work and shared experience to see whether God is there. God in the "sacred" surroundings, yes; but what about God in "the secular city"? To see what people may be up against, at home, on the streets, at the places where they make their living, is to be sure of this: that life can be a very drab and weary business when there is no quickening purpose and no sense of a horizon wider than the crowding facts. But then something else appears. Here is a woman in some shabby little house, nursing a sick child with an unflagging devotion and a tenderness that makes the tired eyes light up with beauty. Here is a man working against heavy odds to earn enough to feed his family, and trying his best not to show to those who depend on him the hopelessness to which sometimes he could almost yield. And here is another who in a close temptation keeps his moral integrity, and in whatever may be the test of loyalty

229

to those who trust him will never let them down. Suppose that one who sees realities like these begins to let his sympathies enlarge, until he becomes so sensitive both to all the wistfulness and to all the wonderfulness that can be in human lives that he wants to bring the best that is in him to those who need what he might give. Then he has found the way in which life, and faith in the Giver of life, expand; and it is thus that we find, and are found by, God.[7]

---

[7] The last two paragraphs repeat part of the final chapter of *Where You Find God* (Harper & Row), in which book I have tried especially to review the thought of Dietrich Bonhoeffer, and to estimate its influence.

XXI. Lights and Shadows

The years at Union covered the whole period of the second World War. Originally it had been planned that Jean and I would go to England and to Cambridge University for the summer and the fall, before settling in for the new life and work on Morningside Heights; but the clouds gathering over Europe in 1939 made the immediate future too ominous for that. In actual event, the storm broke earlier than had been foreseen. On the first of September, 1939, Hitler invaded Poland, and two days later France and England declared war. Even the ignominious pact which Prime Minister Neville Chamberlain had made with Hitler at Munich, and the dismemberment of Czechoslovakia, had not been enough to hold back the Nazi thrust toward the domination of Europe.

In Union Seminary, as everywhere, there was the shocked sense of forces let loose which left no choice that was not to some degree involved in evil. The men in the student body were too young to have lived through the first World War, but they knew the slogan which in that period had been spoken, of "a war to end war." There had been a hope and a possibility of idealism in commitment then which were not present now. If that first World War had been futile so far

231

as any genuine betterment could be reckoned, what likelihood was there that another war would be any less a mockery of human values everywhere? That was what some of the students asked; and a group of them tried to hold aloof from any alignment with either of the sides in conflict; and later, when the United States also was drawn in, they refused to be drafted and in conscientious protest went to jail. A few members of the faculty agreed with them completely, and there were none who did not respect and defend their courageous earnestness. But to the Seminary constituency in general it seemed that to try to keep aloof from the tragic actual choices which a world at war presented was morally more intolerable than involvement in it, and that therefore America must be increasingly aligned with resistance to the Nazi threat.

A year and a half was to go by with the United States still nonbelligerent, but the tension of sympathy and of tragic concern kept mounting. This was the time when in "the Battle of Britain" the fighter squadrons of the British Air Force, with desperate courage and with grievous losses, drove back the German bombers, and the world echoed the words of Winston Churchill, that "seldom in the annals of human warfare has so much been owed by so many to so few." During those months when England stood alone between the threat of Hitler's Germany and the survival of freedom in the West, it could seem true—as again the great voice of Churchill phrased it—that "If the British Empire and its Commonwealth last for a thousand years, men will still say: 'This was their finest hour.' "

Nor is one likely to forget the steady accents of Edward R. Murrow, as he began each night on the radio his bulletins while the bombs were falling: "*This*—is London." Listening to him, one felt deep emotions answering to the courage that he described—not only the courage of men in the armed forces, but the homely and unpretentious courage of the little people who wore no uniforms and would have no decorations, but who by their stubborn patience would see to it that a nation should endure. Through all the suffering and the evil there came the glint of something so indestructible in the human spirit that even the worst ugliness of war was for the moment lightened. Churchill might express the valor of England with Shakespearean nobility of language, but its toughness of resistance in spite of all disaster was no less expressed in the cockney humor of the East-Londoner down by the docks that Murrow told of when houses in all that region were smashed on one night of the bombing. As the Londoner and his wife got out in the streets, she cried: "Ow, Jimes, I must go back. I've left me teeth!" To which he answered, "Old gal, you won't need 'em. It's not sandwiches that Jerry's droppin' tonight."

The staggering attack by the Japanese upon Pearl Harbor brought the United States into the war, and now, of course, all of us in America were more intimately involved. Our Rusty (Walter Russell Bowie, Jr.), who had graduated from Harvard in 1941 and had been president of *The Lampoon*, went in the summer of 1942 to Camp Eustis in Virginia as a private; then being sent to Officers' Training School, he progressed in rank and in assignments of duty until the closing months of the war found him a lieutenant-colonel on the Aleutian Islands. Beverley, in the O.S.S., was in Italy and then in Rumania, where an adventurous pioneering won him the Bronze Medal. Pride and happiness and anxiety and happiness again were mingled in these years. Bev had been married in 1940 to Louise Boynton of Baltimore, and Rusty was married in 1943 to Mary Maenner, of Omaha, and both of them came back safe from the war. And Elisabeth was married to Dwight W. Chapman, Jr., in 1942.

So a new generation was coming to the fore; but also there had been the tolling of bells. In the year before I left Grace Church, Mary-Cooke Branch Munford had died. At the University of Virginia, a new residence hall built for women admitted to the Graduate School was named in her honor, and a tablet recorded her as one "who carried the devotion of a great mind and a flaming spirit into unselfish service to public education throughout Virginia. Her memorial is in numberless young lives set free." In 1944 my sister died in a New York hospital. Her life, which had had its own measure of suffering had had also the joy that came from much unselfish service, and it was to her that in a book entitled *Some Open Ways to God* I wrote this dedication:

> This book is yours—yet not for aught it gives,
> Yours rather for the gain it takes from you,
> Since what you are commends what it would say
> And in your eyes is that which makes it true:
> For through the morn, or through gray mists of tears,
> Where courage led, your steady feet have trod,
> And those who watch that far look on your face
> Know you have found the open ways to God.

Another shadow on those years at Union—though gallantry of spirit brought a brightness to it—was that one day Jean got up from her desk in quick response to answer the telephone, slipped on a rug, fell, and broke her hip. Although we did not know it then, she would never walk freely again; and except with crutches, not at all.

Through our first years at Union, Henry Sloane Coffin as the

President gave to the whole place the spark of his electric personality, and it seemed that the lights would be bound to burn lower when his term came to an end, as it did come to its end in 1945. The Board of Directors tried to persuade him to continue, but he refused to allow a weakening of the retirement rule. Who could worthily succeed him? That seemed the doubtful question—but it got its answer. Henry Pitney Van Dusen, since 1926 a member of the faculty, was the man chosen, and he brought to the presidency outstanding abilities of his own. Also, the gracious spirit which Dorothy Coffin had made familiar in the President's house and communicated to the life of the Seminary was continued by Betty Van Dusen. Her special gift was a flair for dramatics and for all sorts of happy entertainments. She knew how to conscript members of the faculty and students alike for the plays which she produced, and the lively variety of her choices was evidenced by the fact that in successive years she had me once as St. Francis in Laurence Housman's *Brother Juniper* and the next year as one of the murderers in Lord Dunsany's *A Night at an Inn.*

In regard to the war, and the participation of Union men in it, one of the happiest, and certainly the most extraordinary, incidents was what happened to a high-ranking student who graduated just as the war began. He had been awarded a fellowship for further study abroad; instead of that he enlisted as a private in the American Army. In the Battle of the Bulge he was missing and later reported as having been killed. At the Seminary a memorial service was held in his honor. Then one day he appeared—alive and well. He had been captured by the Germans, and had been lost track of until at the German surrender all the captured had been set free. Not only did he make plain that the memorial service had been ahead of time. He became and is now a distinguished member of

the faculty of the Seminary which had been about to enroll
him among its honored dead.

In every seminary there are always men who have not been
in an army, but are conscientiously concerned to be in a war
against what they think are the social evils here at home.
Sometimes their activities, right though they are in purpose,
may be impetuous, and their ideas immature. It was this that
Cyril Richardson of the Union faculty was thinking of, and
with his quick and ready wit expressed, in what he wrote one
day as a paraphrase and parody of Clement Moore's *'Twas
the Night Before Christmas*. At the climax of his production,
this was his substitute for part of the picture in the famous
poem.

When out in the court there arose a great clatter,
I sprang to my feet to see what was the matter.
Away to the window I flew like a flash;
There weren't any shutters, but I threw up the sash.
And as I looked out on the slumbering city,
What should I see but the Social Action Committee!
Here was a Santa most fit for this place,
Democratic and modern with never a trace
Of paternalist ethics and similar shame.
So I shouted with joy and I called them by name:
"Come Helpful, come Hopeful, come Forthright, come
　Curious,
Come Earnest, Sincerity, Eager and Furious."
They came and they looked into this, into that,
And discussed and reported on theory and fact.
They passed resolutions for good and society,
Condemning reaction of every variety,
And accusing old Santa, in tones most emphatic,
Of being complacent and undemocratic,
For he gives to the good and not to the naughty

236

Making absolute judgments, he oughtn't to, ought he?
To the help and the rescue of sundry and all
They dashed through the cloisters, they dashed through the
   hall.
They knocked at the doors of the Dean and the President,
And their goings and comings weren't timid or hesitant.

Then the chairman I heard him blow strong on a whistle,
And away they all flew like the down of a thistle—
And I heard them exclaim, as they rushed out of sight,
"Oh, an uneasy conscience to all, and goodnight!"

Such could be the friendly jest in regard to "social action,"
the social action which of late has taken startling forms in
some colleges and universities. But above the jest stands the
great and commanding fact that there *is* a war that continually needs to be waged at home—the war against poverty
and deprivation and injustice; and in that war Union Seminary
has often been enlisted. Many years ago the Union Settlement
was established on the city's East Side, and in the 1940's there
was a new adventure. The districts of East Harlem, not far
from Union, held some of the most neglected slums of New
York City. In that neighborhood of dilapidated and dirty
tenements, crowded by Negroes and newly arrived Puerto
Ricans ignorant of American life, with dope peddling and
drink, formal churches and conventional ministries could get
nowhere. But a group of students opened a place of welcome,
and ultimately of worship, in a rented store. The leader of
them went to live in a tenement. Out of what they began
has developed the now widely known East Harlem Protestant
Parish, with its varied and wide-reaching ministry which has
brought a saving leaven of hope and new purpose to its whole
section of New York.

The year 1950 would be the time for my retirement from the Union faculty. Jean and I wondered what we should do next. None of the children were now in New York. But where else should we go? Then, without our planning, came the answer—which the next chapter is to give.

XXII. To Virginia Again

Union Seminary had a statutory requirement that when a member of the faculty reached sixty-five years of age his tenure could be continued year by year for three years, but with retirement automatic when he should become sixty-eight. Some other seminaries had not then begun to go by the calendar so regardfully as that. Ever since I had graduated at Alexandria in 1908 I had gone back to the old Virginia Seminary for Commencement every single year except two, because of the love I had for the place and for the men who would be meeting there; and in 1949 I was there again. I had no sooner arrived than Mollegen and Clif Stanley of the faculty looked me up. "When you finish at Union, come back here," they said. "We want your emphasis, maybe your different emphasis, in the message the men here on the Hill are getting."

That word from them was followed up by an official invitation from the faculty and the Board of Trustees to come and have charge of the Department of Homiletics. They would build a new faculty house for Jean and me. Both of us felt the pull of that prospect. The Virginia Seminary of course was familiar ground to me; and Jean had been there several times and knew its warm and friendly spirit. So a year later, in the fall of 1950, we were settled in surroundings which would be our final home. And my mother came from Richmond to be with us, until her death in 1954.

Notwithstanding her lameness from her broken hip, Jean took at once her happy part in the Seminary life and fellowship—the more so because when it was difficult for her to go freely here and there, others came to her; wives of the faculty with their welcome, wives of the married students who began to sense intuitively the sympathy and help that she could give. For some of the younger ones were like uncertain and half-frightened children, and the wives of older men who had decided to come into the ministry after having been lawyers or executives or officers in the army or navy were sometimes bewildered and even half resentful at the sudden shift from the very different surroundings and associations they had been accustomed to before. They needed one who would understand their difficulties, and at the same time inspire their imagination as to what they could look forward to; and that is what they found in her.

One of these student wives tried to express what Jean had meant to her:

I felt the need to be near her—as I once told John, my husband —to recharge my batteries; for when one felt depressed or boxed in with any kind of problem, it seemed the most natural thing in the world to seek out Jean. And here is the interesting thing: when you called on her or talked to her on the telephone, whatever was disturbing you was never mentioned, yet she knew, she knew, and somehow the conversation which did follow spoke directly to your problem. I recall a number of times when, in the middle of a black thought, the telephone would ring and Jean was calling "just to see how you are." She perceived the needs of and was sensitive to everyone around her—and did something about it!

As for me, in my comradeship with the faculty I was back again as one "to the manner born." I knew the spirit of the Seminary, which essentially had not changed in the many years since I knew it first. Because of that, I could take as a passing matter the wave of ideas which—to my curious interest—I found to be dominant among many of the students. They were under the spell of what they supposed to be neo-orthodoxy, and some of them dourly insistent that all proper theological emphasis must be keyed to the demonic, the devil, and doom. Half-digested information can lead to a zeal not really according to knowledge, a zeal which may become belligerent because it thinks that its half-knowledge is the whole truth. Harry Fosdick, in *The Living of These Days*, has written of his experience at Union, in New York. Men who had come to their studies from a background of wide and tolerant thinking often gained from neo-orthodoxy, he said, "valuable emphases and insights," which they presented "with such force and effectiveness as made me grateful. . . . But the men who had never known theology until they learned it first in neo-orthodoxy! In a few cases especially I had never heard . . . such homiletical arrogance, such take-it-or-leave-it assumption of theological finality, such cancellation of the life and words of the historic Jesus by the substitution of a dogmatic Christ. My first contacts with neo-orthodoxy's effect upon the preacher were very disillusioning." [1]

Consequently, I was not unduly surprised when some of the students at Virginia rejected suggestions I tried to give them as to the substance of their sermons, and concluded that I was a naïve newcomer not to be listened to by their more sophisticated understanding. One of the men who happened not to share that view showed me a letter which he had written to

[1] (New York: Harper's, 1956), p. 247.

his bishop, Will Scarlett, of Missouri. This is part of what he said:

I have felt the overpowering emphasis on the sin of man from the time I entered the seminary. And I have seen its effects on many of the students. Of course, I must say there is a certain mentality to which this appeals today. They are glad to grab on to this note and play it for all it is worth. There are also those who find in it a certain consolation for their own feeling of helplessness.

The great danger, as I see it, is that it lulls people into inaction. . . . It undercuts all social action—or is in danger of doing so. Man is helpless to do anything—all his efforts are ultimately frustrated, they say.

Unfortunately, some of the theologians most interested in social action and in doing something about the world are also those who plunge people into the depths of despair about doing anything. They preach so much about sin that their audiences are left without hope. . . .

It has been only since the coming of Dr. Bowie and the return of Dr. Zabriskie that we have seen some clarifying of the situation, and a new note of hope. But unfortunately Dr. Bowie is viewed by many as an oddity out of the past. I understand that some students protested, or were going to protest, his reappointment as professor on the ground that he was irrelevant.

I have written this because I feel the time has come when something must be done about this, or we shall have only a confused ministry.

Of course the men who thought that their sombre mood was the necessary expression of a proper orthodoxy deserved affectionate understanding. They had grown up in a period of history which had been very dark, and their reflection of that fact was desperately serious, if not to say dead serious. It was no wonder that at first I seemed to them to be "irrelevant."

But the trouble was that they had forgotten that even in difficult times—and all the more because the times were difficult
—the Christian gospel, if it is to be true to itself, must somehow be a gospel of good news. My business was to help them
remember that. On the slope of the Hill where some of those
who had embodied the long traditions of the Seminary are
buried there is a shaft over the grave of Bishop Johns, who
died nearly a century ago; and under his name and title are
these five words, "He preached unto them Jesus." That seemed
to me the central emphasis that needed to be recaptured.
There was a *life*, from Bethlehem to Calvary, which had revealed the divine purpose for all life, and had brought a
power of God that could transcend a tragic world. This was
the message men could believe in and could preach with
saving gladness, once it had laid hold upon their hearts.

In the Seminary and after they had left it, it was possible
for men to begin to see that this was true. More than one individual's experience was represented in this letter which
came to me one day:

I've been meaning to write to you ever since some time last August when I began to get settled in my parish and began to consider what my first sermons were going to be about. I thought a
great deal about what was absolutely the first thing you say in
presenting the Christian faith. Being trained as in part I had been,
I began to consider such things as. . . modern meaninglessness, etc.
But the more I thought on these lines, the more I was convinced
that something more basic and concrete (and simple) needed to
be said. The strange part about it was I was not sure what this
"thing" was. Finally, it dawned on me. It was Jesus Christ! ! !
This insight began a train of thought which ended in the conclusion that this is what is wrong with. . . . He has simply no room
for the most elementary and important thing of all—the per-

sonality of Jesus Christ touching the hearts and minds of men. I believe that most of us at the Seminary missed this insight and considered the personality of our Lord a little old-fashioned! But now I want to tell you that you were right, and without that witness we have little chance of getting anywhere in our preaching. I find it coming out again and again in my sermons.

The need was for men to wake up—as the writer of that letter did—to the fact that their preaching was more likely to be real and helpful if it started from "something basic and concrete." The trouble with many men in seminaries—and some more mature men too, for that matter—is that they suppose they must preach on some elaborate idea which they think will sound impressive; but instead of being impressive, they manage only to be pretentious. They may not be expressing something that is vitally their own, but echoing second-hand ideas which they have picked up from a book or from somebody's lecture. And the more abstract the idea is, the more they may be fascinated by it, until they float in a cloud-land far off from where the people are. They are like men in a theological helicopter, setting out to build a house of faith for the people from the top down, instead of from the ground up. But meanwhile in its heart a congregation is saying to the preacher, "Tell us something near and sure about the gospel that *you* have known and felt."

That does not mean to disparage study and respect for scholarship, as though preaching could be an accidental, spur-of-the-moment matter. All the solid thinking, all the careful preparation, a man may be capable of ought to go into the making of a sermon. But the crucial point is that it should be based not upon academic learning, but upon some living conviction—even if it seems a partial conviction—which a man has gained from God when his thought and feeling have gone down deep.

In listening to the men preach, and in watching their general work, it was good to see them grow in their grasp of truth, and in ability, little by little, to express what they felt the truth to be. This satisfaction in their progress was linked with recollection of some of the stumbling early efforts which they had progressed *from:* efforts which one had had to treat tenderly lest there be hurt feelings, but in the presence of which it had been hard at the time to keep a solemn face.

One preacher announced that man, because of his transgressions, is a sinner condemned to execution. "God," he said, "is the executioner, and he stands before the sinner with a rifle in his hands." Then, in a desperate effort to resolve the problem of the seeming contradiction he had read of as between God's justice and his saving mercy, he went on: "God presses the trigger of the rifle aimed at the sinner doomed to die—and then rushes around in time to catch the bullet in his own breast."

Another preacher began with the startling invitation: "Imagine yourself to be a young bull calf." Then he described the calf tied to a tree, and winding the rope tighter and tighter around the tree until he could scarcely move at all. This was supposed to represent man "tied and bound by the chain of his sins." Then the kindly owner, who presumably was God, comes and looses the calf, and lets him go into the pasture. There the calf, who now is the forgiven sinner, is full of happiness; and the sermon came to its triumphant climax of rejoicing in God "in whose service is perfect freedom."

Life and work in the Seminary could not be said to be quite the same as the activities of a young bull calf romping about in a pasture, but the Seminary's life and work did include areas of happy liberty in space and time. One was not always lecturing or listening to sermons or conferring with students as to what their sermons had tried to say. There was a chance also to think, and to put down in writing what one was learning in the stimulating process of trying to teach. So it was natural that soon after I had come back to Alexandria I should begin on a book which might have been described as having to do with "The Principles and Practice of Homiletics," but which actually had the plain title of *Preaching*. A writer is always curious to see whether his publisher recognizes exactly what he has meant to do, and expresses that—and not some fulsome generality—on the paper jacket of the book. In this instance the Abingdon Press did say succinctly what the purpose was. It was to try to answer these plain questions which everybody going into the ministry must sometime ask himself, "*Why Preach—What to Preach—How to Preach.*"

Now and then some seemingly accidental influence may lead to a new train of thought that results in another book. I had a letter one day from the editor of a magazine which had to do with adult religious studies asking me to write nine articles on great figures in the early centuries of the church: from Peter and Paul, through Irenaeus and Tertullian and others, down to Jerome and Augustine. To respond to that invitation led to a good deal of study of the writings of the early fathers, which had the wholesome result of giving me an acquaintance with those men which at least was considerably wider than what I had possessed before. Then it occurred to me that the work which had thus been done might be the beginning for something larger: for remembering the torch-bearers of the gospel not in the first four centuries only but on down to our immediate world and time. And so I wrote on the Monks and Missionaries who arose in the so-called Dark Ages, and then on sixteen of the great figures whose Christian witness has been most heroic and exciting, such as Francis of Assisi, Martin Luther, John Knox, John Wesley, and in our own lifetime, Wilfred Grenfell and Albert Schweitzer. I called it *Men of Fire.*

But why only *Men* of Fire? In the masculine disciples there has been the driving force which fire at first suggests. But the fire in human souls can have many aspects. It can be a flame which has power—and also peril—in it. But it can also be warm and comforting and protecting, and it can shine like a lamp to penetrate the shadows and make a safer progress into the unknown. It is in this gentler way that the flame which burns in the souls of women may be most manifest. Why not therefore a book on women?—on women in whom the power of the spirit has been most intensely shining. I began to meditate on those whose figures rose above all lesser ones in the great succession of the years, beginning with Mary, the mother of Jesus, and including Joan of Arc, Susanna Wesley, Florence Nightingale, Helen Keller, and fifteen others; and the book which grew and was published had for its title, *Women of Light.*

Similar to those two books in having to do with great human personalities and with the mingled lights and shadows of life as dramatized in them was a book including eight figures from the Old Testament, and eleven men and women from the New, with the title which was also an invitation, *See Yourself in the Bible.*

In preaching and in teaching one will ask himself where it is that he himself has been most likely to find such measure of inspiration as has come to him. As a Christian minister he might say of course— in the Gospels. But in which Gospel most? In 1940, William Temple, Archbishop of York and afterward to be Archbishop of Canterbury, published his *Readings in St. John's Gospel,* to express his thoughts as he read what was to him "the profoundest of all writings." Many will agree with the Archbishop in ranking John's Gospel as supreme. But it so happened that for me the Gospel which has made Jesus as Master and Lord and Christ and Savior most vivid and beautiful and compelling is the Gospel of Luke. Because of that, over a considerable period of time and of gradual meditation, I wrote the long book *The Compassionate Christ*, which sought to deal consecutively with all the chapters of the Gospel and with what may be the most immediate significance of the whole Gospel for our faith and hope today. In the same mood I wrote a little book of devotions and prayers for the days of the month, based on the hymn attributed to St. Patrick, and taking its title from the first line of the central verse of the hymn, *Christ Be with Me*.

We had organized at the Seminary when I first came back to Alexandria a Faculty Book Club, similar in its purpose and its program to *Kilin*, which William Norman Guthrie had imagined and created in New York. In one of our monthly meetings we had been reading a profound book on *The Doctrine of the Trinity*. Much of it seemed abstruse and unrelated to our conscious needs; and so I was provoked into trying to think what that doctrine actually meant to me, and what it might mean to contemporary Christians and would-be Christians as linked with religious experience of their own. The result in 1960 was the publication of *Jesus And The Trinity*, dedicated to Paul Sorel, that extraordinary presiding genius of the Seminary Book Service, "Friend and critic, the more helpful because he speaks the layman's mind." And in 1967, faced with the negativism of the "death-of-God" pronouncements, I wrote what cost deeper probings of study and thought than anything I had attempted before, *Where You Find God*.

The Seminary now was in many ways a different place from

the one I had known when I came to it in 1905: with a much larger and more varied faculty, with more than three times as many students, and caught up in a more complicated world. The men who were in it reflected various trends of thought and found themselves involved in intellectual and emotional readjustments which were difficult and sometimes confusing. The clock could not be turned back to what had been a more serene and undistracted time. New ideas and new problems had to be wrestled with. But it seemed to me that in the midst of these there could be, and more than ever there was need to have, a central reality which all fresh thought would illuminate and all growing experience find more commanding. That central reality would be the living spirit of the One who showed what the purpose of God and the power of God for human life are forever meant to be, and in whom men going out to attempted service can know that they have a "Beloved Captain."

Therefore I was glad when the faculty asked me to give a course on *The Life of Jesus as the Foundation of Our Faith*. It required of the men who chose it as an elective four papers, leading up to a conclusion which each man must form for himself. This was the sequence of them:

I. How do we know that Jesus existed; and what do we know of the conditions which surrounded him?

The first part of that question was meant to require of the students some awareness of how to deal factually with the extreme negative criticism which would dissolve the figure of Jesus into a legend; and the second part called for recognition of the forces which the life and decisions of the Man of Nazareth had to reckon with: the Roman occupation; the different hopes and passions in Judaism as represented by the Pharisees, the Sadducees, and the Zealots; the family in Nazareth; the synagogue.

249

II. A. The meaning of the Baptism and of the Temptation in the Wilderness.

B. From the time of the Baptism until the Crucifixion, what did Jesus mean to the disciples?

    as personal companion

    as teacher

    as man of power (including here an
       interpretation of the miraculous element
       in the gospel story)

    as revealer of God.

III. How and why did the Crucifixion and the Resurrection validate and enlarge the conviction the disciples had begun to form of Jesus as the Christ?

IV. A. What now is your interpretation of "was incarnate by the Holy Ghost of the Virgin Mary"?

B. And what will it now mean to you to say, in the words of the Nicene Creed, that Jesus of Nazareth was "God of God, Light of Light, Very God of Very God; Being of one substance with the Father"?

The purpose of the whole study, which by itself may have been staggering in its inclusiveness, was to lead men to think reverently but critically of the whole gospel story; to try to see the human Jesus as the first disciples saw him; and to begin to shape each one his own conviction and interpretation as to how and why it is that men have believed in and been uplifted by a power of God made manifest in him.

Certainly to consider that is to draw near to what is or is not the living heart of Christian faith.

Therefore it brought hope that something real was happening when I read the papers men had written and the notes which sometimes they appended to them.

Such as these:

Our seminar together was a very real turning point in my three years at Virginia. So often, I think, seminary can become merely an academic grind in which the real center—our Lord—becomes beclouded with too many facts and figures. For me this course caught the real meaning of why I was at seminary. . . and what it means to be a Christian.

I have met Jesus as a Friend, Teacher, Man of power, and Revealer of God. . . . Through all the obscurities and ambiguities of human thought, Christian witness seals the unity of Jesus the man and Jesus the Christ. I, for one, have found a Friend. I don't know him well yet but I have met Him. An historical and literary character who had been an eventual concept in a system of thought has now become a living Person. . . . I have discovered not only the humanity of Jesus but more of what it means to be human. This is not an unmixed comfort. For I have also discovered the humanity of a whole host of colleagues: Peter, John, Matthew, Judas, Mary Magdalen, Pilate, Caiaphas, and even Herod. They are all my brothers and sisters, we share a common life. Their ignorance, sin, and betrayal have illuminated my own. These negative attributes are no longer abstract intellectual obstacles to a good life, but personal affronts to one who loves me. . . . But with this personal condemnation has come personal salvation. The objective reality of this salvation has long been accepted by me, but it, too, has been an almost Deistic proposition in theological mechanics. Now I feel growing within my heart the assurance that Jesus knows me personally, knows all about me—good and bad—and still accepts me as a friend he wants to have with Him.

More than any other course in seminary this has caused me to think creatively. First, I have seen that all our words and creeds are an after-the-fact description of an experience with God; and,

251

second, that these words cannot be depended on but must be broken down before you again experience the full meaning of the experience they are trying to describe. By this route I have come to know Jesus as the Christ more clearly and, in knowing him more clearly, have reached into the depths of meaning behind and beyond what we call God. The trip along this route is not over. Moving onward, I feel on the verge of a great discovery—or better yet, of being discovered. God is outreaching my unbelief.

Men who thus felt themselves to be "on the verge of a great discovery" seemed to me to be rediscovering what had always been the deepest witness of the Virginia Seminary. In the Chapel the memorial tablet to Berryman Green, the beloved Dean of a generation ago, speaks of him as "a Christian who both as he taught and as he lived revealed his Master." Through an unusual combination of circumstances, there have been four Deans since I came back to the Seminary in 1950, and all have added to its spiritual values: the present Dean, Jesse M. Trotter, with his wide outlook and his strength in achievement; and before him Alexander C. Zabriskie, with his warmhearted friendliness; the gentle and scholarly Stanley Brown Serman; and E. Felix Kloman, with his gallant courage, who have represented a heritage which outlasts the years.

XXIII. Too Little—and Too Late?

When I came back from New York and joined the faculty of the Virginia Seminary in 1950, there were Negroes in the student body, which had not been a fact in the earlier years. It was a sign of significant change in social relationships, but of a change which had been slow in maturing, and was still so partial and inconsistent as to leave the present and the future shadowed by critical uncertainties.

A century ago, when the War Between the States came to an end and the black people who had been slaves were first made free, it was still assumed as almost a matter of course that Negroes were a secondary people and would naturally continue in a status inferior to that of the master race. They ought to be treated kindly, but it was proper that they should be "kept where they belonged." In Virginia until a few decades ago there was little if any consciousness of a "race problem." Notwithstanding Emancipation, deep-rooted relationships and the assumptions woven round them continued largely as they had been before. The bonds between white families and the Negroes who had been attached to them had a tenacity which altered circumstances could not dissolve. Few then could have had any anticipation of the gulf of alienation that might open or of the inevitable forces which must lead to the collisions of today.

Social calamities may come not from any deliberate wickedness, but from the human inability of many people, even essentially well-meaning people, to change their frame of thought. It is lack of imagination, rather than lack of decent impulse, that may keep the ruling class in a society blind to the overturnings which are bound to come.

One looks back in personal recollection and can see how fixed the old ideas were—and how intertwined with sentiment which made the old seem to have a halo round it. When I was a little boy in Richmond, there lived in my Grandmother Branch's house, as a very old woman long since too old to work but gentle and serene, Mammy Jinnie, who had nursed my Grandmother when she was a child; and also Pendleton, who had been the butler during and before the War. Until 1865, the Branch family had lived in Petersburg; but in the closing period of the War, when the fighting drew continually closer, until at length Petersburg was besieged and parts of the city shelled, my Grandmother, with her children, moved to Richmond, to the home which she had left as a bride in 1856—the home of her father, Dr. William A. Patteson. It stood on East Broad Street opposite to what is now the City Hall; a tall brick house, with a flight of marble steps leading up to the front door; and it was that house which happened to be the scene for something that has come down as enduring witness to the sort of unlimited devotion to their "white folks" which so many of the Negroes exemplified. On April 3, 1865, when the lines around Petersburg had been broken and Richmond was defensible no longer, the Union Army achieved what for four years it had fought for—the capture of the Capital of the Confederacy. From the eastern end of the city and past burning warehouses by the James River, the conquering army marched toward Capitol Square, and past the house of Dr. Patteson. All along Broad Street were crowds of people, caught in the tumultuous emotions of that day. Then at the time when the invading troops appeared and the excitement in the street was greatest, Pendleton came out of the door of Dr. Patteson's house with his pail of hot water, his soap, and scrubbing brush, and washed the marble steps as though it were an ordinary day. When he had finished, he gathered up his things, went into the house, and disdainfully shut the door. It was his way of showing that, as far as he was concerned, nothing had been changed.

And to some who had been bred in the privileged traditions of the old South it seemed that nothing *ought* to be changed. In her *Diary of a Refugee*, Mrs. Judith A. McGuire (the mother of John P. McGuire of Chapter 4), lamenting in 1861 the threat which the War had brought to all that she cherished most, with naïve romanticism described the South as "the fairest land, the purest social order, and the happiest people on earth"; and then she went on: "Under a mysterious Providence, millions of the colored race have been saved from the foulest paganism, millions mentally and morally elevated far above those of their native land, and multitudes saved in Christ forever." [1]

As a matter of fact, at the end of the War it seemed as though very little in the relationship of the races *had* been changed. White people of responsibility and privilege would go on treating their own Negroes—"the good Negroes"—with gratitude and appreciation; and employing the rest as washerwomen or occasional maids and cooks. The Negroes were not slaves any more, but it was taken for granted that they were meant always to be servants. In the Richmond of my

[1] (New York: E. J. Hale and Son, 1867), p. 6.

boyhood, to which my family belonged, if Jackson Ward—on the fringe of the city, where the unattached and disadvantaged Negroes lived—was shabby and bleak, and if the city administration and the public generally paid little attention to conditions there, "Well, Negroes were not accustomed to anything better." Where there needed to be a sensitive social conscience, there was often a blind spot. It was hard for the privileged, even the most kindly ones, to conceive that the Negro might have aspirations equal to their own; and the "poor whites" built up their self-importance by the hard assumption that the Negro was a black subhuman species meant only for the menial jobs which the white man did not want. So it came about in Virginia and the South that many of even "the best people," who were polite and gracious and generally kindhearted, who went to church on Sundays and thought they were good Christians, did little to help the Negroes forward. In my own home for the last twelve years, bound with increasing affection to my Jean and myself, there has been and is a Negro domestic helper and friend who in her integrity and constant faithfulness represents each day a human excellence which not many of any race are seen to equal; but because she grew up in the deep South and never had effective schooling, the consequent limitation to what were and are her full potentialities is an unspoken reproach to all of us in a white power structure that did not sufficiently care about what happened to the disadvantaged.

There were some in that structure who did recognize the need for fresh perception and more exacting purpose. One sensitive and far-seeing man in the post-Civil War generation was Henry W. Grady of Atlanta. He had the devoted loyalty which many had to the values of the past, but he recognized also the inescapable challenge of a different time. In a great oration which reviewed the history of the Civil War and described the almost incredible devotion and faithfulness of the Negroes who had watched over and protected the women and children in the Confederate States while the Southern men were away in the armies, he pled for "A New South" in which the white people who had been the masters should not only remember but express in creative change the gratitude they owed. "May God forget my people," he said, "when my people forget them."

But Henry Grady's hope was only partially fulfilled. Many white people did indeed remember the loyalty which the Negroes had showed during the years of war. But that remembrance was partly clouded by another one: by the recollection of the bitter years following the war's end and the emancipation, when much of the South was still occupied by Federal force and local government was exercised by a combination of carpetbaggers from the North and ignorant Negroes whom they made their tools. If that period of the so-called Reconstruction had never been, those who had power to shape the ultimate thought and policies of the South might have had a wider and more constructive imagination as to the Negroes' future. But as a tragic fact of history, the first experience with the Negro in his freedom seemed to confirm the inherited conviction that the Negro was not qualified for responsibility, and produced a throwback of sentiment and belief to the pre-war days. If the old patterns could be essentially recovered, all might be well. Gratitude and kindness in recognition of all that the Negroes had given, yes; but still the Negro had his place and he should stay in it, since everybody took it for granted that the Negro could never be the full equal of the white man. Under the conditions of the times, even the generous hearted among the social and political leaders believed that. As long as "the right relationship" between the

257

races was recognized from both sides, there would need to be no problem.

But the trouble was that the problem was there, whether or not the white Southerner could yet discern it: the problem of what would happen when the Negro became aware of the potentialities in himself that would not endure to be perpetually suppressed. In the 1800's it was true that the Negroes in general must seem inferior to the whites. Ever since the Negroes had been brought over in the slave ships they had had no status, no education, no unhindered chance to develop such capacities as they might possess, and little encouragement toward racial self-respect. But forces that were stronger than old facts and stronger than inveterate presuppositions were beginning to be at work. The Negro as a human being was beginning to emerge. Whether the words of the Declaration of Independence were originally meant to apply to him or not, a creative power working in humanity that was as invincible as the will of God would manifest for the Negro also "these truths to be self-evident; that all men are created equal; that they are endowed by their creator with certain unalienable rights; that among these are life, liberty, and the pursuit of happiness."

What may have been the critical point of new opportunity came in 1954 with the Supreme Court decision striking down segregation in the public schools, and with the emergence into public notice at that same time of Martin Luther King. The Supreme Court compelled reconsideration of the Negro's status; and Martin Luther King's leadership in 1955 of the patient Negro boycott of the segregated buses in Montgomery, Alabama, set the example for a nonviolent protest against injustice which ought to have appealed to all people of good will, and most certainly to those who supposedly were Christians. Many people in the South and elsewhere did see the creative chance for new spirit and new public policies. As Henry W. Grady had foreseen in the preceding century, they recognized that the time comes when there must be immense readjustments of old ideas and old prerogatives. But human nature being what it is, the majority closed ranks with an almost fanatical determination to defend and maintain white dominance, and to deny to the Negroes the just share in American life and liberties which as human beings they were reaching out for.

Consequently, in the decade and a half since 1954, the collision of opposite influences has grown more acute. White resistance to Negro aspirations, even when these were most moderate and reasonable, has led inevitably to the emergence of new would-be black leadership, bitter and violent and almost ready to be anarchically vindictive. The sad thing is that there might have been a different development. If more of the best minds and spirits of the South had recognized and then deliberately faced what was an unwelcome problem, instead of imagining that somehow it could be suppressed, the problem might not have become the growing peril which it is today.

Being back again in Virginia, one looked with sadness upon what was happening in public affairs. The balances which might have risen toward creative change sank instead toward a darker consequence. Not much large-visioned leadership came forward. Hostility to school desegregation and to anything else that might seem to threaten white privilege and white superiority found its elegant embodiment in Senator Harry Flood Byrd of Virginia, with his slogan of "massive resistance," a failure more lamentable and in the sense of possibility less excusable than the vulgar demagoguery of George C. Wallace of Alabama, with his cruder pandering to the passions of the ignorant and unthinking. Governors of the state and the legislature adopted the Senator's worse-than-futile program. The two newspapers of Richmond, the capital city, echoed it. Even the people of my beloved St. Paul's, who in the earlier years had become the standard-bearers for liberal thought and positive purpose, for the most part dropped back into reaction.

In January, 1957, I wrote to the Richmond *Times-Dispatch* a letter which was published in the correspondence column, a letter protesting against the tame indifference with which it seemed to me the paper had treated outrages upon Negroes that had recently occurred: This was part of it:

Have you no indignation against the shameful facts which have been occurring almost daily during the last two weeks?

A shotgun blast fired on December 23 through the front door of Martin Luther King, the Negro minister of Montgomery, Alabama.

A bomb exploded on December 27 against the house of F. L. Shuttleworth, a Negro minister of Birmingham. . . .

The brutal flogging by five hooded men in Camden, S. C. of a 52-year-old band director of a white high school because—as they said, and apparently falsely said—he had dared to advocate desegregation in the schools.

The beating by a gang of men, not of a man this time but of a colored woman, who had alighted from a Montgomery bus; and the shooting with a rifle bullet of another woman who was inside a bus.

In the light of realities like these, consider the words of one of your columnists on your editorial page who . . . called a unanimous decision of the Supreme Court of the United States—including a Justice from Alabama—"a judicial coup d'etat," language which if some Communist had used it would be considered insolent subversion. . . .

You say, Mr. Editor, that "We have nothing but contempt for rabble-rousers, race-baiters and bullies." But what are you doing except to encourage them when your editorial page carries such inflammatory language as I have quoted concerning the highest legal ruling of the land? Are you not actually contributing to the witches' brew of intemperate speech, crowd violence, White Citizens Councils and Ku Klux Klan revivals which is beginning to boil and bubble?

You and your columnist have the advantage of entrenched white supremacy. Have you then no noblesse oblige? As in Montgomery, Alabama, under the leadership of their minister, so in many of our states Negroes have shown both an integrity of conviction and a patient non-violence which deserve the respect of just and thoughtful men—and may we not say are worthy of the approval of God? Is it admirable that you and your columnist should try to deny them the protection that comes from the highest judicial process which our Constitution has created, when in their localities they have had so little justice?

In personal correspondence the editor was unfailingly courteous and considerate, while at the same time convinced that "massive resistance" must be maintained. So were many others. But the tragic fact is that the passions which have come out of that resistance have led to such poisoning of what might have been a reconciling spirit that now Martin Luther King is dead, and the Stokely Carmichaels and Rap Browns are rising in his place. Constructive effort had been too little. Now that both the state and the churches are waking to new awareness of the threatening facts and to a purpose concerning them which may be both more chastened and more positive, the hope is that it may not be too late.

After the letter to the *Times-Dispatch* had appeared, I had a touching letter from the daughter of Robert Damell, who had been the colored sexton at St. Paul's through all the years when I was rector, and between whom and me there had been a warm and enduring bond. She said she wanted me to know

261

how glad the letter would have made "my Daddy." And her letter ended with words which we who are white, with our unequal privileges, might well wish to make our own: "Pray with me that as a race we may continue to exercise self-control, and exhibit tolerance and Christian brotherhood."

XXIV. Clouds, and the Light Beyond

By the mid-1950's, the Board of Trustees of the Virginia Seminary had brought themselves to the point which the governing boards of most institutions had arrived at long before: namely, of adopting a specified time for retirement of members of the faculty, though even then a later time than has been set in many other places. My 72nd birthday had been in the fall of 1954, and so at the end of that academic year I finished my full-time service at the Seminary. That meant moving from the house which had been built for us in 1950 to one which we bought on the Mount Vernon side of Alexandria, on Windsor Road.

Happily, though, this did not mean any full separation from the Seminary life, or from the friendships which centered there. It was not long before I was invited back for part-time teaching, at first to take over a New Testament course of one of the faculty who had a sudden illness, and then to give the elective course on "The Life of Jesus, as the Foundation of Our Faith" which has been spoken of already. And Jean, notwithstanding her lameness, kept her contacts. By a custom of the Seminary which goes back beyond the twentieth century, each Thursday evening there was "Faculty

263

Meeting," which meant not what the words might seem to mean, the faculty sitting by themselves for routine business; but, rather, a gathering of the whole Seminary family at which one of the faculty spoke on some subject that might be of interest and perhaps of inspiration to everybody. We both liked always to be there, and at dinner with the students in the refectory beforehand. Wives of students who needed a friend and counsellor found their way to Jean on Windsor Road, just as they had come to her when she was nearer. And others came, most constantly Nancy Bell, the widow of Wilbur Cosby Bell, who looked like a more handsome and equally regal Queen Mary of England, and may have been of Queen Mary's age, but no one could know it for she would never tell her own. Her special pleasure was to take Jean out with her to drive; and Jean, who was not afraid of anything, would go—though everybody knew that "Miss Nancy" had a weak heart and now and then might stop the car and take a digitalis tablet. Both of those two took life boldly, and both of them would make a gallant end. As for Mrs. Bell, she was driving one day—fortunately this time alone—through Alexandria, when she found her heart begin to fail. She got her car to the courtyard of the Alexandria Hospital, parked it near the emergency door, turned off the ignition, and died— and they found her there with her hand still on the steering wheel.

It was good that so many friendships still brought enrichment to the life on Windsor Road, for otherwise time might have seemed to have moved a long way since the years when there were the four children, and all the busy Grace Church staff round us, in the rectory on Broadway. Jean and Ted Evans moved from Charlottesville to Worcester, Massachusetts; Elisabeth was in Poughkeepsie; Rusty in Omaha. My mother had died in 1954. The best fact was that Beverley and Louise and their five children were in Hollin Hills, only a few miles away.

Bev had been in the O.S.S. during the second World War; and after intelligence work in Africa and Italy he had been the first American officer to enter Bucharest, having been airlifted into Rumania in the closing days of the war. Now he was a senior editor of the *National Geographic* magazine, and his writing assignments for the *Geographic* took him to exciting places in this country and around the world. He had a gay and glancing mind, and no conversation could be dull when he had part in it. As one of his colleagues said of him, he "could write with tremendous emotional impact, as in his article on the burial of the Unknown Soldier 'Known but to God.' But he particularly delighted in articles that gave full play to his deft humor. Then his words sparkled and his sentences smiled."

He was to show that he could carry on his life, and face death, with light in his eyes even when it was difficult to smile. An obscure lameness in his spine which seemed at first to be a matter to be overcome by exercises turned out to be a malignancy. During weeks spent partly in hospitals, and nearly always in great pain, he began to put into poetry the experiences he was living through. Some of what he wrote dealt poignantly with his own illness and with the realization that he would not be well again. Some reflected his sensitiveness to the tragic contradictions in our general human life, between our stupidities and our evil and the possibilities of the spirit which alone might save us. After he died, some of his friends had his poems published,[1] and the quality of what he wrote is reflected in this part of the poem, "Bom-

[1] *Know All Men by These Presents* (New York: Bookman Associates, 1958).

bardier." It has to do with an aviator who has dropped his bombs upon men and women and little children in a German city—and then comes back presently to his own children who have no consciousness of what it is that he has done.

> Breasting the Fail-Safe Line, his plane
>   meets no recall,
> Shoots past with sucked-in sign of shock,
>   and speeds
> To predetermined ends. At forty thousand feet
> The city holds no people, defines itself
> As blips upon a screen, sterile, inanimate,
> A winking unreality. He leaves
> His card; somewhere below, ten
>   thousand babies burn.

> Luck gilds his wing; and soon he sits at home,
> Knowing quite well the rarity of any home,
> And hears his wren-wife chirrup to the children,
> "Sit closer to the table, sweets, and quiet, please—
> Your daddy's here again, and he'll say . . . grace."

In the *National Geographic*, after Beverley had died in November, 1958, the editors wrote of him as they had known him, and especially as they had known him last while he met "the lengthening shadow" of his illness. "No darkness could quench the light of his personality. He faced death with gallantry, poise, even wit. And in the end he dominated it."

What did those shining words mean? one asks. When a life is cut off at the high point of its possibilities, and when a personality that has been vivid disappears from mortal ken, how can it be said that death is "dominated"? That is the question which human hearts are bound to ask in face of the universal tragedy of personal loss.

Let it be confessed that there is no light and easy answer.

Physical death is too stark a fact to be glossed over. When the eyes of the one we have loved will look at us no more, and the voice will not speak again, it is possible to yield to hopeless resignation, as though this were—the end.

But then comes another answer, an answer that cannot be created at the moment, but grows out of all the deepest convictions of the inner life. There have been those, and we have known them, in whom the spirit *has* "dominated" the flesh. From that experienced fact there grows the faith that *this* is what all existence is meant to witness to, and *this* is the purpose and meaning of life. The universe would be senseless if human personalities, which embody the supreme values that creation has produced, should be no more than the flicker of candles to be blown out by the wind of a wintry night. "Like a man in wrath, the heart"—and the mind also —rise up to proclaim love's intuition that there is in human souls an ongoing power which death cannot destroy.

During Beverley's illness, I gave him a book in which there was included a poem of James Weldon Johnson called "Go Down Death." After he died I found the book with the flap of the paper jacket folded between the pages at verses in which the Negro preacher in the poem is describing how God sent Death down for "Sister Caroline." Beverley had a keen intellect and utter honesty, and he would never pretend to what he did not think. But his imagination was very sensitive; and the emotions can feel reality in expressions which in their form are only naive. I have wondered therefore whether his eyes had lingered on the words in which James Weldon Johnson told of how "Sister Caroline" saw "what we couldn't see."

> She saw Old Death
> Coming like a falling star.

> But Death didn't frighten Sister Caroline;
> He looked to her like a welcome friend.
> And she whispered to us: I'm going home,
> And she smiled and closed her eyes.
>
> And Death took her up like a baby,
> And she lay in his icy arms,
> But she didn't feel no chill.
> And Death began to ride again—
> Up beyond the evening star,
> Out beyond the morning star,
> Into the glittering light of glory,
> On to the Great White Throne.[2]

When Beverley died, the wound was deep in his mother's heart, but with a courage equal to his she was to live for five years more. In the summer of 1962 we had gone again to South Yarmouth, on Cape Cod, near Wianno which was full of her girlhood memories, and where our life together had begun. When we came back to Alexandria that fall, she went to the hospital for an operation, which disclosed a malady that would be fatal. She wanted to know the full truth, and Dr. John E. Roberts, her physician, told her. "She was braver to hear it than I was to tell her," he said. "She made it possible for me to say what I would have given a great deal not to have to say."

The resources which her life had gathered did not fail her. As the end drew near, she would say in the evening to her nurse, between whom and herself there had grown to be a great devotion, "Leave me now for a few minutes as you go out and close the door, and I will be alone a little while with God."

[2] From *God's Trombones* by James Weldon Johnson, copyright 1927 by The Viking Press, Inc., renewed 1955 by Grace Nail Johnson. Reprinted by permission of The Viking Press, Inc.

XXV. The Heart of It All

Now as this book comes to its final chapters, my thought turns back to what was written in the Foreword: "Each one of us is what he is because of the influences from many other lives which have flowed into him. If in some measure he can interpret them, he is dealing with what is much wider than himself. . . . The relationships which any of us have had with those we know and love are what make life meaningful at last"—and help us to know better what this life of ours is meant to be.

As life falls into perspective, events and happenings fade into less importance than once they had. The ambitions achieved or not achieved, the framework built around one's life by this or that, are like the painted scenery on the stage which is of no consequence any more when the curtain finally comes down. But the drama itself in its essential meaning, and the inspiration caught from those who have played their parts so gallantly that what goes on upon this mortal stage is seen to have both depth and dignity—*this* is what is gathered up as precious when the reckoning is made.

There have been many persons who have brought to me the undeserved enrichments which are the gifts of God. I trust that I may have made some of those persons vivid, so that for those who may have read this book, they may—because of our common humanity—seem to belong also to them. Since "no man is an Island, intire of itself," and "every man is a peece of the continent, a part of the maine," those who have been an inspiration to any of us may become an inspiration to us all.

The title of this book is *Learning to Live*, and although I have been a blundering scholar I have at least been made conscious of what I have needed to learn. Many have taught me much as to how life could be lived, but I think it will have grown plain to those who read what I have written that there was one who has taught me most. That one is Jean Laverack, who in her self-giving was willing to become Jean Bowie.

In an earlier chapter I have told how I first heard of her, and of how we met. It was more than a year later that I knew any of her family, but I became bound to them as I was bound to her. She was the youngest of five children: Belle and Gertrude, Howard and William Harold—who disliked the Harold in his name and was always "Jum." Her father, George E. Laverack, had lived all his life in Buffalo. When I first met him, he had retired from business, and because he had lost almost all use of his legs he could walk only painfully, and most of the time he would be sitting by a big window in his Delaware Avenue house, reading or listening to those around him. I say listening, for he was generally a man of few words. He could be outspoken and commanding when he chose to be, but he liked to know what you had to say, and he listened to you with a smiling interest in his eyes. When he could get there, he would go to the Buffalo Club in the afternoons and be among the longtime friends who waited for his coming. It was a great deprivation to him that he could so seldom get about, but that deprivation and the pain he often had were things he never spoke of.

Jean's mother was as eager in speech as Mr. Laverack was silent; active and outgoing and gay. In earlier years, when he was stronger, they went about a great deal among their friends in Buffalo, or had their friends come to them, especially at dinner and for playing bridge afterward, at which both of them were expert. Mrs. Laverack still kept her many contacts, and she was the warm center of the home. Jean would be like her in that, as she was like her father in courage and in her ability—which in later years would be often called upon—to transcend physical pain.

She had her mother's instinctive gaiety, and when I first knew her she had grown up among a circle of friends in Buffalo among whom she found happy response to her own affection, and she was teaching her group of children at the settlement house which Trinity Church had established in the Polish district of the city. In an article which she had written and which was printed in the *Kindergarten Review* in 1904—the year of the summer in Wianno—on "Froebel's Light and Shadow Songs," she unconsciously revealed something about herself when she said about them: "Perhaps the most important idea is the very simple one, that light cannot always come because so often there are barriers to its entrance. The sun and moon and stars can only show their light when the clouds have disappeared. We can only have light in our rooms when the blinds are open and the windows clean. We can always have plenty of light if we only make an effort to let it in."

She did have "plenty of light" in her own spirit, because her attitude to life was always that which let light in. So many of us are self-absorbed, and lack the outgoing spontaneity which sees and registers the sunny aspects of existence, but she seemed to be endowed by nature with a kind of happy expectation which turned instinctively to where the sun might be. She had an alchemy which could find gold in what appeared to be the ordinary events of everyday: talking with a friend about what began as some casual matter of the morning, playing with a child; getting to know all about the girl who waited on her in the grocery store. She could deal the better with serious things because she was so quick to respond to whatever was amusing. Sometimes when she was in her room conversing with someone who had called her on the telephone, I could have no idea from where I was as to what she was talking about, but in the midst of what was indistinguishable there would come the sudden music of her laughter, for which there seemed just one comparison—the remembered sound of sleigh-bells on an exciting winter morning when the sun was shining on the snow.

Since she had been stopped from going to college and therefore had not become accustomed to academic ways of thought, she was not very good at formal arguments, and she was impatient at abstractions. I used to feel sometimes that there was something impossible to fathom in the way her mind was working. Where was any ordered logic in this thing she was saying, and in this decision she seemed likely to arrive at? By what possible rational and certified road was she travelling, and why couldn't she diagram the whole matter in the way I thought I did? But any superior notion I might have assumed I had would often shrivel in the face of her intuitive perception of the truth. Her sure sense of human values and her sympathy carried her to right conclusions about people, and especially about children, while someone else was getting lost in secondary arguments concerning this and that. The reason why she could be so often right, and right in practical as well as emotional matters, was that to a

rare degree she could forget herself and become identified
with another's needs. A tired and troubled social worker in
New York, in a letter of pathetic thanks to Jean for the counsel
and comradeship Jean had given her, wrote this, "*Now*, I can
say, 'Bring on your problems!' We have Jean Bowie."

Out of the heart are the issues of life. When we had been
married and the children were born and growing up—in the
little rectory at Greenwood, in Richmond, at Grace Church
—it was the heart of the wife and mother that made each
one of those homes, in the beautiful words of the Book of
Common Prayer, "a haven of blessing and of peace." "What's
the Use of Mothers?" was the title of an article Jean once
wrote for the *Christian Herald*. Those who knew her could
see in her words not only an ideal of what might be, but a
picture of what was made real in her. "Someone in the home
must have time," she wrote, "somewhere in the week there
must be hours released from routine which can be given to
the children." And then she went on:

To stop and read to a child, or play a game, or listen to a long
and involved account of the latest fight at school, is hard for a
modern mother to do. She is geared by experience, as well as by
the temper of the times, to such activity that it is hard for her
to slow down; and yet it must be done if homes are to continue
and children given the chance to grow. Children thrive in an
atmosphere of leisure—not idle leisure, but in an environment
where there is time to spare.

No one likes extremes. We do not want homes of such "sweet-
ness and light" that the children will grow up selfish and soft,
such delicately nurtured and protected plants as can not stand
the rougher elements outside; but we do need homes where the
spirit is generous and trusting and encouraging, and where there
is time, time to think, and time to talk, and time to share.

Someone asked a mother once what advice she would give on the bringing up of children. "Just love 'em," she said.

The mother Jean quoted as saying "Just love 'em" was also Jean herself. She had the kind of lovingness which all sorts of persons felt—and in it felt also something that they tried, even if blunderingly, to express. "Love is of God;" the disciple who was most close to Jesus wrote, "and every one that loveth is born of God, and knoweth God" (KJV). The reality of that was reflected in what one of the student wives wrote about Jean. Drawn, she said, "by her intelligence, her beauty, her radiance, I knew very quickly that I had met a truly living saint: not in any pious or rigid hands-folded-in-a-constant-attitude-of-prayer sort of way, but one who surely walked with God every minute of every day." That was the fact, and rightly said—except that Jean would have flinched from the one word "saint": flinched from it lest it suggest to someone else what the girl who used it never meant—some separation from the common life. She knew herself to be a woman, with all a woman's humanness in body, mind, and spirit, and the reason why she could give so much to others was because she understood also the humanness in them.

There is a picture of Jean that reveals a part of her many-sidedness in a letter that came to me from one of her friends at Union Seminary.

None of us who knew and loved her can ever forget the very special light that shone through her. After visits with her in McGiffert 401, I would always return to our apartment feeling how blessed I was to know her. Those French classes that she arranged were bright spots in the week, not so much for what we learned as for the joy of being with Jean whose warmth, sparkle and sense of humor put all of us at ease (we were a varied group)

274

and kept us from taking ourselves or our French pronunciation too seriously!

I remember meeting Dr. Kroner one day in the elevator of McGiffert Hall after he had been to see Jean after the second operation on her hip. He said that he had gone to St. Luke's in the hope that he could help to cheer Jean a bit—but that instead he had come away feeling that he was the one who had been uplifted and heartened by her heroic spirit. I will never forget his telling me this because his voice and his words showed how deeply he had been moved by Jean's courage. I think that all of us who went to see Jean felt as Dr. Kroner did—but of course Jean, herself, had no idea how greatly she ministered to all of us by her rare spirit and wouldn't have believed us if we had tried to tell her. What a gift her friendship was. She could weld friends and family together in a circle that was always widening. And her spontaneity and buoyancy, her ability to rise above disappointments and shocks!

Before I knew her well, I can remember walking some distance behind her on Claremont Avenue, thinking as I watched her what a wonderful stride she had. One knew at a glance that she loved to walk. The memory of that impression made me realize in later years what it must have meant to her never to be able to walk again—and what courage and determination it took to accept this deprivation as she did—gallantly, with never a trace of self-pity.

Jean had a kind of radiance that is unforgettable. No one ever described it as aptly as you did in your dedication to her of *Sunny Windows*.

To J. L. B.
Whose heart, with windows to the sun,
is lighted by the Shining One.

Certainly I was the one who most had known what more than one who had loved her thus spoke of as her "radiance." There had been fulfilled in her what Francis of Assisi had voiced in his prayer that began, "Lord, make me an instrument of thy peace." She had sowed love where, without her, love might not have been; where there was sadness, she had sown joy; where there was darkness, light.

When she died, it was on the morning in June when of all days in the year the sunlight is longest. For the deep deprivation of the human heart, it could have seemed that there was only darkness then. But in the service at Immanuel Chapel on the Seminary Hill, we used the prayer which Charles Lewis Slattery had left as a legacy of his ministry at Grace Church: "Lord, we beseech thee, open our eyes to behold the heaven that lies about us, wherein they walk, who being born to the new life, serve thee with the clearer vision and the greater joy; through Jesus Christ our Lord." And on the marble tablet above her grave, under her name, are these twelve words: *In whose soul, and in whose eyes, the heavenly light was shining.*

XXVI. The End, and the Beginning

Toward the end of 1963 the Trustees of the Seminary, to my surprise, voted to me the privilege of building a house on the Seminary grounds. This would mean coming back to the environment with which I had had already such deep associations, and therefore it had immediate appeal. In the spring and summer of 1964 the house was built, and that fall I moved into it. So my ministry had come full circle, and I can look today from my windows across familiar ground to the Seminary Chapel where I was ordained sixty years ago.

The outward scene might produce a reverie and a throwback of consciousness that could make the long interval of time seem almost as though it had not been. The contours of the Seminary hill are the same along which the feet of many generations have come and gone. Some of the great old oaks have outlasted not only my remembered sixty years, but an earlier century before I ever saw them. If I climb up, as now and then I do, to the queer old tower of Aspinwall, I can see the long slopes leading to the same curve of the shining river; and looking beyond the river toward the horizon, say with the psalmist, "I will lift up my eyes unto the hills." The great features of the earth abide; and some also of the things that human hands have built possess a relative permanence that can undergird our individual experience which otherwise might be so fleeting. The older buildings of the Seminary, looking in their major outlines quite unchanged, might seem to say "It is still yesterday. The world you knew then is the world you can know today."

But of course it is not so. The changes have been so vast that it is as though a new universe had come into being—new and different both for the body and for the mind. This Seminary that stood at the far edge of quiet fields is now in the midst of suburbia. The open roads along which one used to walk are the concrete through-ways for a thousand automobiles. That noise coming down from what was once the serenity of the sky is the sound of jet planes which have made Europe and Asia and Africa and all their terrific destinies closer to our consciousness than affairs only a few miles outside our neighborhood might in an earlier day have seemed to be. In a preceding chapter there is the picture, as nearly as I could reproduce it, of the placid Seminary of sixty years ago, and of the uncomplicated ministry which men conceived they were going into, and the gospel which they thought that nearly everybody would understand.

Then came the first World War, with its shock to all that had appeared to be secure. In the face of it there could be no casual assumptions any more as to what men could believe and trust. There needed to be a new dimension for faith and for the formulation of it. So in all the world of religious concern men listened to the word of Karl Barth—with its message of a transcendent Lord who confronted the world with the awful majesty of his moral judgment, and by whose mercy alone, and not by any mortal devices, could human life be saved from the destruction which its prideful sins were bringing near.

Yet movements in theology are often likely to swing to an extreme. From the beginning this seemed to me to be true with what was received and declared as neo-orthodoxy. In the chapters on "Changing Tides in Religious Thinking" and on "To Virginia Again," I have indicated the resistances which I felt needed to be set up against the then prevailing current, lest other elements of truth should be submerged. All during the time of its apparent dominance, I believed that neo-orthodoxy, because of its imbalance, was a passing phase. Its emphasis on a divine will for righteousness which individuals or nations may defy only at their mortal peril is a lasting contribution; but because of that theology's failure to recognize the possibilities for human imagination and devotion as instruments of God's purpose in secular affairs, it cannot satisfy man's permanent need for effective inspiration.

Of late, partly as a reaction against that one-sidedness, a new agnosticism has been spreading, and it was inevitable that sooner or later some would put it into explicit words. There appeared the school of contemporary writers who proclaim that inherited religious beliefs have become impossible. "A . . . radical recasting . . . is demanded, in the process of which the most fundamental categories of our theology—of God, of the supernatural, and of religion itself—must go into the melting." [1] And for a considerable number of others who would reject such words as those, *this* may nevertheless be true: that, as President John C. Bennett of Union Seminary has written, "The present generation is in a kind of theological no-man's-land, not able to appropriate what was so real to its predecessor and yet not able to develop its own confidence concerning the Christian message."

If that were the whole of the fact, then this would be a

[1] John A. T. Robinson, *Honest To God* (Philadelphia: The Westminster Press, 1963), p. 7.

shadowed time. But what has been called "The Shaking of the Foundations" can lead to the rediscovery of the right foundations, and the building upon them of a structure of faith ample enough for the disturbed and questioning to come in. That is what has happened again and again in religious history. Times of confusion which to the shortsighted seemed to be only chaos have proved to be the great times of nobler reconstruction.

So I ask myself, as all of us may do, what are the things I am sure of—sure of not because I can read about them in books, but because they come home to me through the experienced realities of life.

The first thing I know is that there is decisive difference among people, and that when I consider this difference it leads me toward something which is not of this mortal earth.

Superficially people may look alike, and in many aspects of existence they are alike. All of us live in bodies of flesh, and have the body's needs and the body's satisfactions. All of us have concerns that move on the material level. But some people seem to move on that level almost entirely, satisfied if they are comfortable, reaching out for nothing beyond the obvious. They may be decent and respectable, and even agreeable, but they are not inspiring. They seem to be plodding along on roads that have no distant vistas. And then there are the other people who make life have a different dimension. They have larger thought and deeper feeling, they have got hold of something—or Something has got hold of them—which makes them more sensitive both to the joy and the pain of human existence, more understanding, more sympathetic, more outreaching in their helpfulness. It is not as though they were trying to manufacture some peculiar quality in themselves. Rather it is as though they had been open to an influence that comes from beyond the borders of our small selves. There is a spirit in them which seems to bear witness to a mightier Spirit, and to be a gift from a Giver so great that there can be no fitting name but—God.

"The wind blows where it wills, and you hear the sound of it, but you do not know whence it comes or whether it goes; so it is with every one who is born of the Spirit." Thus the influence which makes some people so nobly different cannot always be directly labelled or defined; but as I have looked at human souls it has seemed clear that the influence which has been most transfiguring has been that which was at work in those who have been most aware of Jesus: Jesus in the grandeur of his living, and Jesus in the power of his sacrificial death. It is not only that he has lifted up ideals which the best that is within us wants to try to follow. In his crucifixion he has made us recognize the awful reality of human sin, including each man's own; and at the same time made each one feel himself laid hold upon by a love that will not let us go.

Because, then, of the force let loose in our actual world by one who lived and died and lives again, there can come to pass such a thing as the Kingdom of God which all the gospel dared to promise. If we look for a full definition of it we are baffled. Is the Kingdom of God—which would be the rule of righteousness—to be fulfilled in human history or in some world and age to come? What exactly do the Gospel promises imply? We cannot fully know. But this I think I do know—that I have seen little beginnings of the Kingdom. There are homes where a wife and mother is pouring out a self-forgetting love which makes a family see how uplifting love can be. God is no "Wholly Other" there; he is drawing near in the human love that must have come from him. And wherever in any company, in a church, in a seminary, in a group of friends, there is generosity of spirit, a search for truth, and a common dedication to an ideal of service, some little enclave of the Kingdom has begun.

Again—I have seen the truth of the words of Jesus, "Whoever would save his life will lose it; and whoever loses his life for my sake and the gospel's will save it." I hope that everyone who may have read this book may have recognized the greatness of some of those who have been pictured in it: men and women who in different ways and in different places have given their whole selves to some great loyalty which possessed them; and as they thus gave themselves completely, joy and power in life was given them. Moreover, I believe that in the words of Jesus and in the mind of the eternal Christ, "for my sake and the gospel's" has no narrow or jealous reference. Certainly it is not limited to ecclesiastical service. Perhaps it is not confined either within any of the fixed and narrow limits that the conventionally minded might set up. "Other sheep I have, which are not of this fold" (KJV), said Jesus. Whoever has reflected, in the contexts which were possible for him, that love and that devotion to the needs of others which were supreme in Jesus has belonged within his fellowship. That perhaps is what was sought to be expressed in what has been called "The Secular Meaning of the Gospel"; and in many of the younger generation, including my children and grandchildren, there is often a wideness of outlook and a commitment to constructive causes which may bring to our world more benefit than we older ones have brought.

So one looks at life and at living beings and sees the great realities of the spirit which make him feel the coming-near of God. But there could be a gap through which an ultimate faith might disappear, and that gap does seem to exist in the thinking and the writing of some of those who are supposed to be bringers of a gospel. In many contemporary books about religious beliefs there is no infinite horizon. Something has dropped out of what an earlier generation instinctively believed in, and that something is a warmth of expectation concerning life beyond this mortal life. Instead, there is a kind of chilled shrinking from any consideration of it, as though the hope and faith that glowed in earlier centuries had been damped down by the pressure of a secularistic age which will recognize and acknowledge only that which it can see and touch. Search the index of almost any current book even among those which assume to interpret the Christian gospel, and see how its references are shrunken. Where are the old reminders of the great conviction that life does not have to end at death? They are not there.

Reality to me means more than that sort of negativism. Certainly it is hard sometimes to believe in what we cannot see, hard to look beyond the awful physical fact of dying. But to disbelieve in the victory of spirit would be a tame acceptance of the universe as irrational—as it *would* be irrational if all the highest products of it were meant for nothing except to disappear. The great souls I have known bring home to me a mightier truth than that. I like the sturdy faith that Dr. Wilfred Grenfell—Grenfell of Labrador—proclaimed in his *What Life Means To Me*.[2] "As for life hereafter," he said, "I know little or nothing about it; but that is not of any great importance, because I want it, whatever it is." And then he went on, "I believe Jesus Christ has meant all in this mortal life that he claimed he would mean. . . . So when he says concerning the future, 'Because I live, ye shall live also,' and 'He that believeth in me, though he were dead, yet shall he live,' I simply believe it—and that the more readily and firmly because I want to do so."

[2] (Boston: Pilgrim Press, 1910), pp. 30, 32.

I remember also that William James, when in his latter years he was asked whether he believed in the life to come, answered that what made him come nearest to believing was that he was "just beginning to be fit to live." For myself, I know that I have attained no fitness, and only hope that I may have a further chance to learn. But the one thing I do believe invincibly is that some of those whom I have known and loved have risen so far above all crippling things that they belong in a realm of life imperishable; and that by their intercession the Everlasting Mercy may lead me on the road to where they are.

Index of Names and Places

Abbott, Lyman, 51

Adams, George Plimpton, 49

Alderman, Edwin A., 100, 103, 107

Alexandria, Va., 30, 58, 69, 139, 219, 239, 246, 248, 263

American Mercury, The, 173, 175

Armstrong, Mrs. N. E. ("Miss Arm"), 157, 186, 206

Atwood, Julius W., 180-81

Babcock, Katherine (Mrs. Maltbie D.), 54, 55, 56

Babcock, Maltbie Davenport, 42, 54, 55

Baker, George B., 195

Baker, Myra, 163, 165

Ballantine, Arthur A., 50

Baltimore, Md., 66, 67, 138, 233

Barnwell, Middleton, 68

Barth, Karl, 222, 224, 278

Base Hospital No. 45, 110-11, 112

Batten, L. W., 150

Beaird, Pat, 209, 210

Bell, Nancy (Mrs. W. C.), 264

Bell, Wilbur Cosby, 70, 264

Bellevue School, Va., 34

Bennett, John C., 279

Bewer, Julius A., 69, 206

Bible, Revised Standard Version, 211-18

Bird, Francis William, 50

Black, Hugh, 206

Bleecker, Theophylact B., 152

Bonhoeffer, Dietrich, 227, 230 n.

Bowie, Beverley (son), 93, 94, 157, 186, 187, 192, 205, 233, 264-68

Bowie, Elisabeth. *See* Chapman, Elisabeth Bowie

Bowie, Elisabeth Branch (mother), 9, 24, 78, 80, 85, 93, 240, 264

Bowie, Jean. *See* Evans, Jean Bowie

Bowie, Jean Laverack (wife), 54-57, 58, 72, 73, 79, 81, 82, 85, 86, 88, 94, 101, 140, 150, 151, 179, 181, 182, 187, 188, 189, 192, 204, 206, 207, 234, 238, 239, 240, 256, 263, 264, 270-76

Bowie, John, 9

Bowie, Louise Boynton (Mrs. Beverley), 233, 265

Bowie, Martha. *See* Branch, Martha Bowie

Bowie, Mary Maenner (Mrs. W. R., Jr.), 233

Bowie, Walter (grandfather), 10-12

Bowie, Mrs. Walter (grandmother), 12

Bowie, Walter Russell
   Christ Be with Me, 248
   Compassionate Christ, The, 248
   Jesus and the Trinity, 248
   Master: A Life of Jesus Christ, The, 163
   Men of Fire, 247
   On Being Alive, 163
   Preaching, 246
   Renewing Gospel, The, 164
   See Yourself in the Bible, 247
   Some Open Ways to God, 234
   Story of the Bible, The, 165
   Story of the Church, The, 165
   Sunny Windows, 275
   Where You Find God, 230 n., 248
   Women of Light, 247

Bowie, Walter Russell (father), 9, 22-23

Bowie, Walter Russell, Jr. (son), 94, 157, 187, 188, 206, 233, 264

Branch, Christopher, 9

Branch, Elisabeth Halsted (mother). *See* Bowie, Elisabeth Branch

Branch, James Read (grandfather), 12

Branch, Mrs. James R. (grandmother), 9, 12-13, 27, 254

Branch, Martha Bowie (sister), 16, 80, 85, 101, 187, 234

Branch, Mary ("Mate," niece), 187

Branch, Melville C., 85

Briggs, Le Baron R., 47

Brooks, Phillips, 51, 144

Brooks, Phyllis Langhorne, 75

Brown, Francis, 205

Brown, William Adams, 69, 206

Brunner, Emil, 224

Buffalo, N. Y., 55, 56, 270, 271

Bull, Father, 160

Burrows, Millar, 211, 215

Buttrick, George A., 209, 210

Byrd, Harry Flood, 259

Cabell, Annie (aunt), 17

Cabell, James Branch (cousin), 18

Cabell, John (cousin), 17

Cabell, Robert (cousin), 17, 18

Cadbury, Henry J., 212, 215

Cadman, S. Parkes, 178

Cape Cod, Mass., 54, 55, 56, 268

Carysbrook farm, 19-22

Caswell, Wilbur, 150
Cecil, William (Bishop of Exeter), 181
Cecil, Mrs. William, 182
Chapin School, New York City, 151, 157
Chapman, Dwight W., 234
Chapman, Elisabeth Bowie (daughter), 92, 93, 151, 157, 186, 188, 192, 205, 234, 264
Child, Dick, 49
Christian Herald, 273
Church League for Industrial Democracy, 144
Churchman, The, 197
Clingman, Charlie, 68
Coffin, Dorothy (Mrs. H. S.), 206, 235
Coffin, Henry Sloane, 69, 89, 91, 149, 172, 205, 206, 234
College of William and Mary, 107
Columbia, Va., 20, 22
Conrad, Virginia P., 89
Coordinate College for Women, University of Virginia, 97-108
Craig, Clarence T., 212, 215
Damell, Robert, 261
Danville Register, 104
Daughters of the American Revolution (D.A.R.), 167
Dinwiddie family, 71
Divinity School, Philadelphia, 208
Douglas, Malcolm, 150
Dwelly, F. W., 182, 184, 189
Easton, Burton S., 150
Eisenhower, Dwight D., 169
Eliot, Charles William, 47-48
Eliot, T. S., 222
Emmanuel Church, Greenwood, 72-82
Emmanuel Movement, 179
Evans, Jean Bowie (daughter), 80, 82, 85, 92, 93, 151, 157, 182, 186, 189, 192, 205, 264
Evans, Ted, 188, 190, 191, 192, 205, 264
Federal Council of Churches. See National Council of Churches
Ferris, Theodore, 151
Foakes-Jackson, F. J., 150, 206
Fosbroke, Hughell, 150, 208
Fosdick, Harry Emerson, 149, 160, 206, 241
Fox, Leonard, 74
Garvin, Bertha Maud, 151, 157-58, 163, 165
Gary, Elbert H., 129-30, 131

Geisinger, Joseph F., 111
General Seminary, New York City, 150, 151, 208
Gilkey, Charles W., 69
Gilman, Charlotte Perkins Stetson, 28
Goodspeed, Edgar J., 212, 213, 216, 217
Goodspeed, Mrs. Edgar J., 213, 217
Goodwin, Edward L., 124
Grace Chapel, New York City, 142, 151, 165
Grace Church, New York City, 137, 138, 140-204 *passim*, 234, 264, 273
Grady, Henry W., 256-57, 259
Grant, Frederick C., 206, 212, 213, 215-16
Gravatt, John, 59, 68, 80
Green, Berryman, 61, 62, 163, 252
Greenwood, Va., 71-82, 88, 93, 273
Greer, David Hummel, 171
Grenfell, Wilfred, 283
Grew, Joseph, 45
Guthrie, William Norman, 149, 150, 172, 178, 248
Hancock Pond, Me., 186
Hand, Mrs. Augustus T., 150
Harmon, Nolan B., 210
Harrison, Lewis Carter ("Monk"), 59, 65-67, 78
Harvard University, 44-53, 55, 80, 100, 150, 179, 192, 197, 206, 233
Havens, Catherine Elizabeth, 153
Hawes, Katherine, 101
Hill School, The, Pottstown, Pa., 35-43, 44, 45, 58, 80, 194
Horner, Clarence H. ("Jack"), 199, 200, 203
Huntington, Mrs. Francis C., 151
Huntington, William R., 138, 151, 158
International Council of Religious Education, 211
Interpreter's Bible, The, 209-11
Jackson, John Long, 68
James, William, 46, 284
Jefferson, Thomas, 98, 100, 107
Jesus, 90, 93, 142, 144, 145, 209, 220, 221, 224, 225, 226, 228, 243, 244, 248, 249, 250, 251, 252, 282, 283
John XXIII (Pope), 176, 177
Johns, Bishop, 243
Johnson, James Weldon, 267, 268
Jones, Charlie (cousin), 20
Jones, Julian (cousin), 21, 22

Jones, Tommy (cousin), 21
Jowett, John Henry, 127
Kernochan, J. Frederic, 138, 148
Kilin, 149-50, 178, 248
King, Martin Luther, Jr., 258, 261
Kittredge, George Lyman, 46, 47
Kloman, Edward Felix, 165, 200, 252
Knox, George William, 69
Knox, John, 206, 210
Kroner, Richard J., 206, 207, 275
Krumbhaar, Edward B. (Ned), 195
Lang, Anton, 190
Langdale, John A., 164
Langhorne, Chiswell D., 75, 76-78, 81
Lathrop, John Howland, 179
Laverack, Belle, 270
Laverack, George E., 270, 271
Laverack, Mrs. George E., 271
Laverack, Gertrude, 270
Laverack, Howard, 270
Laverack, Jean. *See* Bowie, Jean Laverack
Laverack, William Harold, 270
Lawrence, William, 146
Leake, James P., 50
Lee, Robert E., 31, 33, 34, 74
Lee, Valentine, 120
Lines, Edwin S., 137
Living Church, The, 127
Lloyd, Bishop, 77
Lodge, Henry Cabot, 48
Lyman, Eugene W., 206
McCarthy, Joseph, 169
McCue, M. L., 72
McCue, Mrs. M. L., 72, 73, 78, 79, 81
McCue, Purcell, 72, 81
McGiffert, Arthur C., 69
McGuire, John Peyton, 30-34, 255
McGuire, Mrs. Judith A., 255
McGuire, Stuart, 110, 112, 113
McGuire's School, Richmond, 30, 32-34
MacKay, John A., 169
McKenney, Virginia S., 101
MacKintosh, H. R., 224 n.
McNeill, John T., 206
Maggie, 78, 79, 80
Manning, William T., 131, 149, 171, 172
Maynard, Douglas Wright, 101
Meigs, John, 35-43, 58, 80
Meigs, Marion Butler (Mrs. John), 38, 39, 40, 41, 80
Meigs, Matthew, 35
Melish, John Howard, 150, 179

Minor, Kate Pleasants, 101
Mitchel, John Purroy, 50
Modern Churchman's Union, 144
Moffatt, James, 206, 212, 214-15
Montgomery Messenger, 104
Mott, John R., 64
Muilenburg, James, 206
Munford, Beverley Bland (uncle), 25, 80, 93
Munford, Mary-Cooke Branch (aunt), 24-29, 80-81, 86, 98, 99, 101, 103, 105, 107, 108, 234
Münsterberg, Hugo, 46
Murray, John Courtney, 175, 176
Murrow, Edward R., 232
National Council of Churches, 128, 137
National Geographic, 265, 266
Nelson, Mammy, 18, 19
Neve, Archdeacon, 73, 76
New York City, 27, 38, 50, 70, 91, 126, 137, 138, 141, 146, 148, 149, 182, 186, 199, 201, 248, 253, 273
New York Times, 142
Nichols, Harry P., 140
Niebuhr, Reinhold, 206
None Dare Call It Treason, 169
Oxnam, G. Bromley, 169
Parks, Leighton, 51, 150
Parson, Artley B., 48
Patteson, William A., 254, 255
Potter, Henry Codman, 138, 151, 171
Quin, "Mike," 68, 71
Randolph, Mrs. Norman V., 101, 106
Red Network, The, 169
Reiland, Karl, 178
Richardson, Cyril C., 206, 236
Richmond, Va., 9, 10, 12, 13-15, 19, 20, 22, 25, 26, 27, 30, 34, 58, 68, 78, 80, 82, 83, 85, 86, 88, 89, 93, 98, 102, 108, 110, 113, 120, 122, 124, 125, 139, 140, 143, 148, 157, 160, 197, 198, 205, 240, 254, 255, 260, 273
Jackson Ward, 97, 257
Richmond Times-Dispatch, 86, 105, 260, 261
Robbins, Howard Chandler, 172
Roberts, John E., 268
Robinson, John A. T.: *Honest to God,* 226, 227, 279 n.
Rogers, Guy, 182-84, 192
Rogers, Martin, 192
Roosevelt, Eleanor, 53, 169

Learning to Live

Roosevelt Franklin D., 45, 51-53
Royce, Josiah, 46
Sachs, Walter, 50
Safford, Mary D., 54, 56, 151
St. Paul's Cathedral, London, 190, 193
St. Paul's Church, Richmond, Va., 9, 15, 81, 83-94, 95-98, 110, 120-24, 132-39, 146, 151, 160, 196, 197, 205, 260
Sanford, Mary R., 54, 56, 151
Scarlett, Will, 242
Scherer, Paul, 206, 210
Scott, Ernest F., 206
Sedgwick, Theodore, 150
Serman, Stanley Brown, 252
Sheerin, James, 143
Sheppard, Dick, 184-85, 192, 193
Sheppard, George Q., 36
Sherrill, Henry K., 114
Shipman, Herbert, 149
Shirley, Armistead, 80, 81
Slattery, Charles Lewis, 137-38, 140, 142, 154, 157, 158, 276
Smith, Kendall K., 49-50
Smith, Roland Cotton, 150
Social Service Commission, Diocese of Virginia, 96
Songs of Praise, 182, 188
Sorel, Paul, 248
Southern Churchman, The, 124, 125, 126, 127, 128, 130, 131, 132, 143
Sparrow, Dean, 220
Spivak, Lawrence E., 173, 174
Stanard, Mary Newton, 101
Stanton, Edwin, 41
Stetson, Caleb, 150
Stevens, Arthur, 164
Stevens, Richard T., 140
Student Volunteer Movement, 64
Taft, William Howard, 124

Temple, William, 247-48
Terrien, Samuel, 206, 210
Theological Seminary in Virginia. *See* Virginia Seminary, Alexandria
Tillich, Paul, 206, 207, 227
Townsend, Howard, 138
Townsend, Mrs. Howard, 150
Trinity Church, Buffalo, 79, 271
Trotter, Jesse M., 252
Tucker, Beverley D., Jr., 139
Union Theological Seminary, New York, 69, 70, 149, 150, 188, 192, 203, 205-9, 212, 213, 231-38, 241, 274, 279
Van Buren, Paul M., 226
Van Dusen, Henry Pitney, 235
Vassar College, 27, 85, 192, 206
Virginia, University of, 30, 97-98, 99, 100, 101, 102, 103-4, 107, 234
Virginia Seminary, Alexandria, 59-70, 80, 139, 163, 188, 219, 239-45, 248-52, 263, 277-78
Wallace, George C., 259
Walsh, Raymond, 179
Washington, D.C., 13, 50, 59, 197, 205
Washington and Lee University, 9, 31
Weigle, Luther A., 164, 212, 214, 216
Wellford, Berta, 26
Wendell, Barrett, 46
Wentz, Abdel R., 212, 216
Wianno, Mass., 54, 55, 56, 57, 58, 268, 271
Wilde, Julia C., 151
Williams, Charles D., 131
Wilson, Woodrow, 48, 110, 123
Winslow, Dick, 188
Woodberry Forest School, Va., 35
Woods, Bishop of Winchester, 181, 188
Worcester, Elwood, 179, 180
Zabriskie, Alexander C., 242, 252

288

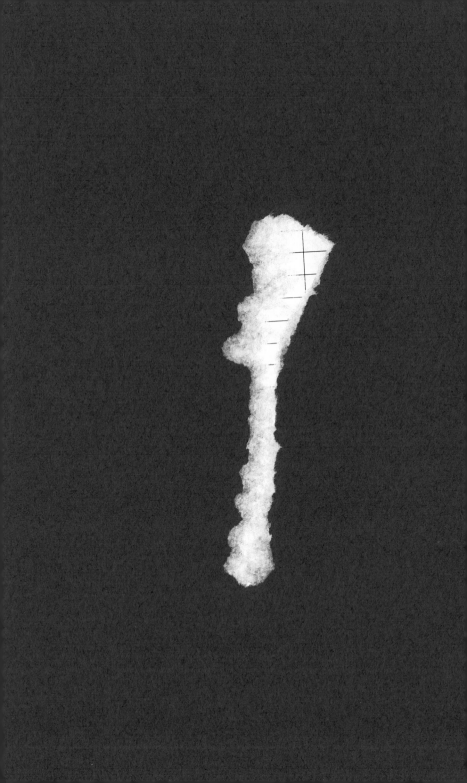